READING, RESPONDING, AND WRITING

SHORT ESSAYS AND STORIES
FOR COMPOSITION

DOMENICK CARUSO
STEPHEN WEIDENBORNER

St. Martin's Press
New York

Library of Congress Catalog Card Number: 86–60658
Manufactured in the United States of America.
10987
fedcba
For information, write:
St. Martin's Press, Inc.
175 Fifth Avenue
New York, NY 10010

Cover design: Darby Downey
Text design: Helen Granger/Levavi & Levavi
Cover photograph: Victor Schrager

ISBN: 0-312-66460-5
Instructor's Edition ISBN: 0-312-00547-4

Acknowledgments

Evelyn R. Fulbright. "Mary and Mrs. Brown," *Today's Education*, February/
   March, 1979. © 1979, National Education Association.
G. Gordon Liddy. "Without Emotion," from *Will: The Autobiography of G.
   Gordon Liddy*. Copyright © 1980 by G. Gordon Liddy, St. Martin's Press,
   Inc., New York.
Henry T. Thomas and Dana L. Thomas. "Beethoven," from *Living Biographies
   of Great Composers*. Garden City Publishing Co., Inc., 1940.
Sylvia Ashton-Warner. "Rolf," from *I Passed This Way*, by Sylvia Ashton-
   Warner. Copyright 1979, Alfred A. Knopf, Inc.
George Orwell. "Henri," from *Down and Out in Paris and London*, by George
   Orwell, copyright 1933 by George Orwell; renewed 1961 by Sonia Pitt-
   Rivers. Reprinted by permission of Harcourt Brace Jovanovich, Inc. and the
   estate of Sonia Bronwell Orwell and Secker & Warburg Ltd.
Langston Hughes. "Father," from *The Big Sea* by Langston Hughes. Copyright
   1940 by Langston Hughes. Copyright renewed © 1968 by Arna Bontemps
   and George Houston Bass. Reprinted by permission of Hill and Wang, a
   division of Farrar, Straus and Giroux, Inc.
Willie Morris. "Our English Teacher," from *North Toward Home*, copyright ©
   1967 by Willie Morris. Reprinted by permission of Joan Daves.
Jean Toomer. "Avey," is reprinted from *Cane* by Jean Toomer by permission

Acknowledgments and copyrights continue on pp. 243–244, which constitute
an extension of the copyright page.

PREFACE

Any instructor who has questioned the mechanistic and prescriptive approaches of most composition textbooks—and who is ready to trust students' natural curiosity and their desire to communicate—should find this reader challenging and refreshing. *Reading, Responding, and Writing* aims to involve students with reading selections to a greater degree than traditional textbooks allow. Prompted by reading selections and by student responses to them, students are encouraged to express their personal concerns in writing. They are motivated to improve their reading and writing skills by learning about themselves and discovering their interests and concerns.

Our approach in this book grew out of our efforts to apply reader-response methods in the classroom. Finding it impractical to follow a "pure" response model under typical classroom conditions, we have adapted the individualized aspects of the method so that students themselves guide each other through discussion and peer editing. They begin by recording their strongest responses to a reading selection, without being guided by preconceived rhetorical or thematic categories. Then, by sharing their responses and getting classmates' reactions, they identify a topic and thesis they care about, and they develop their ideas into a first-draft essay. During revision students again are guided by peers' reactions, and perhaps by the instructor as well, so that the finished essay effectively expresses the point of view they developed in response to the reading.

The Introduction to *Reading, Responding, and Writing* immediately involves students in the process just described. Besides orienting them to this personal approach to reading and writing, the Introduction provides practice in the various classroom procedures that make it work. After the introductory chapter, the book offers four thematic sections of readings: Responding to People, Responding to Situations and Events, Responding to Ideas, and Responding to Language. The first three readings in each of these sections are followed by sample responses and questions about the responses to help students focus their own ideas. The last selections in each part appear without sample responses or questions, as do the Additional Readings in Part Five; students have been prepared for these sections by their work with the guided readings. Finally, Part Six, Improving Your Writing, can be used at any point during the course, either to introduce or to review the main concerns in developing a thesis, drafting the essay, and revising it.

Whether you adhere to the methods described in the Introduction or combine them with your approaches, we believe that the provocative readings and sample responses in this book will result in an active, spontaneous classroom in which students will be challenged to participate—and will take pride in their achievements.

CONTENTS

INTRODUCTION

HOW TO USE THIS BOOK

This book will improve your ability to communicate in nonfiction writing. We want to emphasize the word *ideas* and point out that we are not concerned with teaching creative writing, such as poetry or fiction, or with showing you the proper forms to use for business letters and reports. Instead, the assignments in this book ask you to develop your own ideas into essays that will be clear and effective, essays that your readers will understand and appreciate. The key to becoming an effective writer is, first of all, to come up with an idea that you really want to express. This book will make you aware of some specific ways to discover ideas that are important to you and to develop them into effective essays.

We could, of course, ask you to sit down and "think of a topic that is important to you," but most of our students found this to be one of the most difficult assignments of all. May be the first ideas that come to mind are too personal (a family problem, perhaps) or too "heavy" (preventing nuclear war, or achieving social justice). Or maybe too many ideas pop up at once, making it difficult to choose the best one. At any rate, most writing courses make use of essays or literature and ask students to analyze these as models for their own writing. Assignments in such a course often require the students to write about the same topic as is found in the model or to imitate the form of the model.

This book does provide readings for you to consider, but we ask you to respond freely rather than to analyze them, and the writing assignments in this course do not require you to imitate the forms of the readings. Furthermore, you will be asked to respond not only to the reading selections but also to each other's writing. This reading-responding approach calls for a good deal of active participation, but the interaction between you and your classmates can improve your writing more quickly than an approach in which you must work entirely on your own. By getting feedback from your classmates during the writing process, you will discover what has gone wrong in your writing, or at least what can be improved, *before* you have to prepare your final draft. In addition, by sharing your responses to *other* students' work, you will learn to analyze and criticize writing in general. This, too, will make you a better writer.

You may wonder exactly what we expect when we ask you to "respond." Basically, within each reading we want you to find some idea, large or small, that evokes a strong reaction in you. Whatever that reaction may be, you will be asked to respond by writing down your ideas so that they can be shared with other student writers. The goal is to discover a topic that you care about. Don't try to guess what the instructor is looking for or what your classmates are likely to think. Even if you think your response may come out of "left field," if it represents something meaningful to you, it may well be worth pursuing as a topic for a paper.

Photograph by David M. Grossman

Responding, of course, is a natural part of being alive. We do it all the time, but usually our responses take the form of thoughts or conversation. In this course you will simply record those responses in writing. Let's look at a few examples to show you what we mean.

Examples of Responding

Four college friends who thought they might sign up for a journalism course attended a meeting at which the instructor described the course. Briefly, this is what he said:

> **Professor:** I am looking for intelligent, perceptive students who feel deeply committed to producing a newspaper that readers can respect for its ability to tell the whole story, clearly and without bias, in an appealing style. The paper should be so good that people will feel they have missed something vital any day they fail to read it. I hope you are all fine writers, but if you're too good, I'll have nothing to teach you. At any rate, I am not looking for an Edgar Allan Poe or a John Updike. I want people to be able to read the paper rapidly or at leisure and still come away feeling they have been as well informed as they expected. In this course, you will be required to write something for every class, including one polished article per week, which will be submitted for my comments. Grades will depend primarily on what you get out of the course, for I assume you are all capable of doing the work competently. I am looking forward to getting to know each of you personally and watching you develop your talents in this most exciting field of work.

The four friends met afterward and shared their reactions to the presentation:

> **Betty:** I like this guy. He seems to be more interested in students than in teaching us all the boring details of printing and the history of publishing. I remember all the pressure trying to get a newspaper out in high school, and I sure want someone who cares about me to be there when all the hassling starts.
>
> **Sal:** It sounds like too much work to me. Can you imagine writing three papers a week? On top of all our other classes? No way!
>
> **Betty:** He didn't say ''three papers a week.'' He just wants one article, and that probably wouldn't be as long as an essay in your history course. The other writing isn't even turned in, and it might be quite short. Besides, we're supposed to *like* writing.
>
> **Dan:** He reminds me of this guy I had in high school—same little glasses and peculiar way of thinking. Was he ever nasty when it came to grading! No one could tell what he was looking for.

Janice: I know what you mean, but he seems very sharp to me. He probably has very high standards, but that's what I'm looking for. If I'm going into journalism, I want a teacher who knows what he's doing.

As you can see, people's reactions can come from very different directions. Although some people might not think that a teacher's looks should stop anyone from enrolling in a course, life is filled with such surprising responses. And they are in no way meaningless to those who experience them. What seems like too much work to one person may seem like a worthy challenge to another. Indeed, if all people *did* have the same responses, there would be no reason to write in the first place.

Another example of how people respond differently involved the same students and a decision regarding a photograph proposed for the front page of the college newspaper. The photo is on page 5.

Betty thought the photo was too gruesome, that it would give the paper an image of pandering to ghoulish interests, as horror movies do.

Janice disagreed, saying Betty had missed the point—that the shock effect might save someone's life, since people would think twice before driving recklessly or when drinking.

Sal allowed that the photograph might serve a good purpose, but he objected to putting it on the front page, where news items and the issues of the day should be presented.

What do you think? Does this photograph belong on page 1 of a college newspaper? Take a moment right now to express your opinion briefly in writing.

A Warm-Up Exercise

Before showing you how a sample assignment works, which will entail reading a complete essay, let's warm up by responding to the following newspaper article:

> Mrs. Ivory McInnes, 38, of Greenacres, Kentucky, after having been reported missing by her husband, Ira, six days earlier, showed up at the state police barracks in Wolfsboro, Tennessee, explaining that she had been abducted by alien beings who were operating out of what seemed to be a spaceship. Ennis Air Force Base officials acknowledged that on the night Mrs. McInnes disappeared they had received several reports of strange lights in the sky within a 50-mile radius of Greenacres. Mrs. McInnes said she was walking back home alone from town a little before midnight when a dimly glowing circular aircraft, about 40 feet in diameter, landed vertically in a field about a mile from her house. She was so stunned that she fainted, only to wake inside the craft, which she sensed had taken off, although she had no sense of motion. The figures of the aliens were not distinctly defined in

Caraballo/Monkmeyer Press Photo Service

the eerie light of the ship. She could understand them but does not recall whether they spoke aloud. They began asking general questions about the various kinds of life on this planet and about her species' way of life. Most of their subsequent questions dealt with science and technology. When they realized she could not answer these questions, they returned her to land, though not at the same point they had picked her up. Wolfsboro lies 130 miles southeast of Greenacres. When interviewed on their farm, Mrs. McInnes's husband, Ira, offered no comment when asked about his wife's adventure in space.

Record your response to this story right now, in one or two paragraphs that express whatever ideas or feelings it raised in you.

Reading, Responding, and Writing: An Overview

From the preceding examples and warm-up exercise, you can see that, indeed, you respond to stimuli all the time, and very often your responses are unique. Even when you basically agree with the opinion of others, the way you express that opinion and the intensity of your feelings about it are unique. No one but you can quite say what's on your mind. For that reason alone it's important to be able to express yourself freely and effectively.

Many people have little trouble *saying* what they think, and they usually can make other people understand them—even if they have to shout or repeat themselves. When it comes to *writing*, however, people sometimes find it difficult to share their ideas clearly. In conversations we get feedback from our listeners and can tell when they lose interest or disagree with what we're saying. But writing is usually done in isolation, without readers at hand to tell the author when an idea or opinion or phrase goes over their heads. This book is designed to provide feedback to writers in the form of readers' responses. You and your classmates will share your ideas (1) about reading assignments, (2) about each other's responses to those readings, and (3) about each other's essays. In this way the necessary link between writers and readers will be forged, allowing you to learn firsthand how your written ideas are received.

By learning what others think of your ideas and how you present them, and by telling other student writers where they lost you in a particular paragraph or sentence, your ability to communicate ideas in writing will be improved. Not only will you practice and become comfortable expressing yourself, but your ideas and ways of presenting them will be strengthened. You will write clearly and with conviction, because your readers have helped you to discover an idea that is important to you and have told you whether or not you are conveying it well.

Throughout this book the practice of reading, responding, and writing will lead you to identify your strengths and weaknesses in writing. The entire process is detailed in the next section, but you should know at the outset what to expect. First, you will begin each assignment with a reading selection, to which you will respond briefly in writing. Then you will share your strongest response about the reading with your instructor and classmates—in class discussion or small groups or by trading your paper with someone else. Next, you will give and get feedback by talking with your peers, whose responses will help you to adjust and clarify the ideas you are developing into a paper. At that point, you will expand your ideas into a first draft, which again will be shared with peers. After another round of discussion, you will select the best ideas your classmates have shared, and you will use them to revise your draft into a finished essay.

Before deciding that this process sounds frightening or tedious, consider two thoughts. First, your classmates are in the same situation as you; since everyone is subject to the process of sharing and receiving feedback, no one escapes criticism—and everyone will learn to offer it helpfully. Second, although the pattern of reading, responding, and writing will be repeated throughout the course, the readings you will respond to and write about are all very different. If one reading fails to inspire you, the next one may really spark your interest and have you writing in a frenzy. In addition, within each major part of the book, the readings are related; you may find yourself returning to an earlier reading because a later one presented a different point of view, and you want to consider the two together.

Finally, the first three readings in each part are followed by sample responses written by students in an actual class. The questions we raise about those responses should get you started on the right foot by making you think a little more deeply about your own reactions to the readings. The combination of your own responses, your classmates' feedback, and the sample responses should make you reach for a pen with enthusiasm.

Now let's practice the process we've outlined by going through a sample assignment, complete with students' responses, feedback sessions, and resulting essays.

SAMPLES OF READING, RESPONDING, AND WRITING
(How *Some* Students Have Used This Book)

Now that you are familiar with this book's approach to writing, let's practice the general process that you will follow throughout the course. The best way to demonstrate the process of reading, responding, and writing is to take you through a sample assignment. We will begin with a reading selection and some sample responses of students in a class much like your own. Then we will see how these students developed their responses into an essay through peer editing—by reacting to each other's work and sharing their ideas.

Like the students in this example, you should record your response to an essay as soon as you finish reading it. In this way you are likely to express your strongest ideas, the ones that are truly important to you. Rather than writing a summary—which is unlikely to express what you think about the ideas in the essay—try to respond without deeply analyzing the reading selection. Avoid trying to guess what your instructor may be looking for; *your response* is all that matters at this point. By recording your own thoughts about the essay, you will discover a topic that truly interests you. Then you can develop that topic into a full-length essay by trying out your ideas on classmates, friends, and your instructor.

You may find it difficult at first to let yourself go and record your impressions in writing. But don't worry. You will catch on quickly, and soon you will respond freely and naturally—in class as well as on paper. An important part of this process is to compare your responses with those of other readers. That's why we provide sample responses to the first three reading selections in each part of the book.

Now let's look at an actual classroom example of reading, responding, and writing. After you have read the following essay, record your strongest response to it by writing a short paragraph. Then compare your response to the reactions of the four students in this sample classroom.

MARY AND MRS. BROWN

EVELYN R. FULBRIGHT

It was Valentine's Day. I had just walked into a classroom to observe an experimental reading class. A girl with sparkling eyes caught my attention, mainly because she was larger than the rest of the children and because she had a big valentine on her desk. 1

Then it all came back—the classroom many years earlier when I was a preservice teacher, the place where I had learned one of my most valuable lessons about helping children with behavior problems. It was a lesson that symbolized a child's need for love and self-esteem—but that is getting ahead of the story. 2

Going back to that time, I recall that my professor had assigned my class to observe in elementary classrooms. I was to be with Mrs. Brown's first grade class. 3

The professor had given us all check sheets to record our observations and verbal instructions for marking them, but I was still scared—afraid that I would not see what I was supposed to see. Exactly what I was supposed to see, I did not know. My fellow students seemed equally vague about our purpose. 4

With pencil and paper in hand, nevertheless, I sat in a corner of Mrs. Brown's room, looking as hard as I could, anxious to observe some special secrets of teaching and learning. My eyes came to rest on Mary, who was larger than most of the children. Later I saw on Mrs. Brown's records that she was repeating first grade. 5

As the days passed, I noticed many things about Mary: that her desk seemed too small for her angular body, that her clothes never seemed right—one day they were too big, the next day, too small. Wrinkles were always evident, and what seemed to be a favorite blue sweater had all the buttons missing. 6

In spite of her unkempt appearance, I was drawn to Mary. She was a pretty child, with naturally curly hair—the kind I had always wanted. Unfortunately, it was seldom brushed. Her eyes were bright and flashing—sometimes friendly, sometimes mean. 7

On cold mornings, her chapped cheeks looked almost as if she had gotten into her mother's rouge.

Mary couldn't read very well, but she drew beautiful pictures, 8 and I saw her slip them onto the teacher's desk.

One day I happened to be observing at recess, and I saw Mary 9 give her meat sandwich to a stray dog. I wanted to commend her for that, but I pretended not to notice because she yelled, "I dropped my sandwich." Still I knew what she had meant to do, and I was glad.

Some days, however, I would hear Mary say threatening 10 things as she walked a few steps behind the other children. If anyone laughed, Mary seemed to be pleased.

For weeks she seemed to torment one student in particular, a 11 girl named Jean. I even saw her knock Jean down and then pretend she had done so accidentally.

After that happened, I watched Mrs. Brown talking to Mary 12 with her arm around her. I remember wondering why Mrs. Brown didn't do something more drastic.

Looking back on my own school days, I remembered my 13 teachers' taking immediate action against such offenders. That had certainly seemed right at the time.

Then the holidays came, and I forgot about Mary. When I re- 14 turned to the classroom, she was wearing the same blue sweater she had worn all year. When Mrs. Brown wasn't looking, some of the children made fun of Mary's clothes. That afternoon when I went to say good night to Mrs. Brown, I found her busy with Mary and a package.

On my next visit, Mary had on a different sweater, which ap- 15 peared to be new, and her hair was brushed that day. She was smiling. Her eyes were bright and happy.

But it was not to be Mary's day after all. The mother of another 16 child, Betty, called, and the principal delivered a note to Mrs. Brown that said Mary had been picking on Betty on the way home from school. I sat back to see what Mrs. Brown would do this time.

Just before the dismissal bell, I heard her ask, "Mary, will you 17 be able to stay a few minutes? I've got a lot to do and I need help."

"Yes, Ma'am," Mary grinned.   18

Out of the corner of my eye, I saw Betty's face brighten as she 19 got her books ready to go home.

But another day, as three o'clock drew near, I saw a mean- 20 eyed Mary mutter something under her breath. I also observed the frightened face of Jean. I looked to see if Mrs. Brown noticed.

As the bell rang, Mary smiled unpleasantly, again, and Jean hung back as Mary ran out the door.

Then I saw that Mrs. Brown was getting ready to go out. She 21 called to me, "I'll be back in a minute. I have some things I want to go over with you."

I peered out the window and raised the sash a bit. Sure 22 enough, there was Mary, standing on the playground and waiting for Jean, who was walking very slowly in her direction.

Then Mrs. Brown appeared, and Mary looked up at the 23 teacher, chewed on the corner of her lip, and shivered. Mrs. Brown knelt down, put her arm around Mary, and smiled just as she smiled when she was very happy in the classroom. She brushed back a lock of Mary's hair, and I heard her say, "My, your hair looks pretty today. I want to tell you before you go home." Then she spoke quietly, still smiling at Mary. She buttoned Mary's sweater up right.

Quite often Mary looked away when anyone talked to her, but 24 this time she looked right at Mrs. Brown, blinking her eyes rapidly. I again picked up what Mrs. Brown was saying, "I know I can count on you, Mary." Then she hugged Mary and waved goodbye.

I waited for Mrs. Brown. I wanted to ask her about Mary, but I 25 didn't want to admit I had listened. Anyway, I noticed that she was smiling as if she saw something I couldn't see, so I said nothing.

Some days later I saw Mary and Jean eating lunch together. Af- 26 ter school they went off, laughing and talking.

Then it was Valentine's Day. Everything in Mrs. Brown's 27 room seemed to be covered in lace and red hearts and cupids. The children had decorated individual mailboxes for themselves.

All the children put valentines in one another's boxes. I dis- 28 tributed mine too; for some reason, I "mailed" the prettiest one I had to Mary.

After the other children had read all their valentines, Mary 29 reached into her box and pulled out her last one. It was so big and so pretty that the children murmured "Oh's" and "Ah's" when they saw it.

It was truly the most magnificent valentine of the day. On the 30 inside under the verse, the sender had printed in big letters, "Dear Mary, I love you," but whoever it was had not signed the card.

Mary let the other children hold the card and smell it. It had a 31 delicate fragrance, which they liked. Mrs. Brown smiled approvingly.

In the days that followed, there seemed to be something differ- 32
ent about Mary. Her hair was brushed; her "new" sweater was
buttoned. She had a ribbon in her hair, and her shoes were shiny.

There was more. Mary smiled a lot and offered to help Mrs. 33
Brown. She read aloud with more expression, and Mrs. Brown
called on her often.

I never let Mrs. Brown know that when I was in the card shop 34
buying my valentines, I saw her buy the big valentine Mary had
received. I had been curious about why she was buying such an
expensive card.

I hoped Mrs. Brown knew I was getting the lessons she was 35
teaching me. We never discussed them.

At the end of our classroom observation course, the professor 36
asked, "What was the most significant idea that you have gained
from this course?" I responded, "Teachers must be sensitive to
the hurts and needs of children. Children respond more posi-
tively and learn in a more effective fashion in such an environment." I did not explain about Mary and Mrs. Brown. At the
time, it was not an easy story for me to tell.

Over the years, I have shared bits and pieces of the story with 37
preservice and in-service teachers in various ways, but it has
been many years since I thought of the details.

Not until I walked into the reading classroom that morning 38
and saw the large girl with the big valentine on her desk did I remember the story as it had happened. That is what stirred my
memories and prompted me to wonder whether this reading
teacher also had studied with Mrs. Brown.

Take a moment now to record your personal response to the essay.
When you have finished, your instructor will suggest ways for class members to share their impressions. You may be surprised by some of the responses your classmates have, but you also will discover how many different impressions a single piece of writing can suggest.

By discussing the essay in class or by reading individual responses out
loud, you and your classmates probably arrived at general agreement
about the author's main reason for writing the essay. You might want to
consider your classmates' ideas in evaluating your own response to the essay, but don't feel you have to agree with them when you develop your response into a full-length paper. Your response to the essay may have little
to do with the author's apparent purpose. You may focus on some other

idea instead. But if the essay helped to stimulate your ideas, then it served as an inspiration for finding a writing topic of your own. In other words, many things can help you find and develop your topic: the essay itself, your initial response, other people's responses, and discussion of all these ideas in class.

Now let's look at four students' responses to "Mary and Mrs. Brown" and how one student developed his response into a complete essay.

Sample Responses to "Mary and Mrs. Brown"

Responder 1: Michael

This was one of those phony stories about a dedicated teacher who helps a troubled child to adjust to school and become a better person at the same time. I can tell it's phony because I never had any teachers like Mrs. Brown. Most of the teachers I had couldn't wait to get to the parking lot when the last bell rang. Who does this writer think she can fool? Maybe Mrs. Brown is meant to be an example of what every teacher should be, but there are no Mrs. Browns in the real world.

Responder 2: Carol

At first I liked Mrs. Brown fine, but as the story moved ahead I saw that she was going much too far for a teacher. By going too far, I mean that she should not have bought the girl a sweater. The valentine was a bit too much, too. Yes, Mary was an unhappy girl, and the teacher was smart to notice that. But then she should have sent Mary to a counselor, and they would have talked to Mary's mother. It seems to me that Mrs. Brown was trying to be a good mother for Mary, and that is not a good idea. I also wonder what the other kids thought when they saw what was happening. Some teachers spend too much time worrying about the losers. They need to spend more time with the normal students who may need a little extra help, too.

Responder 3: Stanley

My younger sister is just like Mary. She is driving my parents crazy because they don't know what to do about her. She is always getting into trouble and she is doing badly in school. She hangs out with a bad crowd and listens to them rather than to our parents or to my older sister and me. She really has me worried because I can't see how she is going to avoid getting into worse trouble if she keeps this up much longer.

Responder 4: Elissa

Mrs. Brown was one of those rare, special teachers who just seems to know what a student needs to pull himself or herself together. How Mrs. Brown helped Mary can't really be taught--the teacher either has a special insight with children's problems or she hasn't. It's something like being a great artist--you're either born with outstanding talent or you're not. However, we can't expect all teachers to be great teachers, just as we can't expect all artists to be great artists or all doctors to be great doctors. There are differences among great teachers, just as there are differences among great artists. Mrs. Brown was outstanding in helping the students to overcome personal problems, but other teachers are skilled in other ways--the way they can get students to understand difficult material, for instance. As a mother, I give thanks that there are teachers like Mrs. Brown, teachers who realize the infinite value of every student.

From First Response to Complete Essay

We asked the four students to tell us how they moved from their first responses to the topics they eventually developed into an essay. No doubt their mental processes were more complicated than they were able to recall, but the explanations they offered do give us insights into how the reading-responding approach works. First, though, we promised to look closely at how one of these students (Michael) modified his first response as a result of ideas that came out during class discussion of the essay. Then we'll see how Michael's classmates responded to the first draft of his paper and how their criticism led him to edit and polish his final essay. Look again at Michael's response and notice that, throughout the drafting and revising process, it remains his chief motive for writing.

Michael's first response to the essay was quite negative. In fact, he called it "phony" and characterized Mrs. Brown as a fictitious example of an ideal teacher. When Michael sat down to write his paper, he intended to prove that the author had invented her picture of Mrs. Brown, who, for Michael, was clearly too good to be true. Then he remembered the class discussion, in which a number of students had mentioned teachers from their past who were highly conscientious. Michael realized that his own experience might have been somewhat limited and that teachers like Mrs. Brown might really exist. He reconsidered his plan to expose the phoniness he found in the essay. But he still was not ready to give up his negative response. It made him angry to think about all the less-than-ideal teachers he had encountered in his school years, and so he decided to write a paper about them—teachers who did *not* try to understand, much less to help, their students. Michael began by thinking of all the teachers he had known who "didn't care." Here is the first draft of his paper.

Teachers Who Didn't Care

I've had many teachers in my life who just didn't care about students. Sure, I've had some good teachers, too, but they were definitely in the minority. Most of the teachers I've had couldn't have cared less about helping me to learn and do well in school.

Take my high school geometry teacher for example. His name was Mr. D. That guy hated students--and especially me. I don't know why Mr. D ever became a teacher. Can you imagine someone who can't stand the sight of blood wanting to become a doctor? Well, that's how it was with Mr. D. Why did he become a teacher if he couldn't stand the sight of students?

Mr. D started the term by saying that he didn't expect more than half of us to pass the course. Great! There were about twenty-five of us in the class, so you can imagine how we felt. We had a 50-50 chance of passing, and with my track record in math, the odds were even longer.

Right after the first test, on which I scored a big fat 45, I knew I was in trouble. After he handed back the papers, I asked Mr. D if he was going over the test in class so we could find out where we went wrong. He gave me a look that could have melted a stone statue. Then he said that he didn't want to waste time going over what he had already taught. He told me to study the textbook and help myself. Wonderful! That textbook might have been written in Japanese for all the sense I could make of it. When I told Mr. D that I couldn't understand the text, he replied that my test score was proof enough of that. He said it right in front of the whole class, just to embarrass me, I'm sure.

My father came to school and asked Mr. D if he would give me some extra help. Mr. D was as smooth as cream when he spoke to my father. Of course he would help. He was only too happy to put in extra time with students who needed it. Big deal! His idea of "extra time" consisted of five minutes going over a homework assignment with me. He went through the problems so fast that I couldn't follow a thing he said. Then he told me that he was on his break period and had other, more important things to do.

Naturally, I failed the course and had to take geometry in summer school in order to graduate on time. The summer school teacher was much better at explaining how to solve the problems. And she didn't mind staying after class to give me some extra help with the toughest problems. With her help and some tutoring from my friend Bob, I managed to squeeze out a passing grade.

I also had an English teacher in high school who thought everyone had to write like Shakespeare before they could pass her course. She made me rewrite my first paper five times before she finally broke down and gave it a passing grade. In fact, I had to rewrite each of my essays at least twice in order to meet her so-called standards. She didn't care that she was ruining my weekends and making me a nervous wreck. I really earned the C+ she gave me for the course.

My French teacher was another slave driver. I was pretty good at reading and writing French, but that wasn't good enough for Mrs. L. I also had to speak French with a perfect Paris accent. Whenever I was called on to recite, Mrs. L made me repeat the words over and over until she was satisfied that I sounded "somewhat French." She didn't care how much she made me sweat. Some teachers have no mercy.

So, as you can see, I've had my share of teachers who didn't care about their students. If you ask me, most teachers don't care.

Peer Responses: Constructive Criticism

Michael's instructor asked him if he would mind being the first student to have his essay duplicated and distributed to the class for discussion. The instructor explained that learning how to offer and receive constructive criticism would be a major feature of the semester's work. She emphasized that peer responses can be very helpful in learning what is effective or ineffective in the first draft of a paper. Such feedback, the instructor continued, helps students to find out how well they communicate with each other in writing. Michael did not have to agree with his classmates' comments—whether negative or positive—but the instructor advised him to consider peer responses carefully before revising his draft into the final paper.

Michael agreed to share the first draft with his classmates, realizing that, although peer responses might have an unpleasant side, the feedback would motivate him to improve his writing. Besides, he liked the idea of discovering what his classmates found interesting. By reading each other's essays, everyone would get to know each other better, and the class would be more personal as well as more productive.

A Sample of Peer Responses

The instructor distributed copies of Michael's first draft to the class, and this is what some of his peers had to say.

Instructor: Now that we've all read Michael's paper, why don't we start discussing it by offering our first impressions. Let's not be too analytical right off the bat. Instead, we'll just express how the paper struck us immediately after we read it, and maybe offer a brief explanation for why we felt as we did. Jerry, do you want to begin?

Jerry: I liked it a lot.

Instructor: Okay, by "like" I guess you mean that there was something about the paper that made you feel a certain way?

Jerry: Right. I liked the way Michael told the truth about teachers. I felt he was saying things I've wanted to say for a long time.

Instructor: For instance?

Jerry: How most teachers don't really care about students.

Peggy: I didn't get that from the essay. I think that Michael wasn't very . . . well, fair in his opinion about teachers.

Michael: Fair? What does "fair" have to do with it! I wanted to tell exactly how I felt.

Susan: But you were fair, too. You told us that you had your problems with some subjects in high school.

Michael: That's right. I wasn't trying to pretend I was a perfect student. In fact, I needed a lot of help. But when I asked for help, where were the Mrs. Browns? They weren't in my school, that's for sure.

Carlos: I like the way Michael wrote his ideas. I mean, you could tell he was mad, but he also showed a sense of humor.

Instructor: For instance?

Carlos: Like when he said he didn't know why Mr. D wanted to be a teacher, because it was like someone who couldn't stand the sight of blood wanting to become a doctor. I liked that part.

Stanley: I agree that Michael has a sarcastic sense of humor, but I want to go back to what Peggy said about fairness. I could see where the math teacher didn't care, but the other teachers Michael mentioned aren't in the same category.

Alan: I was thinking about that, too. The English teacher was very strict about what she wanted, but she cared. She made Michael work on his writing. I don't mind a teacher who's strict, as long as she's trying to help me learn.

Bettina: And the same goes for the French teacher, I think.

Instructor: So, what are we saying?

Peggy: That maybe Michael shouldn't mix up strict teachers with those who don't care.

Connie: Also, he said the summer school teacher was great. So how does that fit in with not caring? The title of the paper is "Teachers Who Didn't Care." But that's not what the whole essay is about. Shouldn't all the teachers Michael mentions be ones who didn't care?

Jerry: Yeah. That's right. All the teachers should be examples of bad teachers, not just Mr. D.

Instructor: Michael?

Michael: Well, they were examples . . . in a way . . . but . . . wait. Just let me think about this a minute.

Carol: Can I say something, please?

Instructor: You certainly may.

Carol: We're talking about Michael's paper as if we know better than he does what he wanted to say. That's what bothers me about English classes. "Why did the writer say this? Why did the writer say that?" Michael knows what he wanted to say, so what's the difference what we think? He doesn't need us to tell him how to write his paper.

Instructor: How about that, Michael? Do you feel that some of us are confusing our own ideas with those you have written?

Michael: Sometimes I feel the way Carol just said. But I have to admit that there's a difference between what I thought I said and what my paper actually says. Does that make any sense?

Instructor: I think so.

Michael: I mean, when I write something, I know what I want to say. But I can see that people get confused if you mix up ideas and things in a paper.

Lenny: It's a good paper. It's just that some of your examples don't fit in the way you thought they would.

Michael: Yeah, I see that now. I went overboard because I still get angry whenever I think of Mr. D. I didn't think enough about what I was writing. Maybe I should forget the whole thing and begin all over again.

Stanley: I don't think so. A lot of this paper is good. Maybe you should stick to writing just about Mr. D. You know, build up that part a little more. Then the essay will be better organized.

Instructor: How does Stanley's advice strike you, Michael?

Michael: I like it. There are a few more things I wouldn't mind saying about Mr. D.

Connie: I'm not sure Michael has to limit himself to writing about Mr. D. Couldn't he use the summer school teacher as an example of a teacher who did care? Then he could compare a good teacher with Mr. D, and we'd get a better idea of just how bad Mr. D was.

Michael: That makes sense, too. So what should I do, Professor?

Instructor: You're the writer. Think about these suggestions, and decide which approach you want to take when you revise your first draft. Does anyone have anything else to offer?

Susan: Mostly, I like the way Michael wrote, but in a few places he used some words that just don't sound right.

Instructor: For instance?

Susan: He used "guy" when he talked about the math teacher, which I don't think is right. It's too slangy for an essay like this. And he said the French teacher was a "slave driver" who made him "sweat." Those words just don't sound right to me.

Tony: I agree that "guy" doesn't belong in this paper. But the other words sound all right. What's wrong with them?

Susan: "Perspire" is a better word than "sweat," and "slave driver" is a cliché.

Tony: Oh, come on! Nobody would say a teacher "made me perspire"! Teachers make you *sweat*, man!

This discussion of Michael's first draft continued a bit longer, but you've probably read enough to understand the benefits of peer responses. Notice that Michael's classmates brought up a lot of ideas that he should consider in revising his draft. Besides learning how his peers felt about his ideas and how he communicated them, Michael got feedback about how the essay could be organized better, and he also got suggestions about the words he used.

Imagine yourself as one of Michael's classmates. What comments would you make about his first draft? Are your suggestions as constructive as those offered by Michael's peers? Which comments do you think were most helpful? Which were least helpful?

Now let's see how Michael reacted to peer responses. The second draft of his paper follows.

A Teacher Who Didn't Care

I've had many teachers in my life. Most of them tried to help me to learn, even though there were things about them that I didn't like. Some were so strict about rules that they ran their classes as if the students were soldiers. Others tried to be too friendly, and, as a result, didn't get much done in class. Overall, though, I feel these teachers cared about me as a person and wanted me to learn. But I've also had some teachers who didn't care whether I learned anything or not. The worst of these was my high school geometry teacher, Mr. D.

Mr. D started the term by saying that he didn't expect more than half the class to pass the course. He said this in such a cold, sarcastic way that nobody had any doubt that he meant what he said. With my terrible track record in math, I knew that I was all but doomed. From that first day, I could tell that Mr. D hated students. Can you imagine someone who couldn't stand the sight of blood becoming a doctor? So why did Mr. D become a teacher if he couldn't stand the sight of students?

After the first test, on which I scored an embarrassing 45, I asked Mr. D if he would go over the test in class so we could find out where we went wrong. He gave me a look that could have melted a statue and said that he didn't want to waste time going over what he had already taught. He told me to study the textbook and to figure things out for myself. Wonderful! That book might have been written in Chinese for all the sense I could make of it. When I told Mr. D I couldn't understand the book's explanations, he replied that my test score was proof enough of that. He said it right in front of the whole class, just to embarrass me, I'm sure.

My father came to school and asked Mr. D to give me some extra help. Mr. D, as smooth as cream, said that he was only too happy to put in extra time with students who needed it. I began to think that maybe he wasn't such a hard-hearted person after all. But was I mistaken! Mr. D's idea of "extra time" consisted of five minutes going over a homework assignment with me. He went over the problems so fast, I couldn't follow a thing he said. Then he told me he was on his break period and had more important things to do.

During one part of the term, I actually understood the work more than I had up to that point. I studied hard, because I thought if I could pass one of Mr. D's tests, I might gain some confidence and maybe squeeze out a passing grade for the course. The test wasn't easy, but I felt that I had done enough problems correctly to score at least the 65 that would pass.

When I got my paper back, there was a large 55 on it, but I couldn't believe I had done that badly. I checked my paper against the test of a friend who had gotten a 70. No matter how we figured, I had gotten enough right answers to pass. So I showed my paper to Mr. D the next day and asked if he had made a mistake. He told me there was no mistake. He had deducted ten points because I hadn't shown clearly enough how I had solved the problems. And he wasn't interested in going over the test with me, so I could show him that the figuring was there, even if it was a little sloppy and hard to read. After that I had no confidence at all. I couldn't pass one of Mr. D's tests, even when I passed one.

Naturally I failed the course and had to take geometry in summer school in order to graduate on time. Luckily for me--and for the other fourteen students who failed Mr. D's course--Ms. L taught the geometry class that summer. She had a way of making math much easier to understand. She made up problems of her own that were much more interesting and helpful than the problems in the textbook. And best of all, she didn't mind staying after class to give extra help. Sometimes she became frustrated when I kept coming up with wrong answers to easy problems, but I could tell that she didn't think I was stupid. In fact, she told me I had a perfectly good mind but that geometry wasn't my best subject. What a difference from Mr. D, who went out of his way to make me feel like a hopeless case.

I passed geometry that summer, and so did about ninety percent of the class. It wasn't because Ms. L was an easy marker. Her exams were just as tough as Mr. D's. The difference was that I had actually learned something from Ms. L.

Mr. D was a teacher who didn't care about students. Luckily, Ms. L did care, so my term with Mr. D didn't permanently destroy my confidence. Still, I feel sorry for all the students who have teachers like Mr. D and never get the chance to regain their confidence from a teacher like Ms. L.

Considering the Second Draft

Michael's second draft shows that peer responses had definite effects on his thinking and writing. Consider the following questions and think about the decisions Michael made when he revised his paper:

- Which peer responses did Michael take seriously? To what extent did classmates' suggestions affect the organization of his paper?
- Which peer responses did Michael ignore or not take seriously? Do you agree with his decisions?
- Did all of Michael's changes and additions improve his first draft? Which changes, if any, do you think Michael should not have made?
- What advice would you give Michael if he asked you how he could improve the second draft of his paper?

Other Responses, Other Essays

Earlier in the chapter we showed four responses to the essay "Mary and Mrs. Brown." We then concentrated on Michael's response to show how he benefited from the reading-responding process. Let's return now to those other students. As we will see, Responders 2 and 3, Carol and Stanley, also developed their initial ideas through peer responses to arrive at their essays. But Responder 4, Elissa, switched her topic entirely and ended up focusing on one of her classmate's responses, which she felt took a wrong-headed approach to students like Mary.

Before each of the following essays is a brief description of how the writer arrived at his or her final topic. These essays, along with Michael's, show the variety of responses and topics that can be triggered by a single piece of writing. Each essay reflects the unique response of its writer. Before reading the essays, however, look back at the three students' initial responses to "Mary and Mrs. Brown."

Responder 2: Carol

Most of Carol's classmates agreed with her criticism of Mrs. Brown for buying Mary gifts. They felt that a teacher shouldn't buy things for a student, even if the gifts did somehow help a maladjusted student to feel better about herself. The consensus was that such a practice could get out of hand and could encourage other students to misbehave, hoping to receive a "bribe" from the teacher for good behavior. The class did not agree, however, about how much time and effort a teacher should spend on troubled students. About half the class thought that a good teacher would give extra attention to students whose personal problems interfered with their schoolwork. But there was also strong support for the idea that teachers should be concerned primarily with helping students to understand subject matter, and that they should not see themselves as psychological counselors.

Carol felt uneasy as she read about Mrs. Brown's special acts of kindness toward Mary. She wondered whether the other students were being neglected. The essay made her realize that she has never liked the way our society seems to care more about troublemakers than about the majority who get along nicely and follow the accepted standards of behavior. And as for students who experience difficulty learning their subjects, Carol believed that all of them—not just those who are troubled—should receive the teacher's attention. As a result of peer responses and further thinking, Carol decided to write about the need for teachers to ignore the losers and concentrate on the average and better students. Her first draft follows.

Misplaced Kindness

At first the story of how Mrs. Brown helped Mary made me

feel good because I enjoy reading about kind people. But then I

began to think about the other students in Mrs. Brown's class who also needed help. Maybe they were not as needy as Mary, but they could have used some extra attention to make them good students instead of just average ones. When a teacher spends too much time and energy on the losers, the rest of the students have to improve all by themselves. Most of them cannot do it alone, and so that means Mrs. Brown was not a good example of a perfect teacher.

Many of the students in my classes were like Mary in some way or another, and most of the teachers especially in grade school gave extra time to these "difficult" students. That meant that the rest of us had to sit around very bored, or else we fooled around, while those teachers played Mommy to misbehaving children or those who did not really care about school. I resented the fact that these teachers did not help me to do better in math and science, my worst enemies.

The writer wants us to believe that Mrs. Brown's efforts paid off in a big way for Mary, but I would not bet any money on how well Mary ever did as a result of all that love and TLC. Some of the students in my classes who received extra attention are now unable to hold a job. What good did that special treatment do them? Furthermore, most of those losers never really wanted the extra help; they just did not dare refuse it. But the worst part of all this is that some of my friends who barely managed to pass are now running into trouble as they try to handle college work. If that extra help had gone to them, they would have made good use of it and would not be struggling to survive now.

I think that the article was meant to make teachers feel guilty if they are not giving all of themselves to their students, especially those at the bottom. This writer thinks she knows what is best, but she really does not understand the students. Doesn't she realize that most dropouts just plain do not like school? All they want to do is hang out. They actually resent teachers meddling in their personal lives. My advice to the teachers of the world is to concentrate on those who can really use their help. Let the losers stay lost.

Responder 3: Stanley

In a small-group discussion with classmates, Stanley said that he had not been able to concentrate on the essay very well because he was worried about his sister's behavior. He realized his response may have seemed a little strange because it grew out of his personal distress rather than what the writer of "Mary and Mrs. Brown" was saying. He could not help identifying his sister with Mary, even though his sister was older than Mary and her problems seemed more severe. The group encouraged Stanley to write about his sister, since that was how he responded to the essay.

Stanley was almost convinced, but he thought he should check this idea with his instructor because he wasn't sure it was a proper topic. Stanley's instructor understood why he had responded to the essay as he did, and she added that people are sometimes able to relieve tension and anxiety by writing about their feelings. She encouraged Stanley to develop his response into a paper about his sister's behavior, even though the topic did not follow directly from the essay. The important thing for all writers, she said, is to discover a topic that truly means something to them. Stanley then wrote the following paper.

A Young Woman in Big Trouble

My own adolescence had its ups and downs, but for the most part I enjoyed growing up. Maybe things went well for me because I moved ahead at a normal pace, and I got along pretty well with my parents most of the time. On the other hand, my fourteen-year-old sister, Joann, seems to be having a very rough time. She hardly speaks to Mom and Dad, and she has fallen in with a wild bunch who are always getting into trouble of one kind or another. I wish some understanding person could see Joann's need for help and find some way to reach out to her. I believe Joann's tough attitude is just her way of keeping her personal pain hidden from the world. Somebody outside our family must get through to her before she wrecks her life.

Joann's problem goes back a long way. She came along when I was seven and my older sister Clare was nine. Mother had gone back to her job as a pediatric nurse and did not want to return to the role of housewife/mother. So babysitters were hired to care for Joann until she was old enough to go to kindergarten. None of them stayed very long. When I think back about Joann as a small child, I see a sour-faced brat, whose tears and shouts seemed fake about half the time.

School solved the babysitting problem because Clare and I could be assigned that job when we came home from school. I resented having to look after Joann, and I probably took my frustration out on her some of the time. Then she hit sixth grade, and everything changed.

When Joann, who wins the prize for good looks in our family, turned twelve, she became popular in school for the first time. Not with the teachers--she has never done well on report cards, especially in "attitude"--but with those girls who dress like Brooke Shields and act like they are eighteen. When Mother saw Joann's rapid transformation, she began criticizing her behavior, instead of just complaining as we had all been doing for years. Clare and I felt our parents were being a bit hard on Joann, but we were not worried then because we had fought with them about those things ourselves.

Recently, it became clear to us that the group of girls Joann hangs out with are even more rebellious than we had thought. They spend their afternoons and weekends with guys who are

much older and wilder than is good for someone Joann's age.
When Clare and I try to talk to Joann about the situation, she will
not listen. She tells us to mind our own business.

Since I cannot see Joann responding to any of us, I
desperately hope that someone she can respect will come along
and take note of her troubled condition. She needs a true friend,
and soon!

Responder 4: Elissa

When Elissa heard some of her classmates criticize Mrs. Brown for
"wasting the other students' time on a loser like Mary," she wanted to rise
to the teacher's defense. Having raised a family before returning to college, Elissa believed she had learned something about life, and in her view
the idea of labeling people as "losers" could have grave effects on those
persons' lives. After the class had discussed each other's responses, Elissa
forgot how strongly she felt about this issue, and she proceeded to write
an essay that supported the general idea that teachers like Mrs. Brown are
rare and valuable. However, she found it difficult to say something dis-
tinctly different from what she had read. Even though she added a couple
of examples from her own earlier days in school, the essay as a whole
didn't seem to carry much punch. She felt it sounded like an echo of
"Mary and Mrs. Brown."

When the instructor asked one morning whether anyone was having
trouble writing the essay, Elissa raised her hand and described her predicament. Remembering that Elissa had rather forcefully defended the helping
of so-called losers, the instructor asked Elissa if she still felt as strongly
about that issue. Reminded of her reaction to the other student's response,
Elissa asked whether she could still switch topics. The instructor assured
her that the purpose of sharing responses was to allow each student to find
the best possible topic, and Elissa decided to write about her strongest
feelings. As you will see, her essay came out very nicely.

A Response to the Writer Who Would Abandon "Losers"

When we were asked to present our responses to "Mary and
Mrs. Brown," I expected the usual boring class discussion. But I
was amazed to find that some people felt Mrs. Brown was not an
outstanding teacher. I was especially surprised to hear some
people refer to students with problems as "losers." When I was in

high school, I had trouble in several subjects, and if some teachers hadn't gone out of their way for this "loser," I would not be here today.

The word "loser" is very offensive, for it says the speaker is a "winner." The winner/loser view of life causes many of the problems in our world today. You're not a winner unless you own a huge house, drive expensive cars, have all the latest video and audio systems, spend vacations in faraway places, etc. The winners all use the right soap, drink the right beer, wear the "in" jeans. Anyone else is a nerd and a loser. Winning girls don't even notice losing boys, and vice versa. Sports are fun only if you win; business is full of cheaters competing to be winners. Even Russia and America are thinking about "winning" a nuclear war!

This attitude sees most people as losers. And that means a lot of average people working at everyday jobs, enjoying simple pleasures, are losers who are obviously missing something valuable in their lives. This leaves a lot of people feeling lousy while they are envying the winners. Advertising encourages this attitude in its effort to sell things that promise to make us feel like winners. All this is so wrong. There is no winning in life, only moments of happiness. I'd rather live a happy life, enjoying my relationships with people who mean something to me because they love me and I love them.

School is where this win/lose attitude starts. There, knowing fewer than 65 answers to 100 questions is considered losing. No one asks what difference it makes whether you know all that information. Most of it is soon forgotten anyway. Some people learn more easily than others, generally because they have a special talent (English, math) or because they really like a subject (history, science). That's fine, but the others shouldn't be thought of as losers. Soon they begin to feel like losers, and this negative feeling can carry over to the rest of their lives, unless they have a talent for playing sports or for being popular, which allows them to win a big game or a beautiful girlfriend or boyfriend.

A sensitive teacher like Mrs. Brown knows how important it is to keep children from becoming "losers." She tried to help a troubled student feel she was worth something to someone. Mary may have trouble holding a job after she graduates (and she may not graduate without help from some other Mrs. Browns). But that's not a sign of losing. Who knows where she may end up years later? She may raise a happy family and truly enjoy the simple parts of life--weddings, family picnics, watching TV with family and friends, walking through a park, reading, cooking delicious meals, helping a neighbor out of trouble, feeling close to her husband. If she believes she is a loser, maybe she won't be able to enjoy these experiences, because she'll be reminded by TV and all those would-be winners that the simple joys are not good enough.

A REVIEW OF THE PROCESS
(How *You* Should Use This Book)

Now that you have been through the reading-responding process that forms the basis of this book, let's review the steps and activities that make up the process. The following suggestions about reading and responding will help you prepare to write your essay.

1. Start by reading the assignment and recording your strongest first impressions. Don't analyze the essay or story during this first reading. Instead, let your thoughts run free. At this point you are less interested in what the author had in mind than you are in what comes to *your* mind as you read.
2. Depending on your instructor's guidance, share your impressions and responses through class discussion, by exchanging your ideas with one or more classmates, or by working in small groups. Even friends and roommates who aren't in this class can be helpful during this stage. By trying out your ideas on others, you will think about the essay or story in greater detail and will gain insights into why you responded as you did.
3. When you have a fairly clear idea of what you want to write about, decide upon a topic and begin to write. Remember that the topic you first select may not be the one that you finally write about. Michael, for example, changed the title of his essay because of peer responses to his first draft. In any case, the topic you choose at this point will help you to organize your ideas as you begin to write your first draft.
4. When you have completed your first draft, put it aside for a day or two. This "break" from your work will allow you to reread your draft with the fresh eyes of a reader coming to your words for the first time. When you do reread the draft, you probably will note places where it could be improved through revision. Any time you have to pause or reread a passage in order to remember what you had in mind, you know you need to revise. After all, if you, the writer, have difficulty following the flow of ideas, your readers are certain to have problems. This is your chance to edit any confusing or awkward passages. Now copy your revised first draft neatly and submit it for peer responses to see how well you have expressed your ideas.
5. Peer responses may be gathered through class discussion of your first draft, such as the discussion of Michael's paper. But feedback and constructive criticism can also take place in a small, informal group or in conversations with anyone whose opinions you value. The important point is that you share your first draft and get some sort of peer response, for nothing can replace the insights you will gain from other people's reactions to your writing.

6. After you have discussed your paper with peers, the next step is to decide which of their suggestions and criticism you want to apply in revising the paper. The ability to select suggestions that will strengthen your essays is a vital part of writing, and your ability to do so will improve with each assignment. Be prepared for criticism, and ask yourself *why* your peers responded as they did to your first draft. Even a remark that you consider foolish or insulting may contain a germ of truth—if you listen to it with an open mind.

7. Now you are ready to revise your first draft to reflect those peer responses that you find valuable. Focus especially on suggestions about the organization and wording of your ideas. Did every example you offered contribute to the overall point you wanted to make, or did some readers wonder why you included a particular detail? Did anyone object to your language? Was anyone confused by a point that seemed clear to you? Did your peers find the essay satisfying and complete, or did they feel it just sort of wandered off? Maybe you need to strengthen the conclusion of your paper so that readers will put it down knowing exactly what you meant.

Professional writers know that the process of editing never stops, for the reactions of readers always lead them to see new ideas and ways of saying things. No doubt your second draft also could be improved by seeking further feedback and revising the paper one more time. At some point, however, the writer decides to publish the paper and move on to other things. In this book, too, we encourage you to end the reading-responding process when you have completed your second draft. Move on to the next reading, which will offer a new opportunity to express yourself.

RESPONDING TO PEOPLE

The readings in Part One express writers' ideas and feelings about themselves and about other people. Such essays are likely to stimulate your own ideas and feelings about people you know or have known. You may want to write about someone important in your life, or you may be moved to express something about yourself. As you learned in the Introduction, each reader responds to a piece of writing in unique, unpredictable ways. The best way to discover what impact one of these readings has on you is to record your strongest response to it as soon as you finish reading. Then follow the process illustrated in the Introduction to develop an essay of your own. First, share your response with your classmates, and use their comments to adjust and expand the ideas you plan to write about. Then share your first draft with your peers, and consider their constructive criticism carefully when you revise the draft into your finished essay.

As in the Introduction, the first three essays in Part One are followed by sample responses to help you assess your own ideas. In addition, we have provided comments and questions to guide you in considering the sample responses and how they can be developed into complete essays. You should raise similar questions about your own responses and those of your classmates.

Photograph by David M. Grossman

WITHOUT EMOTION

G. GORDON LIDDY

Squirrel hunting was a popular sport in West Caldwell in the   1
1940s. I loaded my homemade rifle, cocked the spring, and
waited on the steps of the porch. A squirrel was in the top of the
pear tree. I raised the rifle. The movement startled the squirrel
and he jumped to the oak tree and froze as I stepped off the
porch. I sighted along the side of the barrel, aimed for the squirrel's head, and fired.

I missed the squirrel's head and gut-shot him. Bravely, he   2
clung to the tree as long as he could, then started to come down,
clutching piteously at branches as he fell, wounded mortally.

I didn't know it, but the shot alerted my mother. She watched   3
the furry creature's descent until it fell to the ground and I shot it
again, this time through the head at point-blank range, to put it
out of its suffering, then cut off its tail to tie to the handlebars of
my bicycle as an ornament.

When I came into the house my mother told me reproachfully   4
that she had seen from the kitchen window the suffering I had
caused. I went off and wept. The dying squirrel haunted me. I
kept seeing it fall, clutching and clawing from what must have
been a terribly painful wound. I was furious with myself—not
because I'd caused the pain, though I regretted that, but because
I hadn't been able to kill without emotion. How could I expect to
be a soldier in the war? I had to do something to free myself from
this disabling emotionalism.

I cast about for an idea and found it across the street. Bill Jaco-   5
bus's father, to help combat the wartime food shortage and to
supplement rationing, had built a chicken coop in his backyard.

He and his son used to butcher the chickens, then drain, scald, pluck, and clean them for sale.

I asked young Bill if I could help kill the chickens. He was glad 6 to have the help. He showed me how to grasp the bird in such a way as to have control of both wings and feet, lay its neck on an upended stump, and then decapitate it with one chop of an ax held in the other hand. Bill explained that the shock made the corpse convulse and, if I let go, the body would run about, wings flapping, and bruise the meat. I'd need to control the corpse until the shock wore off and the limp body could be hung up by the feet to drain the remaining blood. I should wear my old clothes.

Using the ax tentatively rather than making a bold stroke, I 7 made a mess of my first chicken kill; it took me a number of chops to get the head off. The bird slipped out of my grasp and half flew, half jumped about, blood spurting from its neck all over me and everything else in range. Bill was good about it and gave me another chance.

I got better at it, and over a period of time I killed and killed 8 and killed, getting less and less bloody, swifter and swifter, surer with my ax stroke until, finally, I could kill efficiently and without emotion or thought. I was satisfied: when it came my turn to go to war, I would be ready. I could kill as I could run—like a machine.

Sample Responses to "Without Emotion"

Responder 1: Maria

Liddy has the kind of mentality that keeps the human race going from one war to another throughout all of history. It's people like Liddy who can't wait for the first gun to be fired so they can kill people without going to prison. In fact he wants to kill enough people that he will be awarded a medal saying he's a hero. We must keep our eyes on someone like Liddy to make sure he doesn't get any power if we want to keep the earth from being destroyed in a nuclear war. Squirrels and chickens are just a warmup for a guy who loves war. What he would really like to do is to drop a few H-bombs on small countries that couldn't retaliate. Even if it led to World War III and everybody, including him, was killed, that wouldn't bother a guy like Liddy who's in love with war and death. This character scares the hell out of me.

Responder 2: Atkins

It takes great discipline and training to make good soldiers. Liddy wanted to be prepared for combat just in case his service was needed to defend our country. His childhood happened during the war with Germany and Japan when people believed America was right and were willing to die for democracy. Today many people would say Liddy is crazy because they don't believe in America any more. They want to live here, but they don't want to risk their skin defending the USA. A lot of my friends would leave the country rather than fight in a war. That's terrific! Who do they think will stop the Russians from marching into their houses and killing and raping their families? The world was lucky these guys weren't around when Hitler and Tojo were trying to conquer the world.

Responder 3: Sydney

Sick! Sick! Sick! Sick! Sick! Sick!

Responder 4: Caroline

I despise persons who think animals were put on earth to be tortured and killed for human pleasure. Animals are living things and have feelings just like people. They also feel pain and pleasure. Their lives are valuable to them, and to God, even if brave men like Gordon Liddy don't place any value on them. Brave little Gordon Liddy thought he had the right to decide when animals should die if he felt like having some target practice. Recently, I saw a television picture of baby seals being mercilessly clubbed to death in Canada so that rich women could wear their beautiful fur. That was the most horrible scene I've seen in years. If I were president I'd have those men shot. I know I will never wear a fur coat or anything else made from the skins of innocent animals.

Responder 5: Brad

G. Gordon Liddy was convicted of breaking into Democratic party headquarters during the Watergate scandal which forced Richard Nixon to abdicate. Now this convicted felon writes his memoirs and some immoral publishing company sells them for millions. This disgraceful transaction reveals the profound depths which our once great nation has fallen into. The heads of today's Americans have more holes than Swiss cheese. They read a crook's confessions as if it was another inane soap opera; worse yet, they spend good money on such rubbish. Liddy's rich; Nixon's rich; any criminal can become wealthy if his crime makes the TV news. Corrupt people become heroes in our decadent society. How can we expect America to regain its rightful place as world leader as long as these disgusting people's lives are presented as models for children to look up to and envy.

Considering the Responses

Response 1: Maria

Maria sees Liddy as an example of the kind of people she intensely dislikes and even fears. Notice two phrases that Maria used which reveal the "example" approach: "It's people like Liddy . . ." and "We must keep our eyes on someone like Liddy . . ."

1. Do you think Maria can expand this response into an essay that develops her ideas about people like Liddy? Give reasons to defend your point of view.

2. What other examples can Maria use to support her opinions? Can you think of any problems she might have in using examples to support her opinion?
3. What do you think is Maria's main objection to Liddy and others like him? Is there a better way for her to state her case, other than using the example approach?
4. If Maria followed your advice, would Liddy still be the focus of her essay, or would he appear in a minor role? Why?

Response 2: Atkins

Atkins admired Liddy's determination to be ready for war if America ever needed him. He pointed out the reasons for Liddy's patriotism and contrasted Liddy's attitudes with those of his friends and most young Americans today.

1. Do you believe that patriotism or the lack of it is the main idea Atkins should explore? Why or why not? What other ideas do you see in this response to the Liddy piece?
2. What questions would you ask Atkins to help him develop an essay from his response?
3. What advice would you give Atkins about how to organize his essay?

Response 3: Sydney

Although Sydney's response is unusually brief, it does indicate a strong emotional reaction to the reading.

1. What do you think Sydney felt that caused him to respond by writing the same word six times?
2. What must Sydney do before he can develop his response into an essay?
3. What questions or advice do you have for Sydney?

Response 4: Caroline

Caroline's response shows less concern with Liddy than with an issue which the reading raised in her mind.

1. What do you think is the issue Caroline is concerned about? Do you think she has tied that issue closely enough to Liddy's piece in her response? Why or why not?
2. How would *you* tie Liddy's comments to the issue on Caroline's mind?

3. What is your advice to Caroline as she contemplates writing an essay to persuade us to agree with her stand?

Response 5: Brad

Brad, like Maria, sees Liddy as an example of a kind of person he dislikes.

1. What do you think is the basis for Brad's negative reaction to Liddy? What connection do you see between Brad's response and this portion of Liddy's autobiography?
2. Do you see any way that Brad can express his deep concerns and still focus on Liddy? What approach do you think Brad should take?

BEETHOVEN

HENRY T. THOMAS
DANA L. THOMAS

In keeping with his ardent temperament, Beethoven was al-   1
ways falling in love with some woman or other. He strictly refrained, however, from poaching upon the preserves of married
folk. "It is one of my foremost principles," he said, "never to occupy any other relations than those of friendship with the wife of
another man." Perhaps it is true, as some cynics would have us
believe, that chastity is largely a question of physical appearance
rather than one of spiritual restraint. It is easy for a homely person to remain morally pure. Certainly Beethoven was not the
type of man to conquer the female heart. In his youth he made a
proposal of marriage to the beautiful opera singer, Magdalena
Willmann, but nothing came of the proposal. In later years,
when asked why she had refused Beethoven, she laughingly replied, "Because he was so ugly, and half crazy!"

Added to his other physical defects was his deafness, which   2
had begun to press down upon him shortly before the comple-
tion of his *First Symphony*. Deafness and romance have never
been on speaking terms. Tender words of affection are meant to
be whispered, not shouted. The women of Beethoven's circle admired him, pitied him, at times even adored him; but they never
loved him. They showered him with invitations to give concerts
at their homes. So busy was he at times with these concerts that
he was obliged to begin some of them as early as six o'clock in
the morning. And he always drew audiences to fill "the capacity
of the house." It was an age of musical virtuosity. "In Vienna,"
remarked the famous pianist Hummel, "there are a hundred

ladies who can play the piano better than I.'' And these ladies were anxious to hear and to applaud Beethoven. But not to flirt with him. One does not flirt with a god—especially when he is homely and deaf.

Beethoven's deafness was almost more than he could bear. For   3 it not only isolated him from society but it removed him from the sound of his own music. "This affliction," he wrote, "is more difficult for the artist than for any other man. . . . It was impossible for me to say to my friends, 'Speak louder, shout, for I am deaf.' Ah, was it possible for me to proclaim a deficiency in that one sense which in my case ought to have been more perfect than in all others? . . . For me there can be no recreation in human society, refined conversation, mutual exchange of thoughts and feelings. . . . I must live like an exile. . . . A little more and I should have put an end to my life."

But he soon gave up the thought of death. He had something to   4 live for—his art. "Art alone has detained me. . . . I have emptied the cup of bitter suffering. . . . It shall be transformed into beauty in my soul. . . ." Suffering, and patience, and work. "I owe it to myself, to mankind and to the Almighty. . . . I must write my music . . . to the eternal glory of God."

Sample Responses to "Beethoven"

Responder 1: Jeffrey

This story tells it like it is. Women don't care how intelligent a man is or what a nice person he is--they only care about his looks. Even a genius like Beethoven couldn't find a woman to love him, because he was so ugly. Girls today are just the same. They go crazy over some guy with big muscles or a handsome face who hasn't got a brain in his head. Of course, when you talk with a girl, she says it's personality that counts, but that's a lot of bull. She'd rather be seen with a well-tanned lifeguard type than with an average guy who might really care about her as a human being.

Responder 2: Abby

These authors are extremely mean and nasty. They take great pleasure in ridiculing a man who was unlucky enough to be born without good looks. They also say Beethoven was morally pure only because no woman wanted to love an ugly man. But maybe Beethoven didn't believe in making love to a woman unless he was married. These writers seem to think that great people have to have a weakness of some kind. But why couldn't a genius like Beethoven also be a very moral person? Also, the writers make it sound as though Beethoven was a gorilla. I've seen pictures of him, and I think he looks all right. The writers even make fun of Beethoven's deafness. I don't understand why they would write about a person if they didn't have any respect for him.

Responder 3: Charles

This shows you can't have everything in life. Beethoven had great talent as a composer, but he couldn't get a woman no matter what he did. On the other hand, some men are so good looking that they can get any women they like just by snapping their fingers. So who is better off? Beethoven wasn't happy in love, but he was famous as a musical genius. A handsome dude may get pleasure from all his women friends, but nobody remembers him when he's gone. I think things come out even in the end, and nobody gets everything.

Responder 4: Sylvia

I love classical music, especially the works of Beethoven, and so I don't care how successful the man was as a lover. My interest lies only in his stirring music, which has brought pleasure and inspiration to millions of people throughout history. Perhaps we are fortunate that he wasn't so good looking. Maybe he was able to create such beautiful music as a result of being frustrated in his search for romance. It has been said that all great artists are unhappy. Beethoven seems to have had more than his share of pain and suffering, which may account for the greatness of his musical creations.

Considering the Responses

Response 1: Jeffrey

Jeffrey was quick to associate his own situation and Beethoven's failures with women. (Can you guess how the female students in Jeffrey's class reacted when they heard his response?)

1. In drafting his essay, do you think Jeffrey should stick to this rather extreme view of women? Why or why not?
2. Should Jeffrey rely on his own observations of particular women, or would he do better to explain why he thinks most women behave this way?
3. Do you think Jeffrey's essay can be effective if it leaves out any mention of men's behavior toward women? Why or why not?
4. How would you advise Jeffrey to handle his strong personal response in developing an essay? Do you think it would help if he added humor to his essay? Why or why not?

Response 2: Abby

Abby was unhappy with what she saw as an unpleasant portrait of Beethoven. She especially resented the authors' suggestion that Beethoven's morality reflected his physical unattractiveness rather than his strength of character. In class Abby remarked: "It's ridiculous to think that there is a relationship between a person's physical appearance and morality." She was surprised, however, to learn that several classmates thought there had to be some sort of relationship between "looks" and behavior, although they weren't sure what the relationship was or how much it affected a person's morality. Others believed that the relationship between appearance and morality was very strong, and they tended to agree with the authors' suggestion that an unattractive person has little choice but to be moral, especially in regard to sexual behavior.

Since no one in the class was inclined to admit being both unattractive and sexually immoral, the supporters of the authors' suggestion seemed to carry the discussion. One student did say that he knew a girl who was both beautiful and moral, and another mentioned a friend who was "kind of unattractive" but by no means moral. These examples, however, had little impact on those who believed that looks influence behavior. As one of them put it: "There are always exceptions, but, mostly, how people look is how they act." Abby was astounded that people could support what she called a "false belief," and she began to plan an essay to refute the idea.

1. How might Abby develop an essay that will support her point of view? Which of the ideas in her response should she emphasize?
2. Since Abby wants to persuade people to reconsider their belief that looks influence behavior, will she have to do more than offer examples of people whose behavior seems unrelated to their appearance? What other kinds of evidence can she offer to support her case?
3. Do you think Abby can succeed in changing her classmates' beliefs about looks and behavior? Why or why not?

Response 3: Charles

Charles seems to believe that everybody wins some and loses some in the game called life.

1. How might Charles substantiate and support his position? Do you think he should rely on his own experiences and on examples of people he knows or has read about? Or would such an essay sound something like a sermon that encourages people not to let their occasional losses depress them?
2. Do you think Charles can effectively use Beethoven and the "handsom dude" as examples to support the idea that we all win a little, lose a little? Can two examples prove this idea?
3. Do you think Charles has identified a strong enough topic to develop into an essay? Why or why not? What advice would you give him at this point?

Response 4: Sylvia

Sylvia seems to accept the notion that suffering and pain may inspire great art.

1. Should Syliva do additional research to support her point about suffering and art, or can she stick to Beethoven as an example?
2. Should Sylvia try to explain how Beethoven's particular suffering might have made him so creative? Do you think the reading provides enough evidence for Sylvia to work with?
3. Suppose Sylvia decides to write an essay that describes Beethoven's music and explains why she finds it "stirring" and "inspiring." What problems might she run into with this topic?

ROLF

SYLVIA ASHTON-WARNER

$\mathbf{A}$t school I found a new boy called Rolf Mannington, the 1
same age as me and who rode from across the Taura River on a
fat sleek pony, saddle too. A cared-for and handsome boy with
clear sunned skin, lovely grey eyes and a frequent friendly smile.
From him to us all there emanated a glamour that could not be
ignored, a kind of mystery, my downfall. Even his name was interesting.

Yet he was unacceptable. He was too clever by half at his 2
work, too good-looking, too happy and with too pleasant a natural goodwill. Too fortunate altogether. The mob doesn't like the
exceptional; it distrusts them to the point where it must destroy
them. One lunchtime as we all sat together beneath the pines, as
we watched him open a splendid lunch, we judged and convicted him on every count till resentment reached flashpoint.

I don't know who started it but we ganged up and beat him, 3
with our fists first. We had to break the stranger open, expose his
inside, kill out that in him which was different from us and
which we couldn't understand. Defuse his mystery. The more he
smiled as he sat on the grass the more we hit him until, getting
up, he struggled as far as the horse-paddock fence to try to escape on his pony. But we held his coat and he stuck in the wires
thoroughly at our mercy. Compelled to remove the smile from
him we picked up sticks and thrashed him.

We had to witness the fine one broken to see what he was 4
made of, to gloat on his private tears. We did see the fine one broken but not what he was made of. True, the smile left his face
and tears took its place but we still could not identify the source
of the glamour to eradicate it. As Rolf cried and groaned and

sagged in the wires the charisma remained with him so that as we returned to the pines to our lunches, gratified and justified, we only felt just as hungry for the food and anything but satisfied.

Moreover, this new boy not only did not tell Teacher but turned up the next morning exactly the same, his magnetism intact. The perfect answer to persecution. 5

Sample Responses to "Rolf"

Responder 1: Carrie

Nobody likes someone who has everything. That is why so many people like reading gossip magazines. They feel much better when they see that rich and famous people have serious personal problems and bad luck. They are even happier when they see that someone who is supposed to be very good turns out to be a crook or to mistreat his family. A movie like <u>Mommy Dearest</u> draws large audiences even though it is pretty stupid. Everyone wants to see just how awful a beautiful woman like Joan Crawford was to her child.

Responder 2: Leona

Children don't like goody-goodies because adults always shower them with praise and special favors. A teacher will say, "Why can't you all behave as well as Rolf?" Popular children learn to keep their distance from teachers even if they are good students. They make sure to make a few mistakes in class and to misbehave every once in a while.

Readers may think that the writer and her friends were terribly cruel to Rolf, but this is probably quite normal behavior. And Rolf learned something valuable from the incident. He now understands the way most people really feel.

Responder 3: Matthew

Why can't we accept goodness in others? It all begins with little children. When they are in a group, they become bullies and pick on those children who are somewhat different. This includes those who are very pleasant or very smart as well as those who are a little weird. Maybe kids don't get enough love at home, and that makes it hard for them to love others very much. So they envy anyone who seems really happy most of the time. It's like brothers and sisters; one is always thinking the other is getting more love and attention, and then hating them for it.

Responder 4: Migdalia

I knew a girl in junior high who was disliked by most of the students because she was very sweet and never took part in any activity that was the least bit bad. All the teachers thought Sarah was just splendid, and she constantly won awards. No one ever attacked her physically; in fact, she was elected class secretary; but everyone felt uncomfortable around her. Now she is studying to become a doctor and is planning to work with poor people in some part of the country where few doctors ever go.

My aunt says some people are too good for this world. Sarah and Rolf are like that. They are very confident of themselves and have no interest in doing things that are not right. The world needs more people like them, but most of us don't really like such people because they make us feel ashamed for not living up to our ideals.

Responder 5: Ronald

The writer's final comment is absurd--"The perfect answer to persecution." Is that what the Jews should have done when the

Nazis persecuted them? Most of them did not resist, but the persecution went on. Are black people supposed to come back the next day wearing a smile after being beaten or insulted by bigots? They accepted a hundred years of discrimination before Martin Luther King showed them how to resist persecution effectively. A century of humiliation was no "perfect answer."

Of course, Rolf was different. He was a young god. He seemed to belong to the master race. His refusal to retaliate worked out well because the other children envied him. In fact, his acceptance of the beating added to his perfect image, for the other children wished they could be so strong and cool in the face of adversity. For Rolf, such a response was a "perfect answer." But it would never work for the many victims of persecution in this world.

Considering the Responses

Response 1: Carrie

After reading or hearing about an act of cruelty, most people attempt to explain it, to find an underlying cause. Often they look for some psychological explanation that fits the particular villain, or, if a group perpetrated the cruelty, they search for some truth about human behavior. Carrie's response represents such an effort to explain. She sees Rolf's beating as an example of how people envy someone who is blessed by good fortune.

1. How would you advise Carrie to handle this idea in her essay? Should she present a series of examples to make her point, or should she just offer one major example of how envy affects people?
2. Should Carrie instead write an analysis of envy as a human weakness, explaining its origins and describing its effects? Which of these two approaches do you think Carrie should use? Why?

Response 2: Leona

Leona also wanted to examine the motive behind the attack, but she focused on a narrower topic, the children's dislike of the teacher's pet.

1. Do you think Leona's approach, which covers less ground, is better than Carrie's? Why or why not?
2. Can you suggest a good plan for Leona to follow in developing her essay? How would it differ from the approach you suggested for Carrie?
3. Suppose Leona asked you about this slightly different but broader idea that can be seen in her response: "Occasional cruelty is only natural and can sometimes help its victim in the long run." Which idea do you think Leona should write about, and how should she proceed?

Response 3: Matthew

Matthew chose another path to explain the children's cruelty; he analyzed the event in social and psychological terms.

1. Do you see a clear connection between children's tendency to bully those who are "different" and their jealousy of brothers or sisters who compete with them for parental love? Do you think Matthew can tie these two ideas together to create an effective essay? Why or why not?
2. Do you think Matthew would be better off developing just one of the ideas into an essay? If so, which one?
3. How would you develop this essay if you were Matthew?

Response 4: Migdalia

Midgalia's response covers a good deal of territory.

1. How many ideas can you find in Migdalia's response?
2. Which of her ideas do you think Migdalia should choose for the main thesis of her longer essay? Why?
3. Should Migdalia include the example of Sarah in her essay? If so, how much weight do you think she should give to it? Why?

Response 5: Ronald

This response may have surprised you a bit, since Ronald reacted not so much to the children's cruelty as to the writer's comment about the situation—the insight she hoped to convey to her readers. In fact, Ronald's response comes close to being a summary of a possible paper, for he has thought of several examples and has developed them fairly well. He has also described Rolf's situation at some length.

1. What should Ronald do now to expand his ideas into an essay? Which of the ideas should he explore? Can he use all of them?
2. What questions would you ask Ronald to help him develop his essay?
3. Can you suggest an outline for Ronald to follow in writing his essay?

ADDITIONAL READINGS

HENRI

GEORGE ORWELL

Or there was Henri, who worked in the sewers. He was a tall, melancholy man with curly hair, rather romantic-looking in his long, sewer-man's boots. Henri's peculiarity was that he did not speak, except for the purposes of work, literally for days together. Only a year before he had been a chauffeur in good employ and saving money. One day he fell in love, and when the girl refused him he lost his temper and kicked her. On being kicked the girl fell desperately in love with Henri, and for a fortnight they lived together and spent a thousand francs of Henri's money. Then the girl was unfaithful; Henry planted a knife in her upper arm and was sent to prison for six months. As soon as she had been stabbed the girl fell more in love with Henri than ever, and the two made up their quarrel and agreed that when Henri came out of jail he should buy a taxi and they would marry and settle down. But a fortnight later the girl was unfaithful again, and when Henri came out she was with child. Henri did not stab her again. He drew out all his savings and went on a drinking bout that ended in another month's imprisonment; after that he went to work in the sewers. Nothing would induce Henri to talk. If you asked him why he worked in the sewers he never answered, but simply crossed his wrists to signify handcuffs, and jerked his head southward, towards the prison. Bad luck seemed to have turned him half-witted in a single day.

FATHER

LANGSTON HUGHES

That summer in Mexico was the most miserable I have ever   1
known. I did not hear from my mother for several weeks. I did
not like my father. And I did not know what to do about either of
them.

My father was what the Mexicans called *muy americano*, a typi-   2
cal American. He was different from anybody I had ever known.
He was interested only in making money.

My mother and step-father were interested in making money,   3
too, so they were always moving about from job to job and from
town to town, wherever they heard times were better. But they
were interested in making money to *spend*. And for fun. They
were always buying victrolas and radios and watches and rings,
and going to shows and drinking beer and playing cards, and trying to have a good time after working hours.

But my father was interested in making money to *keep*.   4

Because it is very hard for a Negro to make money in the   5
United States, since so many jobs are denied him, so many un-
ions and professional associations are barred to him, so many
banks will not advance him loans, and so many insurance companies will not insure his business, my father went to Cuba and
Mexico, where he could make money quicker. He had had legal
training in the South, but could not be admitted to the bar there.
In Mexico he was admitted to the bar and practiced law. He acquired property in Mexico City and a big ranch in the hills. He
lent money and foreclosed on mortgages.

During the revolutions, when all the white Americans had to   6
flee from the Toluca district of Mexico, because of the rising na-
tionalism, my father became the general manager of an electric

light company belonging to an American firm in New York. Because he was brown, the Mexicans could not tell at sight that he was a Yankee, and even after they knew it, they did not believe he was like the white Yankees. So the followers of Zapata and Villa did not run him away as they did the whites. In fact, in Toluca, the Mexicans always called my father *el americano*, and not the less polite *el gringo*, which is a term that carries with it distrust and hatred.

But my father was certainly just like the other German and English and American business men with whom he associated in Mexico. He spoke just as badly about the Mexicans. He said they were ignorant and backward and lazy. He said they were exactly like the Negroes in the United States, perhaps worse. And he said they were very bad at making money. 7

My father hated Negroes. I think he hated himself, too, for being a Negro. He disliked all of his family because they were Negroes and remained in the United States, where none of them had a chance to be much of anything but servants—like my mother, who started out with a good education at the University of Kansas, he said, but had sunk to working in a restaurant, waiting on niggers, when she wasn't in some white woman's kitchen. My father said he wanted me to leave the United States as soon as I finished high school, and never return—unless I wanted to be a porter or a red cap all my life. 8

The second day out from Cleveland, the train we were on rolled across Arkansas. As we passed through a dismal village in the cotton fields, my father peered from the window of our Pullman at a cluster of black peons on the main street, and said contemptuously: "Look at the niggers." 9

When we crossed into Mexico at Laredo, and started south over the sun-baked plains, he pointed out to me a cluster of brown peons watching the train slow down at an adobe station. He said: "Look at the Mexicans!" 10

My father had a great contempt for all poor people. He thought it was their own fault that they were poor. 11

OUR ENGLISH TEACHER

WILLIE MORRIS

Our English teacher was the wife of the owner of the barber   1
shop. She had grown up in a small town in Arkansas, and had
even spent some time in New York City before settling down in
Mississippi. In my first year in high school she lectured us for
three weeks on Anglo-Saxon England, and on the Normans, and
then on Chaucer. She made us take notes, because this was the
way it was done in college, and she said she wanted her students
to go to college someday. She had us read *The Canterbury Tales*,
Shakespeare, George Eliot, Thackeray, and Dickens, and Byron,
Shelley, Keats, Coleridge, Wordsworth, Tennyson, and Brown-
ing. Then she would have us give reports on the books and
poems we had read; woe to the unfortunate student who tried to
memorize the outlines of one of her novels by reading it in Classic Comics. She was unsparing in her criticism, and she got
rougher as we moved into the higher grades. I must have parsed
a hundred English sentences on the blackboard of that room, trying to come to reasonable terms with gerundives, split infini-
tives, verb objects, and my own dangling prepositions. It was the
one course in that school where great quantities of homework
were essential: novels, poems, themes, grammar, spelling. She
would give the assignment at the end of every class, and a big
groan would fill the room. She would say, "Well, you want to
learn, don't you? Or maybe you *want* to stay saps all your life."
She had little patience with the slow ones, or the ones who
refused to work, but for those who tried, or who performed with
some natural intelligence, she was the most loyal and generous
of souls. She would talk about their virtues to everyone in town
who would listen, and sometimes take them home to have din-

ner with her and her husband and show them colored pictures of the Lake Country or New England or Greenwich Village.

Among many of the students she was a scorned woman. They bad-talked her behind her back, tried to catch her in contradictions about her travels, and rumored that she worked people that hard out of plain cruelty; I myself sometimes joined in this talk, for it was fashionable. Although she had been teaching there for many years, the students never would dedicate the school yearbook to her, out of simple retaliation, until my senior year when a friend and I managed to get the dedication for her. In the school assembly when the dedication was announced, her acceptance speech was a model of graciousness. She talked about the honor that had been done her, and about the generation of students she had taught in the school, and about how she wanted to stay there in Yazoo the rest of her life. 2

There must be many another small town in America with women like her—trying, for whatever reason, to teach small-town children the hard basics of the language, and something of the literature it has produced—unyielding in their standards, despairing of mediocrity, and incorruptible, and perhaps for all these reasons, scorned and misunderstood. 3

AVEY

JEAN TOOMER

For a long while she was nothing more to me than one of
those skirted beings whom boys at a certain age disdain to play
with. Just how I came to love her, timidly, and with secret
blushes, I do not know. But that I did was brought home to me
one night, the first night that Ned wore his long pants. Us fellers
were seated on the curb before an apartment house where she
had gone in. The young trees had not outgrown their boxes then.
V Street was lined with them. When our legs grew cramped and
stiff from the cold of the stone, we'd stand around a box and
whittle it. I like to think now that there was a hidden purpose in
the way we hacked them with our knives. I like to feel that something deep in me responded to the trees, the young trees that
whinnied like colts impatient to be let free . . . On the particular
night I have in mind, we were waiting for the top-floor light to go
out. We wanted to see Avey leave the flat. This night she stayed
longer than usual and gave us a chance to complete the plans of
how we were going to stone and beat that feller on the top floor
out of town. Ned especially had it in for him. He was about to
throw a brick up at the window when at last the room went dark.
Some minutes passed. Then Avey, as unconcerned as if she had
been paying an old-maid aunt a visit, came out. I don't remember what she had on, and all that sort of thing. But I do know that
I turned hot as bare pavements in the summertime at Ned's
boast: "Hell, bet I could get her too if you little niggers weren't
always spying and crabbing everything." I didn't say a word to
him. It wasn't my way then. I just stood there like the others, and
something like a fuse burned up inside of me. She never noticed
us, but swung along lazy and easy as anything. We sauntered to

1

the corner and watched her till her door banged to. Ned repeated what he'd said. I didn't seem to care. Sitting around old Mush-Head's bread box, the discussion began. "Hang if I can see how she gets away with it," Doc started. Ned knew, of course. There was nothing he didn't know when it came to women. He dilated on the emotional needs of girls. Said they weren't much different from men in that respect. And concluded with the solemn avowal: "It does em good." None of us liked Ned much. We all talked dirt; but it was the way he said it. And then too, a couple of the fellers had sisters and had caught Ned playing with them. But there was no disputing the superiority of his smutty wisdom. Bubs Sanborn, whose mother was friendly with Avey's, had overheard the old ladies talking. "Avey's mother ont her," he said. We thought that only natural and began to guess at what would happen. Some one said she'd marry that feller on the top floor. Ned called that a lie because Avey was going to marry no-body but him. We had our doubts about that, but we did agree that she'd soon leave school and marry some one. The gang broke up and I went home, picturing myself as married.

Nothing I did seemed able to change Avey's indifference to 2 me. I played basketball, and when I'd make a long clean shot she'd clap with the others, louder than they, I thought. I'd meet her on the street, and there'd be no difference in the way she said hello. She never took the trouble to call me by my name. On the days for drill, I'd let my voice down a tone and call for a compli-cated maneuver when I saw her coming. She'd smile apprecia-tion, but it was an impersonal smile, never for me. It was on a summer excursion down to Riverview that she first seemed to take me into account. The day had been spent riding merry-go-rounds, scenic-railways, and shoot-the-chutes. We had been in swimming and we had danced. I was a crack swimmer then. She didn't know how. I held her up and showed her how to kick her legs and draw her arms. Of course she didn't learn in one day, but she thanked me for bothering with her. I was also somewhat of a dancer. And I had already noticed that love can start on a dance floor. We danced. But though I held her tightly in my arms, she was way away. That college feller who lived on the top floor was somewhere making money for the next year. I imag-ined that she was thinking, wishing for him. Ned was along. He treated her until his money gave out. She went with another feller. Ned got sore. One by one of the boys' money gave out. She left them. And they got sore. Every one of them but me got sore. This is the reason, I guess, why I had her to myself on the top deck of the *Jane Mosely* that night as we puffed up the Potomac, coming home. The moon was brilliant. The air was sweet like clover. And every now and then, a salt tang, a stale drift of sea-weed. It was not my mind's fault if it went romancing. I should have taken her in my arms the minute we were stowed in that old lifeboat. I dallied, dreaming. She took me in hers. And I could feel by the touch of it that it wasn't a man-to-woman love. It made me restless. I felt chagrined. I didn't know what it was, but I did know that I couldn't handle it. She ran her fingers through my hair and kissed my forehead. I itched to break through her tenderness to passion. I wanted her to take me in her arms as I knew she had that college feller. I wanted her to love me passionately as she did him. I gave her one burning kiss. Then she laid me in her lap as if I were a child. Helpless. I got sore when she started to hum a lullaby. She wouldn't let me go. I talked. I knew damned well that I could beat her at that. Her eyes were soft and misty, the curves of her lips were wistful, and her smile seemed indulgent of the irrelevance of my remarks. I gave up at last and let her love me, silently, in her own way. The moon was brilliant. The air was sweet like clover, and every now and then, a salt tang, a stale drift of sea-weed . . .

The next time I came close to her was the following summer at   3 Harpers Ferry. We were sitting on a flat projecting rock they give the name of Lover's Leap. Someone is supposed to have jumped off it. The river is about six hundred feet beneath. A railroad track runs up the valley and curves out of sight where part of the mountain rock had to be blasted away to make room for it. The engines of this valley have a whistle, the echoes of which sound like iterated gasps and sobs. I always think of them as crude music from the soul of Avey. We sat there holding hands. Our palms were soft and warm against each other. Our fingers were not tight. She would not let them be. She would not let me twist them. I wanted to talk. To explain what I meant to her. Avey was as silent as those great trees whose tops we looked down upon. She has always been like that. At least, to me. I had the notion that if I really wanted to, I could do with her just what I pleased. Like one can strip a tree. I did kiss her. I even let my hands cup her breasts. When I was through, she'd seek my hand and hold it till my pulse cooled down. Evening after evening we sat there. I tried to get her to talk about that college feller. She never would. There was no set time to go home. None of my family had come down. And as for hers, she didn't give a hang about them. The general gossips could hardly say more than they had. The boarding-house porch was always deserted when we returned. No one saw us enter, so the time was set conveniently for scandal. This worried me a little, for I thought it might keep Avey from getting an appointment in the schools. She didn't care. She had finished normal school. They could give her a job if they wanted to. As time went on, her indifference to things began to pique me; I was ambitious. I left the Ferry earlier than she did. I was going off to college. The more I thought of it, the more I resented, yes, hell, thats what it was, her downright laziness. Sloppy indolence. There was no excuse for a healthy girl taking life so easy. Hell! she was no better than a cow. I was certain that she was a cow when I felt an udder in a Wisconsin stock-judging class. Among those energetic Swedes, or whatever they are, I decided to forget her. For two years I thought I did. When I'd come home for the summer she'd be away. And before she returned, I'd be gone. We never wrote; she was too damned lazy for that. But what a bluff I put up about forgetting her. The girls up that way, at least the ones I knew, haven't got the stuff: they don't know how to love. Giving themselves completely was tame beside just the holding of Avey's hand. One day I received a note from her. The writing, I decided, was slovenly. She wrote on a torn bit of note-book paper. The envelope had a faint perfume that I remembered. A single line told me she had lost her school and was going away. I comforted myself with the reflection that shame held no pain for one so indolent as she. Nevertheless, I left Wisconsin that year for good. Washington had seemingly forgotten her. I hunted Ned. Between curses, I caught his opinion of her. She was no better than a whore. I saw her mother on the street. The same old pinch-beck, jerky-gaited creature that I'd always known.

Perhaps five years passed. The business of hunting a job or something or other had bruised my vanity so that I could recognize it. I felt old. Avey and my real relation to her, I thought I came to know. I wanted to see her. I had been told that she was in New York. As I had no money, I hiked and bummed my way there. I got work in a ship-yard and walked the streets at night, hoping to meet her. Failing in this, I saved enough to pay my fare back home. One evening in early June, just at the time when dusk is most lovely on the eastern horizon, I saw Avey, indolent as ever, leaning on the arm of a man, strolling under the recently lit arclights of U Street. She had almost passed before she recognized me. She showed no surprise. The puff over her eyes had grown heavier. The eyes themselves were still sleepy-large, and beautiful. I had almost concluded—indifferent. "You look older," was what she said. I wanted to convince her that I was, so I asked her to walk with me. The man whom she was with, and whom she never took the trouble to introduce, at a nod from her, hailed a taxi, and drove away. That gave me a notion of what she had been used to. Her dress was of some fine, costly stuff. I suggested the park, and then added that the grass might stain her skirt. Let it get stained, she said, for where it came from there are others.

I have a spot in Soldier's Home to which I always go when I   5 want the simple beauty of another's soul. Robins spring about the lawn all day. They leave their footprints in the grass. I imagine that the grass at night smells sweet and fresh because of them. The gound is high. Washington lies below. Its light spreads like a blush against the darkened sky. Against the soft dusk sky of Washington. And when the wind is from the South, soil of my homeland falls like a fertile shower upon the lean streets of the city. Upon my hill in Soldier's Home, I know the policeman who watches the place of nights. When I go there alone, I talk to him. I tell him I come there to find the truth that people bury in their hearts. I tell him that I do not come there with a girl to do the thing he's paid to watch out for. I look deep in his eyes when I say these things, and he believes me. He comes over to see who it is on the grass. I say hello to him. He greets me in the same way and goes off searching for other black splotches upon the lawn. Avey and I went there. A band in one of the buildings a fair distance off was playing a march. I wished they would stop. Their playing was like a tin spoon in one's mouth. I wanted the Howard Glee Club to sing "Deep River," from the road. To sing "Deep River, Deep River," from the road . . . Other than the first comments, Avey had been silent. I started to hum a folk-tune. She slipped her hand in mine. Pillowed her head as best she could upon my arm. Kissed the hand she was holding and listened, or so I thought, to what I had to say. I traced my development from the early days up to the present time, the phase in which I could understand her. I described her own nature and temperament. Told how they needed a larger life for their expression. How incapable Washington was of understanding that need. How it could not meet it. I pointed out that in lieu of proper channels, her emotions had overflowed into paths that dissipated them. I talked, beautifully I thought, about an art that would be born, an art that would open the way for women the likes of her. I asked her to hope, and build up an inner life against the coming of that day. I recited some of my own things to her. I sang, with a strange quiver in my voice, a promise-song. And then I began to wonder why her hand had not once returned a single pressure. My old-time feeling about her laziness came back. I spoke sharply. My policeman friend passed by. I said hello to him. As he went away, I began to visualize certain possibilities. An immediate and urgent passion swept over me. Then I looked at Avey. Her heavy eyes were closed. Her breathing was as faint and regular as a child's in slumber. My passion died. I was afraid to move lest I disturb her. Hours and hours, I guess it was, she lay there. My body grew numb. I shivered. I coughed. I wanted to get up and whittle at the boxes of young trees. I withdrew my hand. I raised her head to waken her. She did not stir. I got up and walked around. I found my policeman friend and talked to him. We both came up, and bent over her. He said it would be all right for her to stay there just so long as she got away before the workmen came at dawn. A blanket was borrowed from a neighbor house. I sat beside her through the night. I saw the dawn steal over Washington. The Capitol dome looked like a gray ghost ship drifting in from sea. Avey's face was pale, and her eyes were heavy. She did not have the gray crimson-splashed beauty of the dawn. I hated to wake her. Orphan-woman . . .

RESPONDING
TO SITUATIONS
AND EVENTS

The readings in Part Two are about situations and events that authors have found interesting or significant. They are likely to stimulate you to write about particular events or on-going situations that have affected your life or the lives of others. Based on your work with this book so far, however, you know that a reading arouses different responses in people. The best way to discover how an essay or story affects you is to record your strongest response as soon as you have finished reading it. Your response probably will contain the germ of an idea that matters to you and can form the basis of an essay that others will want to read.

Again, the first three readings of Part Two are followed by sample responses that should help you think about your own reaction to the essay or story. By considering these sample responses and answering the questions we ask, your own writing will become more effective. And don't forget to share your ideas with classmates and friends. Their reactions to your work will strengthen your writing.

Photograph by David M. Grossman

YOU SHOULD HAVE BEEN A BOY!

ELIZABETH CADY STANTON

When I was eleven years old, two events occurred which 1
changed considerably the current of my life. My only brother,
who had just graduated from Union College, came home to die.
A young man of great talent and promise, he was the pride of my
father's heart. We early felt that this son filled a larger place in
our father's affections and future plans than the five daughters
together. Well do I remember how tenderly he watched my
brother in his last illness, the sighs and tears he gave vent to as he
slowly walked up and down the hall, and, when the last sad moment came, and we were all assembled to say farewell in the silent chamber of death, how broken were his utterances as he
knelt and prayed for comfort and support. I still recall, too, going
into the large darkened parlor to see my brother, and finding the
casket, mirrors, and pictures all draped in white, and my father
seated by his side, pale and immovable. As he took no notice of
me, after standing a long while, I climbed upon his knee, when
he mechanically put his arm about me and, with my head resting
against his beating heart, we both sat in silence, he thinking of
the wreck of all his hopes in the loss of a dear son, and I wondering what could be said or done to fill the void in his breast. At
length he heaved a deep sigh and said: "Oh, my daughter, I wish
you were a boy!" Throwing my arms about his neck, I replied: "I
will try to be all my brother was."

Then and there I resolved that I would not give so much time 2
as heretofore to play, but would study and strive to be at the
head of all my classes and thus delight my father's heart. All that
day and far into the night I pondered the problem of boyhood. I
thought that the chief thing to be done in order to equal boys was

to be learned and courageous. So I decided to study Greek and learn to manage a horse. Having formed this conclusion I fell asleep. My resolutions, unlike many such made at night, did not vanish with the coming light. I arose early and hastened to put them into execution. They were resolutions never to be forgotten—destined to mold my character anew. As soon as I was dressed I hastened to our good pastor, Rev. Simon Hosack, who was always early at work in his garden.

"Doctor," said I, "which do you like best, boys or girls?"   3

"Why, girls, to be sure; I would not give you for all the boys in   4 Christendom."

"My father," I replied, "prefers boys; he wishes I was one,   5 and I intend to be as near like one as possible. I am going to ride on horseback and study Greek. Will you give me a Greek lesson now, doctor? I want to begin at once."

"Yes, child," said he, throwing down his hoe, "come into my   6 library and we will begin without delay."

He entered fully into the feeling of suffering and sorrow which   7 took possession of me when I discovered that a girl weighed less in the scale of being than a boy, and he praised my determination to prove the contrary. The old grammar which he had studied in the University of Glasgow was soon in my hands, and the Greek article was learned before breakfast.

Then came the sad pageantry of death, the weeping of friends,   8 the dark rooms, the ghostly stillness, the exhortation to the living to prepare for death, the solemn prayer, the mournful chant, the funeral cortège, the solemn, tolling bell, the burial. How I suffered during those sad days! What strange undefined fears of the unknown took possession of me! For months afterward, at the twilight hour, I went with my father to the new-made grave. Near it stood two tall poplar trees, against one of which I leaned, while my father threw himself on the grave, with outstretched arms, as if to embrace his child. At last the frosts and storms of November came and threw a chilling barrier between the living and the dead, and we went there no more.

During all this time I kept up my lessons at the parsonage and   9 made rapid progress. I surprised even my teacher, who thought me capable of doing anything. I learned to drive, and to leap a fence and ditch on horseback. I taxed every power, hoping some day to hear my father say: "Well, a girl is as good as a boy, after all." But he never said it. When the doctor came over to spend the evening with us, I would whisper in his ear: "Tell my father how fast I get on," and he would tell him, and was lavish in his praises. But my father only paced the room, sighed, and showed that he wished I were a boy; and I, not knowing why he felt thus, would hide my tears of vexation on the doctor's shoulder.

Soon after this I began to study Latin, Greek, and mathematics 10 with a class of boys in the Academy, many of whom were much older than I. For three years one boy kept his place at the head of the class, and I always stood next. Two prizes were offered in Greek. I strove for one and took the second. How well I remember my joy in receiving that prize. There was no sentiment of ambition, rivalry, or triumph over my companions, nor feeling of satisfaction in receiving this honor in the presence of those assembled on the day of the exhibition. One thought alone filled my mind. "Now," said I, "my father will be satisfied with me." So, as soon as we were dismissed, I ran down the hill, rushed breathless into his office, laid the new Greek Testament, which was my prize, on his table and exclaimed: "There, I got it!" He took up the book, asked me some questions about the class, the teachers, the spectators, and, evidently pleased, handed it back to me. Then, while I stood looking and waiting for him to say something which would show that he recognized the equality of the daughter with the son, he kissed me on the forehead and exclaimed, with a sigh, "Ah, you should have been a boy!"

Sample Responses to "You Should Have Been a Boy!"

Responder 1: Celia

What a father! How could he be so mean to his daughter! She tried to take the place of the son, but the father didn't care. All he wanted was the boy. I'm glad my father is different. He tells me I'm the one who should continue my education because I do well in school. He tells my brother that he should start thinking about learning some sort of trade because "Ronnie and books don't get along." If the father in the story had been more like my father, the girl would have been appreciated for what she did. Ugh! What a father!

Responder 2: Leona

It's the same old story. Boys are the pride and joy of the family, while girls are just supposed to be nice, get married, and not have any ambitions about being somebody. That's the way my family reacts to me. I told my mother the other night that I was thinking about becoming a doctor. I didn't tell her that I was certain since I know that it isn't easy to become a doctor. I only said I was <u>thinking</u> about it. She just sort of smiled and said that I'd probably change my mind when I met some nice fellow. I felt like screaming, but my mother, even though she's not that old, was brought up in a very traditional family. So, for her, a woman's place is in the kitchen. On the other hand, when my brother told my father he wanted to be a physical therapist, my father got mad and said he was aiming too low. He thinks my brother has what it takes to be a doctor. When I asked my father, "What about me?" he said that only certain women are able to do it--become doctors, he meant. In other words, only superwomen can compete with men when it comes to the higher jobs. The whole thing drives me up the wall, but there's not much I can do about it right now.

Responder 3: Sonia

I know the other women in the class will make a big thing out of this essay. They'll talk about women's lib and how men have kept women suppressed all through history. As a woman I should probably agree with them, but my experiences tell me different. When I was ten years old, my mother decided that being a housewife and mother wasn't good enough. She wanted a career, and she wanted to earn her own money. My father had a good job, and so we really didn't need extra money. But my mother kept saying that she didn't want to spend the rest of her life trapped in a house. So my mother got a job selling real estate, which she liked. She liked her job so much that she came home late almost every night. And all she ever talked about was how exciting her job was and how she was working her way up the ladder. All this was fine for her, but it wasn't fine for me.

I had to take over her housework. My brother was five years old at the time, and so I had to be a mother for him. My father would come home hungry from work, and I had to cook for him, even though I wasn't very good at it. My father tried to help, but he wasn't much of a cook either, and besides, he was usually too tired. My life became a mess. I couldn't go out with my friends or even spend much time talking to my friends on the phone or watching TV. The whole thing ended in a divorce, which I don't even like to think about. But you can see why I'm not so sure about women's lib.

Responder 4: Randy

God set up the way men and women should live. When people try to live their own way and not God's way, things go wrong. The daughter tried to be a boy, which was wrong. God created her a woman, and she tried to be a man. That's why her father said what he said. He knew she could not change God's plan for her. True, if she had been a boy, then what she did would have been all right. But wanting to be a different sex than you are is a sin.

A lot of the problems in the world today are caused by women trying to act like men. Instead of being mothers and housewives as God intended them to be, they want to do the work that God intended men to do. That's why so many young people are on drugs or are involved in all kinds of crime and violence. These kids don't know right from wrong. How could they, when their mothers don't know right from wrong? If women don't start acting the way God made them to act, there's a lot more trouble coming to this world.

Considering the Responses

Response 1: Celia

Celia compared her father's attitude toward her academic success with the attitude of Elizabeth Cady Stanton's father toward Elizabeth's success. An obvious strategy for Celia in planning an essay might be to expand on the portrait of her father as a person who understands and appreciates his daughter's academic success.

1. If Celia decides to follow this strategy, how might she develop her essay?
2. Would an essay composed almost entirely of her father's compliments about Celia's schoolwork prove interesting and convincing? Why or why not?
3. How else might Celia support her contention that her father is unbiased in his attitude toward women and intellectual achievement?

During class discussion of Celia's response, several students took exception to what they saw as a "put down" of Celia's brother by his father. These students were disturbed by the implication that learning a trade is somehow inferior to doing well in school.

4. Is there a possible essay topic in the feelings these students expressed? How would you summarize that topic?
5. What difference of opinion seems to be at the heart of these students' objections about the father's attitude toward the brother? Do you agree or disagree with these students? Why?

Response 2: Leona

Leona evidently feels that, because she is female, her parents do not take her career aspirations seriously. She complains that her mother's attitude toward her reflects her mother's traditional upbringing.

1. If Leona decides to write an essay that might help readers get a clear idea of just what it's like to grow up in a "traditional" family, how might she relate her topic to Elizabeth Cady Stanton's piece?
2. Do you think Leona should write an essay showing that her treatment by her parents is typical of how parents react to sons and daughters? Or would she be safer to confine her essay to her particular situation? Explain your answer.

Response 3: Sonia

Some students felt that Sonia's rather lengthy response put her well on the way to writing a complete essay, and they suggested that all she needed to do was to provide more detail about the "misery" she went through because of her mother's decision to pursue a career. Other students, however, thought that Sonia was somewhat unfair to her mother. Why, they wondered, couldn't someone have been hired to help with the cooking and the housework, especially since both parents earned a good salary? They asked whether something about the father's attitude prevented the couple from working out a satisfactory plan that would have relieved Sonia of the housework at the same time it allowed her mother to pursue her career. In other words, they advised Sonia to go more deeply into the problems that led to the eventual breakup of the family.

1. If Sonia does decide to explore the breakup of the family, how much of her initial response do you think she can use in her essay? Which ideas would still fit the new topic?
2. If Sonia decides to stay with her original response, does she need to add details about the hard life she led in order to make a strong case for her personal objection to women's liberation? Or has she already proved her case in her original response? Explain your answer.

Response 4: Randy

Randy takes a truly traditional view of the events Elizabeth Cady Stanton described.

1. Do you think Randy can support his idea that God set up the way men and women should live? What kind of supporting details should he offer to convince readers that he is correct?
2. What questions might some readers raise about Randy's belief that much of the trouble in the world results from women's trying to act "like men"?
3. Do you think Randy can develop an essay based on the ideas expressed in his original response? Why or why not?

SALVATION

LANGSTON HUGHES

I was saved from sin when I was going on thirteen. But not 1
really saved. It happened like this. There was a big revival at my
Auntie Reed's church. Every night for weeks there had been
much preaching, singing, praying, and shouting, and some very
hardened sinners had been brought to Christ, and the member-
ship of the church had grown by leaps and bounds. Then just before the revival ended, they held a special meeting for children,
"to bring the young lambs to the fold." My aunt spoke of it for
days ahead. That night I was escorted to the front row and placed
on the mourners' bench with all the other young sinners, who
had not yet been brought to Jesus.

My aunt told me that when you were saved you saw a light, 2
and something happened to you inside! And Jesus came into
your life! And God was with you from then on! She said you
could see and hear and feel Jesus in your soul. I believed her. I
have heard a great many old people say the same thing and it
seemed to me they ought to know. So I sat there calmly in the
hot, crowded church, waiting for Jesus to come to me.

The preacher preached a wonderful rhythmical sermon, all 3
moans and shouts and lonely cries and dire pictures of hell, and
then he sang a song about the ninety and nine safe if the fold, but
one little lamb was left out in the cold. Then he said: "Won't you
come? Won't you come to Jesus? Young lambs, won't you
come?" And he held out his arms to all us young sinners there on
the mourners' bench. And the little girls cried. And some of them
jumped up and went to Jesus right away. But most of us just sat
there.

A great many old people came and knelt around us and 4
prayed, old women with jet-black faces and braided hair, old
men with work-gnarled hands. And the church sang a song about
the lower lights are burning, some poor sinners to be saved. And
the whole building rocked with prayer and song.

Still I kept waiting to *see* Jesus. 5

Finally all the young people had gone to the altar and were 6
saved, but one boy and me. He was a rounder's son named Westley. Westley and I were surrounded by sisters and deacons praying. It was very hot in the church, and getting late now. Finally
Westley said to me in a whisper: "God damn! I'm tired o' sitting
here. Let's get up and be saved." So he got up and was saved.

Then I was left all alone on the mourners' bench. My aunt 7
came and knelt at my knees and cried, while prayers and songs
swirled all around me in the little church. The whole congrega-
tion prayed for me alone, in a mighty wail of moans and voices.
And I kept waiting serenely for Jesus, waiting, waiting—but he
didn't come. I wanted to see him, but nothing happened to me.
Nothing! I wanted something to happen to me, but nothing happened.

I heard the songs and the minister saying: "Why don't you 8
come? My dear child, why don't you come to Jesus? Jesus is waiting for you. He wants you. Why don't you come? Sister Reed,
what is the child's name?"

"Langston," my aunt sobbed. 9

"Langston, why don't you come? Why don't you come and be 10
saved? Oh, Lamb of God! Why don't you come?"

Now it was really getting late. I began to be ashamed of my- 11
self, holding everything up so long. I began to wonder what God
thought about Westley, who certainly hadn't seen Jesus either,
but who was now sitting proudly on the platform, swinging his
knickerbockered legs and grinning down at me, surrounded by
deacons and old women on their knees praying. God had not
struck Westley dead for taking his name in vain or for lying in
the temple. So I decided that maybe to save further trouble, I'd
better lie, too, and say that Jesus had come, and get up and be
saved.

So I got up. 12

Suddenly the whole room broke into a sea of shouting, as they 13
saw me rise. Waves of rejoicing swept the place. Women leaped
in the air. My aunt threw her arms around me. The minister took
me by the hand and led me to the platform.

When things quieted down, in a hushed silence, punctuated 14 by a few ecstatic "Amens," all the new young lambs were blessed in the name of God. Then joyous singing filled the room.

That night, for the last time in my life but one—for I was a big boy twelve years old—I cried. I cried, in bed alone, and couldn't stop. I buried my head under the quilts, but my aunt heard me. She woke up and told my uncle I was crying because the Holy Ghost had come into my life, and because I had seen Jesus. But I was really crying because I couldn't bear to tell her that I had lied, that I had deceived everybody in the church, that I hadn't seen Jesus, and that now I didn't believe there was a Jesus any more, since he didn't come to help me.

Sample Responses to "Salvation"

Responder 1: Joel

I hate it when people expect me to perform. When I was a little boy, my mother wanted me to thank my aunt for an ugly sweater that only a girl would wear. She told me to go over and make a little speech. I ran upstairs and hid, and later I was punished for being rude. And when I was in seventh grade, the teacher chose me to recite a poem on Parents Day. I couldn't face standing up in front of all those people, and so I stayed home pretending I was sick. You have to let people do things on their own and not force them.

Responder 2: Erika

Religion is for hypocrites, as Langston Hughes so rightly states. That revival meeting was packed with persons just like Westley. But the others were quicker than Westley and Langston to catch on and play the game. When anyone goes along with religion by saying they love Jesus or any other deity, they feel they need to force everyone else to join their club so that no one will know they were lying. Eventually, they begin to believe what they are saying because they say it so often. As history has shown, these groups of believers often become angry that not everyone agrees with them, and they go to war to force the rest of the world to say that their way is the right way. Most of the problems in this world can be traced to some people trying to make other people accept their religion.

Responder 3: Clark

Life presents us with many problems which we cannot cope with alone without divine assistance. I was miserable when I was in high school. No one liked me, and I was always in a lot of trouble. My parents said I was no good, and it was all because I had not found Our Lord. I was arrested when I was seventeen, and I guess that scared me enough to think about what I was doing to myself. My sister had been trying to get me to go to meetings, and I finally did. At first I was most uncomfortable because all the other people seemed so good. But one time I heard people confessing their sinful ways and telling how they had found peace, and I began to feel something inside. When I finally took Our Lord to me, I knew my troubles were over. Now I am happy, and I'll never be unable to face any problems that come along.

Responder 4: John

Langston Hughes was the only honest one. He admitted to himself that he had lied--about seeing Jesus. I bet everybody in that church lied too. Everybody went along with the show, though, because nobody wanted to be different. When you're different, people go against you or think you're weird. I'll bet half the students in this college don't want to be here, but are just conforming to what their parents want or what society wants. At least Langston had the guts to hold out until the crowd almost went crazy. I don't think I could have held out that long.

Considering the Responses

Response 1: Joel

Joel's experiences were quite different from the author's, but they represent a topic that holds great interest for him. When the class asked him how he planned to create an essay from this response, he said he remembered other embarrassing times when he was under pressure to perform, and he could add more details to the two incidents already mentioned. The class advised him to discuss at some length the general situation—adults forcing children to do something that seems "good" or "right." Once the general discussion had finished, he could determine how many examples would be useful. One classmate warned Joel of the dangers of "overkill" that might result from offering too many similar examples.

1. Should Joel's essay include a look at the situation from the adults' point of view? Or should he stick to his own feelings and what he supposes other children would have felt?
2. Depending on your answer to question 1, advise Joel about how to plan his essay.

Response 2: Erika

Erika faced the opposite problem from Joel, for she had too many wide-reaching ideas for a short essay. The other students noticed that Erika's response contained two rather large topics: (1) her view that most religious people are hypocrites and (2) her ideas about religious wars. In addition, many classmates challenged Erika's opinions. Since she could count on having an interested audience when her essay was completed, she was under no small pressure to construct her argument carefully. The class seemed more receptive to the topic of religious wars, but Erika preferred to explore the issue of hypocrisy.

1. Which of the two topics do you think would be easier to develop into an effective essay? Why?
2. Depending on your answer to question 1, what kinds of supporting detail should Erika include?

Response 3: Clark

Clark's response contained plenty of material for an essay, and the class thought that his essay could be divided into three major sections.

1. What three sections do you think the class found in Clark's response?
2. Should Clark develop all three sections in his essay or focus on only one or two? Why?

Response 4: John

John's response triggered a lively discussion about the issue of conformity. The class was especially interested in John's contention that half the students in the school didn't want to be there. Many classmates agreed with John, saying that they were in college in order to conform to their parents' desires or to social pressures. Other students claimed that they were in college because they wanted to be there. And some students weren't quite sure why they were in college.

1. How might John's essay be organized to cover all three of the attitudes expressed by his classmates?
2. What ideas in "Salvation" caused John to write about college rather than religion? Is John's response closely connected to Langston Hughes's piece? Why or why not?

THERE'S ONLY LUCK

RUTH REICHL

My mind went numb when I saw the gun pointing against 1
the car window as we pulled out of the garage: This can't be happening to me. Then I felt the gun, cold, against my head, and I
heard my friend Jeremy saying, "What do you want? Take my
wallet," but at the time nothing registered. I didn't question why
they wanted us to go into the house; only later did I realize that
there must have been more than money on their minds.

I remember being only vaguely annoyed when the man with 2
the gun pulled me from the car by my hair, and annoyed at being
called a bitch. I remember the walk up to the house and, behind
us, Jeremy and another man with a gun. I remember the fear and
anger in both men's voices because Jeremy was being so slow,
and I remember wondering *why* he was being so slow. I did not
realize that Jeremy had thrown the keys into the shrubbery, but I
do remember Jeremy sinking to his knees saying, "I'm sorry, I'm
sorry." And I remember the sound of the gun hitting Jeremy's
head and the feeling as the man who had hold of my hair re-
leased me. And I remember the split second when I realized that
he had not only let go of me but that he was looking at Jeremy
and the man who was hitting him, and I remember that tiny
question in my mind about how far I could run, how fast and
how likely it was that I could make it to the car parked across the
street before he pulled the trigger. But I was already running as I
thought these things, and when I got to the car I didn't crouch behind it but screamed instead.

I remember thinking that there was something absurdly melo- 3
dramatic about screaming, "Help, help!" at eight o'clock on a

Tuesday evening in December in the Hollywood Hills, and then seeing, in my mind, the man behind me with the gun, and changing my plea to a more specific one. "Help, let me in, *please* let me in!" But the houses were cold, closed, unfriendly, and I ran on until I saw a screen door, thinking that I could leap right through it if I had to. But by then I had heard Jeremy's screams behind me, and I knew that our attackers had fled.

The neighbors who had not opened their doors to us came out   4 with baseball bats and helped Jeremy find his glasses and keys. In a group they were very brave. We waited for the cops to come, until someone said to someone else that the fettuccine was getting cold, and I said politely, "Please go and eat. I'm all right."

I was happy to see the neighbors go. They had been talking of   5 stiffer sentences, of bringing back the death penalty and how Reagan is going to clean up the country. I was thinking, they could be saying all of this over my dead body, and I *still* feel that stiffer sentences wouldn't change a thing. All the rage I should have felt for my attackers came out in a rush against these complacent people standing in front of their snug homes talking about all the guns they were going to buy. What good would guns have been to us?

People all over the neighborhood had called to report our   6 screams, and the police turned out in force. When the cops arrived twenty minutes later they were grumpy and disgusted at so much ado about what was, to them, nothing. After all, Jeremy was hardly hurt, and we were hopeless when it came to identification. "Typical," snorted one cop when we couldn't even agree on how tall the men were. Both of us were able to describe the guns in horrifying detail, but the two policemen who stayed to make the report didn't think that would be much help.

The cops were matter-of-fact about the whole thing. The fat   7 one went off to take a call, and his thin partner took our depositions. "That was a stupid thing to do," he said, "throwing away the keys. When a man has a gun against your head you do what you're told." Jeremy looked properly sheepish.

Then the fat cop came back, and the thin one went off to prowl   8 around the house, "That was the best thing you could have done, throwing away your keys," he said. "If you had come in the house with them . . ." His voice trailed off. "They would have hurt her"—he jerked his head toward me—"and then killed you both." Jeremy looked happier. "Look," said the fat cop kindly, "there's no right or wrong in the situation. There's just luck." He arranged to get Jeremy to the hospital, and I sat there and waited for the horror of it all to overcome me.

All night I replayed the moment those black gloves came up 9
against the car window, and I saw, over and over, the ugly snout
of the gun peering greedily in at me. I wondered why I had felt so
calm. I had not been afraid—ever. I was hardly even there. All
night the loop of the gloves and the gun and the voice replayed
itself in my mind, and I waited for the right emotions to come
and claim me.

How long did the whole thing last? Three minutes, five, eight? 10
How many hours of my life will I spend reliving it? Knowing that
no matter how many I do, there is no way to prepare for the next
time, no intelligent response to a gun. The fat cop was right:
There's only luck. The next time I might end up dead.

And there will be a next time—I'm sure of that now. It can 11
happen anywhere, anytime, to anyone. Security is an illusion;
there is no safety in locks or in numbers—or in guns. Guns make
some people feel safe and some people feel strong, but they're
fooling themselves.

Sample Responses to "There's Only Luck"

Responder 1: Alan

The neighbors didn't help her, like everyone else these days.
We're all too scared to get involved. The more people are attacked,
the more scared we are. Horror movies always contain scenes in
which someone is running from evil men and finds every door
locked. I think this scene is more frightening than bloody ax
murders, which never seem real to me. But being unable to get
help from people when you're running for your life is a real
nightmare. If just one door would open and a light shine out, the
killers would run away. But no one wants to be involved. This is a
sad comment on our country. We all need to help each other. We
all must take a chance when we hear someone call for help.
Someday that someone could be you!

Responder 2: Toni

I know I'd like to have a cop around if I were being attacked, just to scare the guy away. But I don't want to have anything else to do with police. They're too cold, and they try to seem tough, and they have nothing but contempt for women. I had a flat tire one night last summer, and I couldn't turn the screws to get the tire off because they were on too tight. Two police cars passed me by--I guess I didn't look like their type of woman. The third cop stopped, but he sneered at me and said he couldn't help with the tire; that wasn't his job; he wasn't a garage mechanic. So he called a tow truck which cost me $35, not for a tow, just for some kid to change the tire. He really sweated over the screws and said they used air pumps to do the job quickly and they're careless and do it too much. He had to take out a very large tool to do the job because mine wasn't any good in this case. But I can't forget that cop's sneering face.

Cops think all rape victims asked for it, too. They don't believe there are any lunatics out there just waiting to hurt women. Yet some people make excuses for policemen being so hard-hearted, saying they see so much violence they have to be tough or they wouldn't survive. We need doctors who are not just interested in making money, and we need cops who can have some feeling for average people, especially for women.

Responder 3: Bob

People have been attacked by criminals ever since history began. But in today's affluent society, we cry out in anguish when we are robbed by people who enjoy none of the benefits of our society. I sympathize with the victims for whatever pain they endure, but I can't stand their griping about the "terrible state of affairs we have come to." They talk about the horror of living in a civilized society and still being terrorized by violent criminals. Well, they ought to ask themselves how civilized our country really is when 20 million of us live in poverty! Poor people see how disgustingly rich so many other people are today. And they see how little talent most of these successful people have. So it's no wonder that they become angry and try to obtain their fair share of the pie by using their wits or physical strength.

Aren't landlords who let their poor or old tenants freeze really "violent"? Isn't it "violence" to leave bag persons and derelicts starving and freezing on the streets? Isn't trying to overthrow unfriendly foreign governments "violent"? True civilization can only be seen on public television. The world may seem civilized because its weapons are so advanced they can vaporize people from a thousand miles away, and we have computers and VCRs and SSTs and little robots who can bring us a cold drink when we call their name. But underneath all this civilization is the same old human animal--selfish, violent, intolerant. We're dressed better than our ancestors in the jungle, but it's still the survival of the fittest in this dog-eat-dog world.

Considering the Responses

Response 1: Alan

Alan said he had no more to say beyond his response. He couldn't think of any reason why people remained safely in their houses except for the obvious fear of injury. And he couldn't see any way to change their behavior except by appealing to their sense of brotherhood. One classmate suggested that Alan could write about why the streets have become so dangerous and what the government or individual neighborhoods can do to reduce the dangers. Another challenged Alan to write an editorial aimed at reluctant citizens, trying to convince them that the danger is greater when they refuse to help.

Alan showed so little enthusiasm for these ideas that another student urged him to write about horror movies, suggesting that he discuss why they are so popular and what makes some of them better than others. Alan asked the instructor whether this topic was acceptable, since he knew that it is not directly related to the story they had read. The instructor was glad Alan had found a topic that interested him.

1. Can you see any way for Alan to tie the popularity of horror movies to this author's comments about crime? What topic sentence might Alan use to begin his essay?
2. Can you see any other connections between Alan's response and the story? What do *you* think Alan should write about? Why?

Response 2: Toni

Toni's response has all the ingredients for a rousing essay attacking policemen's attitudes toward women. She has even mentioned a common explanation for why the police seem so hard. (In fact, her response caused another student to switch his topic and write an essay defending policemen.)

1. How broad an essay should Toni write? Should she include all aspects of policemen's attitudes toward women, or should she limit her topic to their attitudes about rape? Why?
2. Do you think Toni's response is directly related to the author's point in this story? Why or why not?

Response 3: Bob

Bob, too, had a strong response to the story, but he wasn't sure which topic to explore in his essay: The Plight of the Bag People? Inconsistencies in U.S. Foreign Policy? The Falseness of Our Civilization? The True Nature of Man? Nor could the class help Bob select a topic, because he had not gone far enough with any of these ideas in his response.

1. Do you see any general theme running through Bob's response that could be developed into an effective essay? How would you state that theme?
2. Which ideas in his response should Bob use to develop the theme you suggest? Which ideas should he drop from the essay?

Before you expand your own response into an essay, look again at the story and consider these three sample responses to it. Do you think Alan, Toni, and Bob responded to the story as a whole? Or did they miss the author's main point? Reconsider your response to this story by asking what the author intended.

ADDITIONAL READINGS

YOUR EYES
CAN DECEIVE YOU

ARTHUR BARTLETT

George Smith got home from a date with his girl about mid-   1
night. His mother was not at home. Probably she was out playing
cards with friends, George thought. That had been her favorite
recreation ever since her divorce, when George was six. Working all day in the candy factory, she liked to relax in the eve-
nings. Now that George was 20, and working, and had a girl to
occupy his attention, she often stayed out fairly late. So George
went up to his own front room, undressed, got into bed and lay
there reading the newspaper.

A bus stopped across the street, and George pulled aside the   2
window shade and looked out. Under the street light, he could
see his mother descending from the bus. A tall, heavy-set man
got out behind her. The bus moved on. George was about to drop
back on his pillow when his startled eyes stopped him. The man
was reaching for his mother, trying to put his arms around her.
George saw her push at him and try to step back off the curb;
saw him grab her again and start pulling her towards him.

George leaped out of bed, pulled on his trousers and rushed   3
down the stairs to the front door. Across the street, the man was
still attempting to embrace his mother and she was struggling
against him. George dashed to the rescue. Clenching his fist as he

ran, he leaped at the man and punched with all his strength, hitting him squarely on the jaw. The man toppled backward and uttered a groan as his head hit the sidewalk. Then he lay there, still.

What happened next filled George with utter confusion. Dropping to her knees beside the unconscious man, his mother looked up at him with anguish in her eyes. "George," she cried, "what have you done? This is Howard Browser. . . . Howard, the candymaker at the factory . . . the man who asked me to marry him." . . .   4

The boy stared at his mother across the crumpled figure on the pavement. "He wasn't attacking you?" he demanded, dully.   5

"Of course not," she told him. "We'd been out together all evening. He brought me home. He wanted a good-night kiss, that's all. I was just teasing him."   6

An ambulance took Howard Browser to the hospital, but he never regained consciousness. He died the next day. George Smith spent that night in a jail cell.   7

The authorities finally decided not to prosecute. George, the investigation proved, didn't know Browser; had never seen him before. He had honestly thought that what he saw was a man attacking his mother.   8

But he had been misled by what he saw. His imagination exaggerated the evidence presented by his own eyes and converted it into something that wasn't true at all. As a result he had killed his mother's suitor. . . .   9

A GHASTLY STAB!

MARK TWAIN

It is hard to forget repulsive things. I remember yet how I ran   1
off from school once, when I was a boy, and then, pretty late at
night, concluded to climb into the window of my father's office
and sleep on a lounge, because I had a delicacy about going home
and getting thrashed. As I lay on the lounge and my eyes grew
accustomed to the darkness, I fancied I could see a long, dusky,
shapeless thing stretched upon the floor. A cold shiver went
through me. I turned my face to the wall. That did not answer. I
was afraid that that thing would creep over and seize me in the
dark. I turned back and stared at it for minutes and minutes—
they seemed hours. It appeared to me that the lagging moonlight
never, never would get to it. I turned to the wall and counted
twenty, to pass the feverish time away. I looked—the pale square
was nearer. I turned again and counted fifty—it was almost
touching it. With desperate will I turned again and counted one
hundred, and faced about, all in a tremble. A white human hand
lay in the moonlight! Such an awful sinking at the heart—such a
sudden gasp for breath! I felt—I cannot tell *what* I felt. When I recovered strength enough, I faced the wall again. But no boy
could have remained so, with that mysterious hand behind him.
I counted again, and looked—the most of a naked arm was exposed. I put my hand over my eyes and counted till I could stand
it no longer, and then—the pallid face of a man was there, with
the corners of the mouth drawn down, and the eyes fixed and
glassy in death! I raised to a sitting posture and glowered on that
corpse till the light crept down the bare breast—line by line—
inch by inch—past the nipple,—and then it disclosed a ghastly
stab!

I went away from there. I do not say that I went away in any 2
sort of hurry, but I simple went—that is sufficient. I went out at
the window, and I carried the sash along with me. I did not need
the sash, but it was handier to take it than to leave it, and so I
took it. I was not scared, but I was considerably agitated.

When I reached home, they whipped me, but I enjoyed it. It 3
seemed perfectly delightful. That man had been stabbed near the
office that afternoon, and they carried him in there to doctor
him, but he only lived an hour. I have slept in the same room
with him often, since then—in my dreams.

GROWING UP IN THE SHADOW OF AN OLDER BROTHER OR SISTER

SALLY HELGESEN

Being the oldest child in a family is coming into the world 1
tubula rasa, with a clean slate; there is no model, no outline, no
course one is expected to follow. Being the oldest is being a pio-
neer who must explore the tame uncharted territories so that set-
tlers who come afterward may find life better-defined, more secure. "I always felt I was born old, born *knowing*, the youngest of
five once told me, explaining that she had witnessed enough mistakes by her older siblings to know just what to avoid.

I felt envious. As the oldest of five, I always felt as if I'd been 2
born young, born *not* knowing. Nobody made my mistakes for
me. The advantages of having an older brother or sister have always been apparent to me, but it wasn't until recently that I began to understand that this particular blessing could be a mixed
one, like most good things in life.

The influence of an older child in the family may be so strong 3
that a younger spends a lifetime trying either to escape it or to
live up to imagined expectations. Although it's rare to encounter
an older child who's been profoundly influenced by a younger's
opinion, it's common to find those who, even in their forties and
fifties, are still enslaved by the opinions of a sibling only a year
or two older. A younger child may learn from an elder's blun-
ders, but often pays for the knowledge with a loss of freedom.

Let's listen again to that youngest child of five, the eighteen- 4
year-old who says she was born knowing, born old. "My brother
is three years older, and he had the most influence over me," she
says. "He had three older sisters, so when I came along he tried
to make me into a little brother. If I played with dolls, he laughed
at me, so I tried to be good at what he respected—mainly sports.

He had a crush on a girl in his class, Jody, who was a tomboy. She was my idol, too, so whenever he thought I wasn't trying hard enough to win, he'd yell and say, *don't you want to be like her?* If I got hurt, he'd make me get up and keep my mouth shut. Because of him, I learned to take pain and not cry. I'm glad of that—most girls seem like crybabies to me—but he also taught me that I had to stifle my feelings, so I learned to keep my emotions a secret. Sometimes I feel like I'm part guy because I understand so well how guys think. That makes me feel isolated from other kids. I can't imagine what I'd be like if I hadn't had a brother.''

I can't imagine what I'd be like—how often younger children say 5 that when referring to the influence of an older! And indeed, it's hard for me to imagine my friend without that peculiar code of toughness that she adopted under her brother's tutelage. Another young woman I know—recently married and still living in her small home town—spoke of a similar inability to conceive of herself without her two older sisters.

''My whole world view was shaped by them,'' she said. ''For 6 one thing, both of them moved away from town when they were eighteen, so I always assumed that's what people should do. I've never wanted to leave town, but I feel like a failure because I haven't. My husband can't understand.

''When I first learned to walk, my sisters stood me in the mid- 7 dle and made me come to whomever I liked best. I guess I've always felt torn between them. The oldest one grew up before the hippie era; she was popular, wore pleated skirts and matching sweaters, and went to all the dances and football games. I just assumed I'd be like that, but when I got into high school, everyone was a hippie, and what I'd taken for granted didn't happen. My second sister had been a hippie—she sat in her room all day, writing poetry and listening to Bob Dylan. So again, I felt as though I had to choose between my sisters. The choice was a conflict, and I didn't realize there could be a way in between, just for myself.''

Prompted by her second sister, this young woman rushed into 8 sexual relationships before she felt ready or even wanted to have them, in order to win approval. I mention this because in talking to younger brothers and sisters, I found that older children exert a surprising influence upon younger ones in regard to sex. But although this is quite common, it's rarely talked about, so people feel peculiar in their experience, and resent it. Girls seem particularly influenced by older brothers.

One high-school girl described it this way: "When my brother 9
started tenth grade, I was afraid he wouldn't hang around with
me anymore because he began to like girls. But he spent more
time with me than ever. Mostly, he'd talk about sex—what guys
liked, what made them feel good. I felt self-conscious at school,
because I knew so much more than the other kids. I felt older
than them, so I started having sex younger. Sometimes I blame it
on my brother, that my innocence was spoiled."

This girl might be much comforted if she were to learn how 10
common her experience is. She might resent her brother less.
Youngest children usually grow up fast—often faster than they
would like to. They learn lessons simply because older children
are eager to teach them. Parents seem unable to stop this; often,
they're oblivious to what's going on. But, while the lessons
younger children learn may propel them into a life for which
they don't feel ready, the insights they gain by watching older
kids at close range usually prepare them for more than they realize. Big brothers and sisters are, as I said, a mixed blessing. They
may map out your path instead of allowing you to follow your
own inclinations, but you can use their experience to move down
that path more directly.

THE STORY OF AN HOUR

KATE CHOPIN

Knowing that Mrs. Mallard was afflicted with a heart trou- 1
ble, great care was taken to break to her as gently as possible the
news of her husband's death.

It was her sister Josephine who told her, in broken sentences, 2
veiled hints that revealed in half concealing. Her husband's
friend Richards was there, too, near her. It was he who had been
in the newspaper office when intelligence of the railroad disaster
was received, with Brently Mallard's name leading the list of
"killed." He had only taken the time to assure himself of its truth
by a second telegram, and had hastened to forestall any less careful, less tender friend in bearing the sad message.

She did not hear the story as many women have heard the 3
same, with a paralyzed inability to accept its significance. She
wept at once, with sudden, wild abandonment, in her sister's
arms. When the storm of grief had spent itself she went to her
room alone. She would have no one follow her.

There stood, facing the open window, a comfortable, roomy 4
armchair. Into this she sank, pressed down by a physical exhaus-
tion that haunted her body and seemed to reach into her soul.

She could see in the open square before her house the tops of 5
trees that were all aquiver with the new spring life. The delicious
breath of rain was in the air. In the street below a peddler was
crying his wares. The notes of a distant song which some one
was singing reached her faintly, and countless sparrows were
twittering in the eaves.

There were patches of blue sky showing here and there 6
through the clouds that had met and piled above the other in the
west facing her window.

She sat with her head thrown back upon the cushion of the 7 chair quite motionless, except when a sob came up into her throat and shook her, as a child who has cried itself to sleep continues to sob in its dreams.

She was young, with a fair, calm face, whose lines bespoke re- 8 pression and even a certain strength. But now there was a dull stare in her eyes, whose gaze was fixed away off yonder on one of those patches of blue sky. It was not a glance of reflection, but rather indicated a suspension of intelligent thought.

There was something coming to her and she was waiting for it, 9 fearfully. What was it? She did not know; it was too subtle and elusive to name. But she felt it, creeping out of the sky, reaching toward her through the sounds, the scents, the color that filled the air.

Now her bosom rose and fell tumultuously. She was beginning 10 to recognize this thing that was approaching to possess her, and she was striving to beat it back with her will—as powerless as her two white slender hands would have been.

When she abandoned herself a little whispered word escaped 11 her slightly parted lips. She said it over and over under her breath: "Free, free, free!" The vacant stare and the look of terror that had followed it went from her eyes. They stayed keen and bright. Her pulses beat fast, and the coursing blood warmed and relaxed every inch of her body.

She did not stop to ask if it were not a monstrous joy that held 12 her. A clear and exalted perception enabled her to dismiss the suggestion as trivial.

She knew that she would weep again when she saw the kind, 13 tender hands folded in death; the face that had never looked save with love upon her, fixed and gray and dead. But she saw beyond that bitter moment a long procession of years to come that would belong to her absolutely. And she opened and spread her arms out to them in welcome.

There would be no one to live for during those coming years; 14 she would live for herself. There would be no powerful will bending her in that blind persistence with which men and women believe they have a right to impose a private will upon a fellow-creature. A kind intention or a cruel intention made the act seem no less a crime as she looked upon it in that brief moment of illumination.

And yet she had loved him—sometimes. Often she had not. 15 What did it matter! What could love, the unsolved mystery, count for in face of this possession of self-assertion which she suddenly recognized as the strongest impulse of her being!

"Free! Body and soul free!" she kept whispering.   16

Josephine was kneeling before the closed door with her lips to 17
the keyhole, imploring for admission. "Louise, open the door! I
beg; open the door—you will make yourself ill. What are you doing, Louise? For heaven's sake open the door."

"Go away. I am not making myself ill." No; she was drinking 18
in a very elixir of life through that open window.

Her fancy was running riot along those days ahead of her. 19
Spring days, and summer days, and all sorts of days that would
be her own. She breathed a quick prayer that life might be long.
It was only yesterday she had thought with a shudder that life
might be long.

She arose at length and opened the door to her sister's impor- 20
tunities. There was a feverish triumph in her eyes, and she carried herself unwittingly like a goddess of Victory. She clasped
her sister's waist, and together they descended the stairs. Richards stood waiting for them at the bottom.

Some one was opening the front door with a latchkey. It was 21
Brently Mallard who entered, a little travel-stained, composedly
carrying his grip-sack and umbrella. He had been far from the
scene of accident, and did not even know there had been one. He
stood amazed at Josephine's piercing cry; at Richards's quick motion to screen him from the view of his wife.

But Richards was too late.   22

When the doctors came they said she had died of heart dis- 23
ease—of joy that kills.

RESPONDING TO IDEAS

In Part Three the readings focus especially on ideas and are likely to trigger your own ideas in response. Although all reading and writing involve ideas in one way or another, the essays and stories in this part explore particular ideas that interested the authors. These readings, then, are like your own essays: The authors chose a topic and developed lines of argument and examples to support their ideas. The authors take a stand and express themselves, just as you have been doing in your essays for Parts One and Two.

When writing about ideas, it is especially important to select and limit your topic carefully and to organize your supporting examples and details to good effect. Whether you simply want to express your ideas or want to persuade your readers to accept your point of view, by sharing your work with classmates and friends you can learn whether your ideas are clear and convincing.

In responding to the readings that follow, remember that the goal is to discover your own ideas—not necessarily those which might be popular with your classmates or acceptable to your instructor. If you identify ideas that are important to you, you should be able to present them in an interesting, persuasive manner.

Photograph by David M. Grossman

INTELLIGENCE

ISAAC ASIMOV

What is intelligence, anyway? When I was in the army I re- 1
ceived a kind of aptitude test that all soldiers took and, against a
normal of 100, scored 160. No one at the base had ever seen a figure like that, and for two hours they made a big fuss over me. (It
didn't mean anything. The next day I was still a buck private
with KP as my highest duty.)

All my life I've been registering scores like that, so that I have 2
the complacent feeling that I'm highly intelligent, and I expect
other people to think so, too. Actually, though, don't such scores
simply mean that I am very good at answering the type of academic questions that are considered worthy of answers by the
people who make up the intelligence tests—people with intellectual bents similar to mine?

For instance, I had an auto-repair man once, who, on these in- 3
telligence tests, could not possibly have scored more than 80, by
my estimate. I always took it for granted that I was far more intelligent than he was. Yet, when anything went wrong with my
car I hastened to him with it, watched him anxiously as he explored its vitals, and listened to his pronouncements as though
they were divine oracles—and he always fixed my car.

Well, then, suppose my auto-repair man devised questions for 4
an intelligence test. Or suppose a carpenter did, or a farmer, or,
indeed, almost anyone but an academician. By every one of those
tests, I'd prove myself a moron. And I'd *be* a moron, too. In a
world where I could not use my academic training and my verbal talents but had to do something intricate or hard, working

with my hands, I would do poorly. My intelligence, then, is not absolute but is a function of the society I live in and of the fact that a small subsection of that society has managed to foist itself on the rest as an arbiter of such matters.

Consider my auto-repair man, again. He had a habit of telling   5 me jokes whenever he saw me. One time he raised his head from under the automobile hood to say: "Doc, a deaf-and-dumb guy went into a hardware store to ask for some nails. He put two fingers together on the counter and made hammering motions with the other hand. The clerk brought him a hammer. He shook his head and pointed to the two fingers he was hammering. The clerk brought him nails. He picked out the sizes he wanted, and left. Well, doc, the next guy who came in was a blind man. He wanted scissors. How do you suppose he asked for them?"

Indulgently, I lifted my right hand and made scissoring mo- 6 tions with my first two fingers. Whereupon my auto-repair man laughed raucously and said, "Why, you dumb jerk, he used his *voice* and asked for them." Then he said, smugly, "I've been trying that on all my customers today." "Did you catch many?" I asked. "Quite a few," he said, "but I knew for sure I'd catch *you.*" "Why is that?" I asked. "Because you're so goddamned educated, doc, I *knew* you couldn't be very smart."

And I have an uneasy feeling he had something there.   7

Sample Responses to "Intelligence"

Responder 1: Alex

Right on! This writer said what I've been saying for a long time, but he said it better. This whole society is going nuts over putting people in school and keeping them there. They think that because a person reads some books and swallows information about different subjects, that person is going to be intelligent. No way! Book learning is okay for some people, but other people are smart in different ways. Like Asimov told us--his auto repairman was a genius at fixing cars, but he probably couldn't score 80 on an intelligence test. I have friends who are going to college and friends who aren't. Some of the friends who aren't going are, in my opinion, smarter than the ones who are going. So what am I doing in college? I made a deal with my father. He said, "Go for a year, and if you don't like it, you can quit and work full time." I think he was sure I was going to like it. But I don't. In fact, I'm droppping out (how horrible!) after this semester. This essay was the only interesting thing I've read since I've been here.

Responder 2: Jerry

It's nice when somebody's so successful he can pretend that he's not so great. Isaac Asimov is a famous and rich writer. He's written a lot of science-fiction books and even factual books about science. I've read two or three of his science-fiction books, and I enjoyed them. So I'm not saying Asimov isn't a good writer, because he is. What I'm saying is that he <u>knows</u> he's very intelligent and successful, and so he can make fun of himself without worrying that anybody will take him seriously. Oh, yeah, he can say his mechanic is smart when it comes to fixing cars. But so what? The mechanic will be a working stiff all his life, and he'll never have a small fraction of the money that Asimov has. Asimov probably makes more money from one of his books than most people make in their lifetimes. Why should he worry about having his car fixed? He could buy a new car every month if he wanted to. I wish people wouldn't be so phony. Don't you love it when rich people, like famous movie or TV stars, tell us that money isn't everything. For them it isn't, because they've got plenty. It's nice for Asimov to say that his intelligence isn't any better than his mechanic's. Oh, sure, it isn't. It's only a million dollars better.

Responder 3: Millie

In high school there was a girl I have to describe as a real genius. She was a wiz in every subject. The math teacher even admitted that Phyllis (that was her name) knew more than he did.

But talk about sick. I mean that girl was the weirdest kid in school. She had no friends, even though some of us tried to be friendly with her. I asked her if she would like to eat lunch with me. I figured she really wanted a friend but was too shy. You know, she never even said anything. Just shook her head and walked away. And she wasn't bad looking. A couple of boys asked her if she would like to go out sometime. She told them she wasn't interested in going out because she had other things to do. One of the boys told me she was the coldest fish he ever talked to.

So I guess Phyllis was smart, but if being smart makes you so weird, you can have it. I'd rather be just average in intelligence but also a human being.

Responder 4: Jean

Society decides how valuable something is. That's why a smart auto mechanic doesn't get as much respect as a doctor or a lawyer. People may respect a mechanic's skill at fixing things, but nobody invites him on television to give his opinions about what's going on in the world. Maybe a mechanic has the intelligence to solve some of the problems in our society. However, we'll never hear his opinions, because no one will ever ask him.

I think we kid ourselves when we talk about all the opportunities in our country. Most of the important positions are filled by people who come from the ''right'' families and go to the ''best'' schools. Two people may have a college degree. However, a

degree from a prestigious college is worth more than a degree from
an ordinary college. Things aren't equal, because some people are
born with a head start over the rest of us. We can all dream about
reaching the top, but very few of us will be able to crack the
system that the ruling class has set up for its own benefit.

Considering the Responses

Response 1: Alex

Apparently, Alex doesn't value a college degree very highly. He claims
that some of his noncollege friends are smarter than his college friends.
Furthermore, he questions society's emphasis on education or, at least, on
schooling. He seems to have gotten little from his classes so far, and he expresses his intention to drop out and go to work full time.

1. Based on his response, do you think Alex can write a convincing essay on the idea that a college education isn't needed by everyone in
   our society? Do you think he can support his contention that some of
   his noncollege friends are smarter than his college friends? What
   problems do you see in planning an essay which might convince us
   that his observation is reasonable?
2. Do you see another possible topic in Alex's personal reasons for
   wanting to drop out of college? Which ideas in his response should
   he expand to develop this topic?

Response 2: Jerry

Jerry thinks that successful people are so secure that they can play down
their talents. He sees a streak of phoniness in Asimov's praise for his auto
mechanic's intelligence, as well as in the pronouncements of rich people
who tell us that money isn't everything. In fact, Jerry seems to equate intelligence with the ability to make money.

1. To write an essay defending the idea that intelligent people are also
   people who have a great deal of money, would Jerry have to present
   a somewhat different definition of intelligence than the one most
   people use? How do you define intelligence? Could that definition
   be the basis of Jerry's essay?
2. Do you think an essay *can* be written defending the ideas in Jerry's
   response? Why or why not? Would an essay that argues against Jerry's ideas be easier to write?

Response 3: Millie

Millie's experiences with Phyllis lead her to suggest that highly intelligent people have problems fitting in socially. Millie calls Phyllis "the weirdest kid in school," a judgment which later leads her to imply that—when it comes to being a human being—her own "average" intelligence is preferable to Phyllis's "genius."

During discussion many students supported the idea that high intelligence often leads to social and psychological problems. Like Millie, some students offered examples of bright people who were unable to lead "normal" social lives. Other students disagreed, citing examples of people they knew who were extremely bright and very popular as well.

1. Since some students gave examples of people who were very bright and well adjusted, and others gave examples of highly intelligent but abnormal people, do you think Millie can support her idea that high intelligence leads to social maladjustment? Why or why not?
2. If Millie still wants to write about Phyllis, what topic sentence or controlling idea might she use to guide her essay?
3. If Millie wants to explore the relationship between intelligence and social adjustment more broadly and more objectively, what should she do to learn more about this relationship? What advice would you give her?

Response 4: Jean

Jean's response contains several ideas that might be developed into an interesting essay.

1. Does the idea that a person's profession may *automatically* confer respect and status seem like a promising topic? Why or why not? What difficulties do you foresee in planning such an essay?
2. In Jean's opinion, a degree from one of the "best" schools is more valuable than a degree from "an ordinary college." How might this line of reasoning be pursued in an essay?
3. Jean also feels that it is difficult for someone to "crack the system" unless that person is born into the "right" family. What arguments could she offer to support this idea? Can you think of examples that would undercut such arguments? Do you think that a writer *can* convince readers of this idea? Why or why not?

NO ALLUSIONS
IN THE CLASSROOM

JAIME M. O'NEILL

Josh Billings, a 19th-century humorist, wrote that it is better   1
"not to know so much than to know so many things that ain't
so." Recently, after 15 years of teaching in community colleges, I
decided to take a sampling to find out what my students know
that ain't so. I did this out of a growing awareness that they don't
always understand what I say. I suspected that part of their failure to understand derived from the fact that they did not catch
my allusions. An allusion to a writer, a geographical locality or a
historical episode inevitably produced telltale expressions of be-
wilderment.

There is a game played by students and teachers everywhere.   2
The game goes like this: the teacher tries to find out what students don't know so that he can correct those deficiencies; the
students, concerned with grades and slippery self-images, try to
hide their ignorance in every way they can. So it is that students
seldom ask pertinent questions. So it is that teachers assume that
students possess basic knowledge which, in fact, they don't possess.

Last semester I broke the rules of this time-honored game   3
when I presented my English-composition students with an 86-
question "general knowledge" test on the first day of class.
There were 26 people in the class; they ranged in age from 18 to
54. They had all completed at least one quarter of college-level
work.

Here is a sampling of what they knew that just ain't so: 4

Creative: Ralph Nader is a baseball player. Charles Darwin in-   5
vented gravity. Christ was born in the 16th century. J. Edgar

Hoover was a 19th-century president. Neil Simon wrote "One Flew Over the Cuckoo's Nest"; "The Great Gatsby" was a magician in the 1930s. Franz Joseph Haydn was a songwriter during the same decade. Sid Caesar was an early Roman emperor. Mark Twain invented the cotton gin. Heinrich Himmler invented the Heimlich maneuver. Jefferson Davis was a guitar player for The Jefferson Airplane. Benito Mussolini was a Russian leader of the 18th century; Dwight D. Eisenhower came earlier, serving as a president during the 17th century. William Faulkner made his name as a 17th-century scientist. All of these people must have appreciated the work of Pablo Picasso, who painted masterpieces in the 12th century.

My students were equally creative in their understanding of geography. They knew, for instance, that Managua is the capital of Vietnam, that Cape Town is in the United States and that Beirut is in Germany. Bogotá, of course, is in Borneo (unless it is in China). Camp David is in Israel, and Stratford-on-Avon is in Grenada (or Gernada). Gdansk is in Ireland. Cologne is in the Virgin Islands. Mazatlán is in Switzerland. Belfast was variously located in Egypt, Germany, Belgium and Italy. Leningrad was transported to Jamaica; Montreal to Spain.

And on it went. Most students answered incorrectly far more often than they answered correctly. Several of them meticulously wrote "I don't know" 86 times, or 80 times, or 62 times.

They did not like the test. Although I made it clear that the test would not be graded, they did not like having their ignorance exposed. One of them dismissed the test by saying, "Oh, I get it; it's like Trivial Pursuit." Imagining a game of Trivial Pursuit among some of today's college students is a frightening thought; such a game could last for years.

But the comment bothered me. What, in this time in our global history, is trivial? And what is essential? Perhaps it no longer matters very much if large numbers of people in the world's oldest democratic republic know little of their own history and even less about the planet they inhabit.

But I expect that it does matter. I also suspect that my students provide a fairly good cross section of the general population. There are 1,274 two-year colleges in the United States that collectively enroll nearly 5 million students. I have taught at four of those colleges in two states, and I doubt that my questionnaire would have produced different results at any of them. My colleagues at universities tell me that they would not be surprised at similar undergraduate answers.

My small sampling is further corroborated by recent polls 11
which disclosed that a significant number of American adults
have no idea which side the United States supported in Vietnam
and that a majority of the general populace have no idea which
side the United States is currently supporting in Nicaragua or El
Salvador.

Less importantly, a local marketing survey asked a sampling of 12
young computer whizzes to identify the character in IBM's
advertising campaign that is based on an allusion to Charlie
Chaplin in "Modern Times." Few of them had heard of Charlie
Chaplin, fewer heard or knew about the movie classic.

Common Heritage: As I write this, the radio is broadcasting the 13
news about the Walker family. Accused of spying for the Soviets,
the Walkers, according to a U.S. attorney, will be the Rosenbergs
of the '80s. One of my students thought Ethel Rosenberg was a
singer from the 1930s. The rest of them didn't know. Communication depends, to some extent, upon the ability to make (and
catch) allusions, to share a common understanding and a common heritage. Even preliterate societies can claim this shared as-
sessment of their world. As we enter the postindustrial "information processing" age, what sort of information will be
processed? And, as the educational establishment is driven
"back to the basics," isn't it time we decided that a common understanding of our history and our planet is most basic of all?

As a teacher, I find myself in the ignorance-and-hope business. 14
Each year hopeful faces confront me, trying to conceal their ignorance. Their hopes ride on the dispelling of that ignorance.

All our hopes do.   15

We should begin servicing that hope more responsibly and dis- 16
pelling that ignorance with a more systematic approach to im-
parting essential knowledge.

Socrates, the American Indian chieftain, would have wanted it 17
that way.

Sample Responses to "No Allusions in the Classroom"

Responder 1: Gary

Why do teachers think everything they know is so
important? And why does this one believe the answers that the

students gave to his questions? I know I'd give a flip answer if I wasn't sure what the test was all about.

Who'd feel stupid if he didn't know the name of some old comedian on early television or a Nazi police officer who's been dead forty years? This teacher lived back in those days, and so he remembers it all from the movies and the news when he was growing up. We'll remember Son of Sam and Steve Martin, but our grandchildren won't have any idea who they were. I won't expect them to, either, but then I'm not a teacher.

And geography! That's like knowing the names of all the stars and the constellations. I bet he wouldn't know Sirius is the nearest star (Oops, I forgot the sun) or what the Pleiades look like. And he'd never guess what Dragon Slayer is.

If he's going to publish all those wrong answers before a national audience, then no wonder so many of the students answered "no comment." I sure wouldn't want to be in his class. But I'm afraid I've got a couple of teachers just like him this semester.

Responder 2: Gwen

I can't believe anybody in college doesn't know most of the things on this teacher's questionnaire. Nobody could be expected to know them all, but everybody should know some of them, like Jesus, Darwin, and Socrates. I guess some people find it hard to remember for very long the things they learn for tests. Maybe they have to keep hearing about someone or some place for it to stick in their minds. Maybe he should have given them multiple choices to jog their memories. Then he wouldn't have gotten wild guesses. But still, we forget so much because there is so much we are expected to learn, and it's hard to tell what's really important.

Even his test might confuse someone from another country. They might think all the names and places are very important. But Neil Simon, William Faulkner, Cologne, and Bogota are not nearly as significant as Beirut, Eisenhower, Mark Twain, and Picasso. And some names might be recognizable if they came up in our reading, where our attention would be pointed in the right direction by the topic. Also, if I wasn't sure how to spell Beirut, I might have been fooled. Some people are truly ignorant, and they won't last long in college unless they learn an awful lot and very fast. But I think the test doesn't mean all that much.

Responder 3: Yvette

I thought I came to college to learn, but this man thinks I should know everything right now. I was encouraged to return to school now that my family are all in their teens or married. My son is also going to college, but not this one. But if I had been tested like this on the first day, I'd have quit right then and there. I'm supposed to know all these names? Actually I did know some of the ones that he put on the test just to show he isn't a snob (Neil Simon and Sid Caesar). I suppose the list of things the students didn't know is full of answers that would seem humorous if I knew who the people and places really are. But I didn't know most of them. And I don't think it is funny that someone didn't know when Christ lived. Maybe he was Jewish or a Hindu. I've forgotten some things he says I should know, like whose side we were on in the Vietnam War. I only know we were on the wrong side, since they lost. Also, I'm a little confused by his last quotation. I thought Socrates was the name of an ancient Greek philosopher. If it is also an Indian chief, history is going to be much harder than I expected.

Considering the Responses

Response 1: Gary

Gary felt at a loss for a topic. He realized that just criticizing the test questions one by one would not result in an "essay," but he couldn't see how his objections to this teacher's approach could be turned into a topic that would interest anyone.

1. What do you think is the main idea in Gary's response? Does any sentence in his response sum up that idea? What topic sentence would you advise Gary to use in focusing his ideas?
2. Depending on your answers to question 1, help Gary plan his essay. What kinds of examples should he use to develop his main idea? Will those examples prove his point, or does he need to go beyond his own observations?

Response 2: Gwen

Gwen's response revealed mixed feelings about this essay. She tended to agree that students should be better informed, but she also made excuses for their poor performance on this questionnaire. Her last sentence—"The test doesn't mean all that much"—sums up her defense of students. She seems to believe that the fault lies in Professor O'Neill's test, both in how the questions were presented and in the kinds of information he expected students to know. But she also includes a lot of ideas about why students do poorly on tests.

1. Should Gwen develop a paper about poorly designed tests or about poorly prepared students? Which topic is a better response to O'Neill's essay? Why?
2. Of the two topic ideas in question 1, which is easier to develop in an essay? Why?

Response 3: Yvette

Yvette was intimidated by Professor O'Neill's questionnaire, because she is not as well informed as she would like to be. In fact, most of her response is about why she herself would do poorly on this test.

1. What do you think Yvette should write about? Is her response about the essay or about herself? What topic sentence should she explore?
2. Depending on your answers to question 1, how should Yvette develop her essay? What ideas and examples should she offer, and how should she organize them?

MEMORIES AREN'T
MADE OF THIS

ERIC ZORN

Something terrible has happened to popular music in this   1
country. Over the last few years it has touched its finger to the
Tar Baby of television and now finds itself unable to pull away.
Consider the following depressing news:

- There are 200 regular television programs in America that   2
  feature nothing but the combination of film clips and rock
  songs.
- Warner Amex's Music Television (MTV), the cable net-   3
  work based solely on these music videos, hits nearly 20
  million homes and is the hottest basic cable operation in
  history.
- The marriage of music and television has proved to be so   4
  popular that it is credited with almost singlehandedly
  snapping the recording industry out of a four-year slump
  in 1983 and changing the face of popular music by intro-
  ducing the new bands and new sounds radio wouldn't
  touch.
- Today's pop-music groups find that they must produce   5
  video versions of their songs if they wish to survive. Many
  are making video-cassette albums that customers buy instead of records.
- Really cool people now speak of "seeing" the latest songs   6
  as opposed to hearing them. More than a majority of MTV
  viewers recently sampled say they "play back" the video
  in their minds when they hear a song on the radio.

This all indicates strongly that music videos are no passing fad.   7
They're here to stay, just like TV itself when it first came along in
the late 1940s to add pictures to the old radio dramas.

I find this all terribly sad. The proliferation of music videos 8
threatens to produce an entire generation of people who will all
but miss out on the sublime, extremely personal element of
music.

What nobody has bothered to point out in the course of all this 9
hoopla attendant upon rock video is that music has always had a
visual element of a sort: the images, people and places that the
listener sees in his mind's eye when a favorite song or symphony
comes on.

One of the truly great but least understood components of mu- 10
sic is the way it can tap long-forgotten emotions and unlock unconscious memories. Many feelings and old visual impressions
are so deeply hidden in the recesses of the mind that sometimes
only the sudden surprise of a melody can lead the way to them.

Special songs can act for us like the tea and madeleine cake in 11
Marcel Proust's huge novel, "A Remembrance of Things Past,"
as a simple spark that sets off a blaze of recollections.

"Mr. Tambourine Man" by Bob Dylan brings back the long 12
walks my best buddy and I used to take on the beach near his
mom's cottage on Cape Cod; "Mrs. Robinson" by Simon and
Garfunkel conjures up the kitchen in the first house my parents
ever owned; "Amie" by Pure Prairie League reminds me of
springtime in the old college dormitory and my first train trip to
Chicago.

When I hear someone fiddle "Lamplighter's Hornpipe," I 13
think of a particular section of Altgeld Street near DePaul University where I first heard that tune on tape; and "Seasons in the
Sun" by Terry Jacks, a terrible song, brings on the delightful
memory of a young woman named Martine for whom I yearned
so tragically in 11th grade I could scarcely move myself to speak
to her.

For Martine, wherever she is, it is safe to say "Seasons in the 14
Sun" has entirely different associations. That's the great thing
about music. No matter how many millions of people bought
that record or heard it on the radio, there will always be something about its smarmy lyrics that will be special only to me.

Not every song still has this power, however. I've already had 15
a few of them ruined when, in idle moments, I have lingered too
long in front of a TV set showing music videos. When, for example, I hear Michael Jackson's "Billie Jean," the first, overwhelm-
ing image I get in my mind is of the lithe little Mr. Jackson caper-
ing around and pointing his lithe little finger every which way.
No good memories. No bad memories. Nothing but the exact
same memories that everyone else will have of this song for decades to come.

Who can hear "Suicide is Painless," the theme song from 16
M*A*S*H," and think of anything else but helicopters? Who can
hear "Yellow Submarine" by the Beatles and not be flooded with
thoughts of the brightly colored Peter Max cartoons that
splashed through the movie of the same name?

Antiseptic Music: What we're really talking about here is the 17
wholesale substitution of common, shared memories for individual memories; a substitution that ends up robbing us of pieces of
our own lives. The personal side of music is steadily being replaced by the corporate side, so that the associations and mental
pictures that go along with songs for the MTV generation don't
relate to *their* lives, but to the lives of the people who conceived
the videos.

We're left with popular music that has the same distant, anti- 18
septic feel as network television: you may enjoy it, but you must
admit that it doesn't, in any meaningful way, feel as though it *belongs* to you. The combination of sight and sound not only pro-
motes passive viewing, but serves to depersonalize the entertain-
ment offered.

Young lovers today, I suspect, do not elbow each other excit- 19
edly when an old Duran Duran clip comes on the TV screen and
coo, "Look, darling, they're showing our video."

And that's depressing news: future generations will be locked 20
into the prefabricated memories of a false musical experience,
restricted by monolithic visual interpretations of songs that pre-
empt and defy the exercise of individual experience, motion and
memory.

Videos will not be the death of pop music, radio or the old rock 21
groups that never thought to film themselves moving their lips to
the words. But ultimately the insidious combination of film and
song will sap away some of the great power of music and change
how we feel about it in a very fundamental way.

I wonder how many of us are really ready for that?   22

Sample Responses to "Memories Aren't Made of This"

Responder 1: Lillian

My parents always say that the music I listen to doesn't

make any sense. They like the music from their generation when

they were younger, which, if you ask me, is kind of dull. But I guess you like the music you listened to when you were young. At weddings I notice that the older group really gets into those old songs, and they get up and dance as though they were still young. I don't particularly like their music, but I think it's nice to see my parents and my uncles and aunts and their friends acting like they were falling in love for the first time. It makes me think that life isn't really over just because you get older. Maybe music videos will make my generation all have the same picture in mind when we hear one of today's hits later, when we are a lot older. But I don't think so. By the time we're old enough to get sentimental over one of our old favorites, we probably won't remember the pictures that went with the song. But I could be wrong.

Responder 2: Richard

I'm ashamed to be part of this so-called younger generation, and rock videos make me even more ashamed. It seems that any kind of senseless gadget becomes a big seller because young people these days are idiots. They start out by becoming hypnotized by TV even before they learn how to talk. After years of watching TV, their minds are destroyed as far as concentration and learning are concerned. So why shouldn't they think rock videos are terrific? Here's another gadget to keep their minds from thinking or worrying about anything that might be important. Eric Zorn is wasting his time if he thinks he can persuade this generation to give up its rock videos and to let their own minds create the pictures that will be part of their memories. Most young people today don't have good enough minds to create anything, not even their own memories. In fact, the people addicted to rock videos would find this essay too hard to read.

Responder 3: Vito

This essay is ridiculous. My older brother and his girlfriend are intellectual types. They love to go to the opera because that kind of music and singing really turns them on. But just because they see an opera performed on a stage doesn't mean that they don't listen to recordings of the same opera. Sometimes I see them listening to the stereo with an opera on and their eyes closed as if they were in another world. I'm sure they don't see the opera the way it was performed on stage when they listen at home. The same with rock videos. Sometimes I think of the video when I hear a song on the radio, but sometimes I don't. It depends on the mood I'm in. Also, I've seen many movies that had European locations--France, Italy, Spain--but that doesn't mean that when I go to Europe I won't see it in my own way. According to this writer, when I go to Europe I'll only think of the movies I saw, not the real thing. What I really think is that this writer is like all older people. Everything the younger generation likes, the older generation finds something wrong with. Just because this writer didn't have videos when he was growing up, videos must be no good. It's the same old story.

Considering the Responses

Response 1: Lillian

Lillian apparently wasn't as interested in discussing Zorn's thesis as she was in speculating about what it is like to grow older. Her response indicates that she has thought about what her world will be like when she is part of the "older group."

1. Based on her response, do you think Lillian has a positive attitude, a negative attitude, or an ambivalent attitude toward aging?

2. Do you think Lillian can write an essay in which she explores all of her attitudes. What might be the purpose of such an essay? How might it be organized?
3. Suppose Lillian entitles her essay "My Life When I Am 45." What advice can you give her about developing this topic? How can she make her speculations about the future convincing?

Response 2: Richard

Richard categorizes rock videos as "senseless gadgets," which, like television, allow young people to close off their minds to thought and worry. He says he is "ashamed" to be part of the younger generation, and he disparages the intellectual and creative abilities of his peers.

1. Does Richard's response convey enough about his ideas and feelings so that we can understand why he is so negative toward his generation? What would you ask Richard about his response?
2. Assume that you agree with Richard's perceptions of young people. Do you think he is ready to develop his response into an essay? What advice can you give him about focusing his ideas and developing a main purpose for writing?
3. How would you defend the younger generation against Richard's charges? Which of Richard's ideas and comments would you focus on? Why?

Response 3: Vito

Vito went so far as to label this essay "ridiculous." He presents an opposing view based on the behavior of his brother and his brother's girlfriend when they listen to opera recordings. Then he extends his argument by doubting that movies will affect his impressions of Europe when he travels there. He closes by saying that Zorn's criticism of videos stems from the prejudice that older people show toward anything that younger people enjoy.

1. Do you think Vito's argument can be developed into an essay defending rock videos? How could he expand his argument? What other kinds of support could he use to defend his point of view?
2. Could Vito's remarks about the older generation's attitudes toward young people be developed into an effective essay? How could Vito support his idea that older people automatically dislike anything younger people like? What advice would you give Vito about supporting this line of argument?

ADDITIONAL READINGS

HOW ABOUT LOW-COST DRUGS FOR ADDICTS?

LOUIS NIZER

We are losing the war against drug addiction. Our strategy   1
is wrong. I propose a different approach.

The Government should create clinics, manned by psychia-   2
trists, that would provide drugs for nominal charges or even free
to addicts under controlled regulations. It would cost the Government only 20 cents for a heroin shot, for which the addicts
must now pay the mob more than $100, and there are similar
price discrepancies in cocaine, crack and other such substances.

Such a service, which would also include the staff support of   3
psychiatrists and doctors, would cost a fraction of what the nation now spends to maintain the land, sea and air apparatus necessary to interdict illegal imports of drugs. There would also be a
savings of hundreds of millions of dollars from the elimination of
the prosecutorial procedures that stifle our courts and overcrowd
our prisons.

We see in our newspapers the triumphant announcements by   4
Government agents that they have intercepted huge caches of
cocaine, the street prices of which are in the tens of millions of
dollars. Should we be gratified? Will this achievement reduce the
number of addicts by one? All it will do is increase the cost to the
addict of his illegal supply.

117

Many addicts who are caught committing a crime admit that 5
they have mugged or stolen as many as six or seven times a day
to accumulate the $100 needed for a fix. Since many of them
need two or three fixes a day, particularly for crack, one can understand the terror in our streets and homes. It is estimated that
there are in New York City alone 200,000 addicts, and this is typical of cities across the nation. Even if we were to assume that
only a modest percentage of a city's addicts engage in criminal
conduct to obtain the money for the habit, requiring multiple
muggings and thefts each day, we could nevertheless account for
many of the tens of thousands of crimes each day in New York
City alone.

Not long ago, a Justice Department division issued a report 6
stating that more than half the perpetrators of murder and other
serious crimes were under the influence of drugs. This symbol-
izes the new domestic terror in our nation. This is why our citizens are unsafe in broad daylight on the most traveled thorough-
fares. This is why typewriters and television sets are stolen from
offices and homes and sold for a pittance. This is why parks are
closed to the public and why murders are committed. This is
why homes need multiple locks, and burglary systems, and why
store windows, even in the most fashionable areas, require iron
gates.

The benefits of the new strategy to control this terrorism 7
would be immediate and profound.

First, the mob would lose the main source of its income. It 8
could not compete against a free supply for which previously it
exacted tribute estimated to be hundreds of millions of dollars,
perhaps billions, from hopeless victims.

Second, pushers would be put out of business. There would be 9
no purpose in creating addicts who would be driven by desperate
compulsion to steal and kill for the money necessary to maintain
their habit. Children would not be enticed. The mob's macabre
public-relations program is to tempt children with free drugs in
order to create customers for the future. The wave of street
crimes in broad daylight would diminish to a trickle. Homes and
stores would not have to be fortresses. Our recreational areas
could again be used. Neighborhoods would not be scandalized by
sordid street centers where addicts gather to obtain their supply
from slimy merchants.

Third, police and other law-enforcement authorities, domestic 10
or foreign, would be freed to deal with traditional nondrug
crimes.

There are several objections that might be raised against such 11 a salutary solution.

First, it could be argued that by providing free drugs to the ad- 12 dict we would consign him to permanent addiction. The answer is that medical and psychiatric help at the source would be more effective in controlling the addict's descent than the extremely limited remedies available to the victim today. I am not arguing that the new strategy will cure everything. But I do not see many addicts being freed from their bonds under the present system.

In addition, as between the addict's predicament and the 13 safety of our innocent citizens, which deserves our primary concern? Drug-induced crime has become so common that almost every citizen knows someone in his immediate family or among his friends who has been mugged. It is these citizens who should be our chief concern.

Another possible objection is that addicts will cheat the system 14 by obtaining more than the allowable free shot. Without discounting the resourcefulness of the bedeviled addict, it should be possible to have Government cards issued that would be punched so as to limit the free supply in accord with medical authorization.

Yet all objections become trivial when matched against the cri- 15 sis itself. What we are witnessing is the demoralization of a great society: the ruination of its school children, athletes and executives, the corrosion of the workforce in general.

Many thoughtful sociologists consider the rapidly spreading 16 drug use the greatest problem that our nation faces—greater and more real and urgent than nuclear bombs or economic reversal. In China, a similar crisis drove the authorities to apply capital punishment to those who trafficked in opium—an extreme solution that arose from the deepest reaches of frustration.

Free drugs will win the war against the domestic terrorism 17 caused by illicit drugs. As a strategy, it is at once resourceful, sensible and simple. We are getting nowhere in our efforts to hold back the ocean of supply. The answer is to dry up demand.

PROBLEMS AND PAIN

M. SCOTT PECK

Life is difficult.   1

This is a great truth, one of the greatest truths. It is a great   2
truth because once we truly see this truth, we transcend it. Once
we truly know that life is difficult—once we truly understand
and accept it—then life is no longer difficult. Because once it is
accepted, the fact that life is difficult no longer matters.

Most do not fully see this truth that life is difficult. Instead   3
they moan more or less incessantly, noisily or subtly, about the
enormity of their problems, their burdens, and their difficulties
as if life were generally easy, as if life *should* be easy. They voice
their belief, noisily or subtly, that their difficulties represent a
unique kind of affliction that should not be and that has somehow been especially visited upon them, or else upon their families, their tribe, their class, their nation, their race or even their
species, and not upon others. I know about this moaning because
I have done my share.

Life is a series of problems. Do we want to moan about them   4
or solve them? Do we want to teach our children to solve them?

Discipline is the basic set of tools we require to solve life's   5
problems. Without discipline we can solve nothing. With only
some discipline we can solve only some problems. With total discipline we can solve all problems.

What makes life difficult is that the process of confronting and   6
solving problems is a painful one. Problems, depending upon
their nature, evoke in us frustration or grief or sadness or loneliness or guilt or regret or anger or fear or anxiety or anguish or despair. These are uncomfortable feelings, often very uncomfortable, often as painful as any kind of physical pain, sometimes

equaling the very worst kind of physical pain. Indeed, it is *because* of the pain that events or conflicts engender in us that we call them problems. And since life poses an endless series of problems, life is always difficult and is full of pain as well as joy.

Yet it is in this whole process of meeting and solving problems that life has its meaning. Problems are the cutting edge that distinguishes between success and failure. Problems call forth our courage and our wisdom; indeed, they create our courage and our wisdom. It is only because of problems that we grow mentally and spiritually. When we desire to encourage the growth of the human spirit, we challenge and encourage the human capacity to solve problems, just as in school we deliberately set problems for our children to solve. It is through the pain of confronting and resolving problems that we learn. As Benjamin Franklin said, "Those things that hurt, instruct." It is for this reason that wise people learn not to dread but actually to welcome problems and actually to welcome the pain of problems.

REFLECTIONS ON
A HOCKEY HELMET

GREGORY BAYAN

I was in the middle of a hockey game recently when I over- 1
heard two young spectators arguing about the way I play. I heard
the words "very brave" and "very foolish," attributes I would
never use to describe myself. Yet every year at this time I am be-
sieged by ever-increasing numbers of well-meaning people who
suggest or plead that I cease my sacrilege and start to play it safe.
The cause of this concern is simple: I refuse to wear a protective
helmet.

This expression of individuality does not come cheaply or friv- 2
olously. Bareheaded ice-hockey players are banned from all offi-
cially sanctioned amateur play, including school, college, junior
and international competition. I am forever banished to the neth-
erworld of semiprivate club hockey in men's amateur leagues,
the only refuge where my vanishing species is still allowed to
exist.

The decision not to wear a helmet involves intensely personal 3
feelings that transcend safety. I find the helmet to be physically
uncomfortable, but more important, it strikes me as being anti-
individual and esthetically repellent. Look at film clips of the
1960 U.S. Olympic hockey team's gold-medal victory at Squaw
Valley, when not even the Russians wore helmets. Now watch a
clip of any of this year's hockey matches, where helmets are
mandatory. There's something missing. The human element of
daring independence is gone. As much as I love the sport, I can
no longer watch televised hockey. I simply cannot relate to the
players as human beings when they all resemble identical au-
tomatons.

Like a dorsal fin that breaks water and heralds the presence of 4 a leviathan, so the helmet is a metaphor for something deeply wrong in America.

Protection: Helmets are a sign we've entered the era of the 5 Hardhead. A Hardhead is one who seeks to protect us not only from others, but from ourselves. He is creating a Huxley-like world where all irritating incongruities among individuals are being conveniently erased in the name of safety. Americans are afraid, afraid of risk. We want absolute personal safety, and we want it guaranteed and mandatory.

Perhaps it's because we now enjoy such an unprecedented de- 6 gree of safety, compared with the past, that previously disregarded risks stand out in such bold relief. The great population destroyers of rampant disease, impure food and unduly hazardous working conditions have been largely brought under control, reducing the average person's daily contact with death and injury to a level thought impossible only a few decades ago. This is obviously a good thing. I shed no tears for smallpox and polio. I feel better having the Food and Drug Administration monitor the presence of rodent hairs in my frozen pizza, rather than being forced to take up a microscope and do the job myself. Government should try to protect its citizens from external malice and negligence beyond the individual's control, but there is a fine line between necessary protection and unwarranted interferences.

When the Hardheads go to work on dismantling freedom of 7 choice, that's when I put my skate down. When the phrase *it's for your own good* determines every direction of personal initiative, then I know we've embraced the philosophy of the Pringle's potato chip—uniformity and monotony. Domed sports stadiums are springing up like mushrooms to protect us from the unpredictable. Speedometers read no faster than 85 mph to protect us from the temptations of curiosity. U.S. amateur boxers must now wear headgear for their own good. Our automobiles now buzz us to buckle up for our own good. CBS is even taking the scissors to The Bugs Bunny/Road Runner cartoon show, lest scenes of excessive "violence" feed our latent homicidal impulses. All for our own good.

America is being smothered by safety. Sometimes I think if 8 Henry Hudson were to suddenly reappear in New York Bay, he would be arrested and placed under observation, and the leaky old Half Moon would be impounded for innumerable construction violations.

There is no such thing as complete safety. When Astroturf first 9 came out, its uniform surface was touted as a way to reduce injury. There now exists an entire lexicon of Astro-turf-induced injuries, such as "Astro-burn" and "Astro-knee." There are examples of people who have been thrown from their cars and spared from death in terrible accidents because they were *not* wearing their seat belts. Motorcycle helmets have been known to cause whiplash. Government statistics tell us that the leading cause of personal injury in the United States is people falling down—in bathtubs, on stairs, off ladders, everywhere. Despite our best efforts to the contrary, the universe still appears to be firmly in the grip of Murphy's Law (if something can go wrong, it will).

Mandatory armor, worn at all times, and a life spent huddled 10 in a bomb shelter may result in longevity—but what kind of life is that? To those who demand an utterly protected and predictable existence I say fine, good luck, but don't include me in your mandate.

Mavericks: Freedom of choice is the only thing that separates 11 the living from the dead. We need it, with all of its inherent dangers. We need the risk taker, the maverick, the thorn in the side of conformity. We need Martin Luther, John Lennon, George Willig, Sir Thomas More, Jack Paar and Wile E. Coyote. And ice hockey's Hobey Baker. We need every last bit of individuality we can get. Without it, life loses the glorious zest of freedom and diversity, of fantasy and change.

Which brings me back to the helmet. I would never impose my 12 personal preference on others. All I claim is the same consideration for myself.

I realize the risk involved in the simple act of playing ice 13 hockey without wearing a helmet, and I accept it, the same as I accept the fact that I won't live forever. When the Hardheads change that fact, when they finally succeed in loading life's dice, that's when I'll hang up my skates.

For my own good. 14

THE LAST JUDGMENT

KAREL ČAPEK

The notorious multiple-killer Kugler, pursued by several   1
warrants and a whole army of policemen and detectives, swore
that he'd never be taken. He wasn't either—at least not alive.
The last of his nine murderous deeds was shooting a policeman
who tried to arrest him. The policeman indeed died, but not before putting a total of seven bullets into Kugler. Of these seven,
three were fatal. Kugler's death came so quickly that he felt no
pain. And so it seemed Kugler had escaped earthly justice.

When his soul left his body, it should have been surprised at   2
the sight of the next world—a world beyond space, gray, and infi-
nitely desolate—but it wasn't. A man who has been jailed on two
continents looks upon the next life merely as new surroundings.
Kugler expected to struggle through, equipped only with a bit of
courage, as he had in the last world.

At length the inevitable Last Judgment got around to Kugler.   3

Heaven being eternally in a state of emergency, Kugler was   4
brought before a special court of three judges and not, as his previous conduct would ordinarily merit, before a jury. The courtroom was furnished simply, almost like courtrooms on earth,
with this one exception: there was no provision for swearing in
witnesses. In time, however, the reason for this will become apparent.

The judges were old and worthy councillors with austere,   5
bored faces. Kugler complied with the usual tedious formalities:
Ferdinand Kugler, unemployed, born on such and such a date,
died . . . at this point it was shown Kugler didn't know the date
of his own death. Immediately he realized this was a damaging
omission in the eyes of the judges; his spirit of helpfulness faded.

"Do you plead guilty or not guilty?" asked the presiding judge.   6

"Not guilty," said Kugler obdurately.   7

"Bring in the first witness," the judge sighed.   8

Opposite Kugler appeared an extraordinary gentleman,   9
stately, bearded, and clothed in a blue robe strewn with golden
stars.

At his entrance the judges arose. Even Kugler stood up, reluc-   10
tant but fascinated. Only when the old gentleman took a seat did
the judges again sit down.

"Witness," began the presiding judge, "Omniscient God, this   11
court has summoned You in order to hear Your testimony in the
case against Kugler, Ferdinand. As You are the Supreme Truth,
You need not take the oath. In the interest of the proceedings,
however, we ask You to keep to the subject at hand rather than
branch out into particulars—unless they have a bearing on this
case.

"And you, Kugler, don't interrupt the Witness. He knows ev-   12
erything, so there's no use denying anything.

"And now, Witness, if You would please begin."   13

That said, the presiding judge took off his spectacles and   14
leaned comfortably on the bench before him, evidently in prepa-
ration for a long speech by the Witness. The oldest of the three
judges nestled down in sleep. The recording angel opened the
Book of Life.

God, the Witness, coughed lightly and began: 15

"Yes, Kugler, Ferdinand. Ferdinand Kugler, son of a factory   16
worker, was a bad, unmanageable child from his earliest days.
He loved his mother dearly, but was unable to show it; this made
him unruly and defiant. Young man, you irked everyone! Do you
remember how you bit your father on the thumb when he tried
to spank you? You had stolen a rose from the notary's garden."

"The rose was for Irma, the tax collector's daughter," Kugler   17
said.

"I know," said God. "Irma was seven years old at that time.   18
Did you ever hear what happened to her?"

"No, I didn't."   19

"She married Oscar, the son of the factory owner. But she con-   20
tracted a venereal disease from him and died of a miscarriage.
You remember Rudy Zaruba?"

"What happened to him?"   21

"Why, he joined the navy and died accidentally in Bombay.   22
You two were the worst boys in the whole town. Kugler, Fer-
dinand, was a thief before his tenth year and an inveterate liar.
He kept bad company, too: old Gribble, for instance, a drunkard

and an idler, living on handouts. Nevertheless, Kugler shared many of his own meals with Gribble."

The presiding judge motioned with his hand, as if much of this 23 was perhaps unnecessary, but Kugler himself asked hesitantly, "And . . . what happened to his daughter?"

"Mary?" asked God, "She lowered herself considerably. In 24 her fourteenth year she married. In her twentieth year she died, remembering you in the agony of her death. By your fourteenth year you were nearly a drunkard yourself, and you often ran away from home. Your father's death came about from grief and worry; your mother's eyes faded from crying. You brought dishonor to your home, and your sister, your pretty sister Martha, never married. No young man would come calling at the home of a thief. She's still living alone and in poverty, sewing until late each night. Scrimping has exhausted her, and patronizing customers hurt her pride."

"What's she doing right now?" 25

"This very minute she's buying thread at Wolfe's. Do you re- 26 member that shop? Once, when you were six years old, you bought a colored glass marble there. On that very same day you lost it and never, never found it. Do you remember how you cried with rage?"

"Whatever happened to it?" Kugler asked eagerly. 27

"Well, it rolled into the drain and under the gutterspout. As a 28 matter of fact, it's still there, after thirty years. Right now it's raining on earth and your marble is shivering in the gush of cold water."

Kugler bent his head, overcome by this revelation. 29

But the presiding judge fitted his spectacles back on his nose 30 and said mildly, "Witness, we are obliged to get on with the case. Has the accused committed murder?"

Here the Witness nodded his head. 31

' "He murdered nine people. The first one he killed in a brawl, 32 and it was during his prison term for this crime that he became completely corrupted. The second victim was his unfaithful sweetheart. For that he was sentenced to death, but he escaped. The third was an old man whom he robbed. The fourth was a night watchman."

"Then he died?" Kugler asked. 33

"He died after three days in terrible pain," God said. "And he 34 left six children behind him. The fifth and sixth victims were an old married couple. He killed them with an axe and found only sixteen dollars, although they had twenty thousand hidden away."

Kugler jumped up. 35

"Where?" 36

"In the straw mattress," God said. "In a linen sack inside the 37 mattress. That's where they hid all the money they acquired from greed and penny-pinching. The seventh man he killed in America; a countryman of his, a bewildered, friendless immigrant."

"So it was in the mattress," whispered Kugler in amazement. 38

"Yes," continued God. "The eighth man was merely a pass- 39 erby who happened to be in Kugler's way when Kugler was trying to outrun the police. At that time Kugler had periostitis and was delirious from the pain. Young man, you were suffering terribly. The ninth and last was the policeman who killed Kugler exactly when Kugler shot him."

"And why did the accused commit murder?" asked the presid- 40 ing judge.

"For the same reasons others have," answered God. "Out of 41 anger or desire for money; both deliberately and accidentally— some with pleasure, others from necessity. However, he was generous and often helpful. He was kind to women, gentle with animals, and he kept his word. Am I to mention his good deeds?"

"Thank You," said the presiding judge, "but it isn't necessary. 42 Does the accused have anything to say in his own defense?"

"No," Kugler replied with honest indifference. 43

"The judges of this court will now take this matter under ad- 44 visement," declared the presiding judge, and the three of them withdrew.

Only God and Kugler remained in the courtroom. 45

"Who are they?" asked Kugler, indicating with his head the 46 men who had just left.

"People like you," answered God. "They were judges on 47 earth, so they're judges here as well."

Kugler nibbled his fingertips. "I expected . . . I mean, I never 48 really thought about it. But I figured You would judge, since—"

"Since I'm God," finished the Stately Gentleman. "But that's 49 just it, don't you see? Because I know everything, I can't possibly judge. That wouldn't do at all. By the way, do you know who turned you in this time?"

"No, I don't," said Kugler, surprised. 50

"Lucky, the waitress. She did it out of jealousy." 51

"Excuse me," Kugler ventured, "but You forgot about that 52 good-for-nothing Teddy I shot in Chicago."

"Not at all," God said. "He recovered and is alive this very 53 minute. I know he's an informer, but otherwise he's a very good man and terribly fond of children. You shouldn't think of any person as being completely worthless."

"But I still don't understand why You aren't the judge," 54 Kugler said thoughtfully.

"Because my knowledge is infinite. If judges knew everything, 55 absolutely everything, then they would also understand everything. Their hearts would ache. They couldn't sit in judgment— and neither can I. As it is, they know only about your crimes. I know all about you. The entire Kugler. And that's why I cannot judge."

"But why are they judging . . . the same people who were 56 judges on earth?"

"Because man belongs to man. As you see, I'm only the wit- 57 ness. But the verdict is determined by man, even in heaven. Believe me, Kugler, this is the way it should be. Man isn't worthy of divine judgment. He deserves to be judged only by other men."

At that moment the three returned from their deliberation. 58

In heavy tones the presiding judge announced, "For repeated 59 crimes of first degree murder, manslaughter, robbery, disrespect for the law, illegally carrying weapons, and for the theft of a rose: Kugler, Ferdinand, is sentenced to lifelong punishment in hell. The sentence is to begin immediately.

"Next case, please: Torrance, Frank. 60

"Is the accused present in court?" 61

RESPONDING
TO LANGUAGE

The readings in Part Four are about how language affects our attitudes and behavior. We are all "language experts" to some extent, because we spend so much of our time using language and responding to it. Based on your experiences, then, you probably will find yourself agreeing with some of the observations in these essays, disagreeing with some, and wondering about others. Whatever your responses, however, look on them as opportunities to explore how language affects your perceptions of yourself, other people, and the workings of society.

When we consider language as a broad subject, many possible writing topics arise. We may be moved to write directly about the effects that certain kinds of words or phrases have on us. At other times, we may want to delve into how language affects our cultural and social experiences, such as the effects of advertising language or bureaucratic jargon. And there is always the strong possibility that reading about language may generate responses that have little to do with the direct concerns of a particular author. Your immediate responses to these readings should indicate what kinds of feelings are aroused when you read about language, and this should lead you to express yourself in language of your own.

Photograph by David M. Grossman

LETTER TO THE EDITORS

NAME WITHHELD ON REQUEST

Dear Editors:

Your November issue contained an article praising the world 1
of advertising for its "essential contribution to the betterment of
our way of life." According to the writer, our modern economic
growth "would never have reached its present spectacular state
except for the creative partnership between American inventor/
entrepreneurs and the brilliant wordsmiths and idea-men who
fill our lives with colorful and witty works of art." Balderdash! as
Grandad used to say.

True, over the last 75 years, our economy has grown exponen- 2
tially, and advertising has helped many small enterprises become enormously successful by rapidly spreading the word
about valuable new products and services. But, with the advent
of television, we, the public, have been subjected to a psycholog-
ically sophisticated assault upon our eyes and ears, an assault
that cannot be avoided without depriving ourselves of programs
we enjoy. Being visually seduced into buying new cars or beer is
bad enough, but the ad industry, in the service of the soap
makers, set about creating artificial needs; and these false needs
have drastically affected the ways we relate to each other and
even the way we feel about ourselves. I am speaking now of
those "personal care" products which supposedly keep us from
offending the people we work and play with—such products as
mouthwash, deodorant, and toothpaste, for example.

The admen's attack, designed by unscrupulous psychologists, 3
strikes us where we are most vulnerable—raising fears of rejec-

tion or, at least, of nonacceptance by other people. Think of all
the products being advertised today whose only purported value
lies in saving us from offending the hypersensitive noses of potential friends and lovers. Not only do we constantly worry
about our own bodies' betraying us, but we have been trained by
these insidious ads to be keenly aware of everyone else's odor
quality.

As a child, I saw many western movies in which a snake-oil   4
salesman promised crowds of townspeople that his "superior
elixir cures most any ailment known to man, from lumbago to
clubfoot." Well, the con men of Madison Avenue went one step
further. They invented a new disease, "bad breath," for which
their employers were ready to sell a cure, "mouthwash." The
medicinal-smelling concoction they offered supposedly killed
germs that cause bad breath, or *halitosis* (a high-sounding word
they invented by translating "bad breath" into Latin, the language of doctors). A torrid ad campaign then created a social crisis by telling us that our mouths—which we employ both to
whisper sweet nothings to our loved ones and to confer with our
bosses—might betray us. Since then, an endless flood of mouthwash ads has kept Americans sufficiently unsure of themselves
to keep the product on drugstore shelves forever.

Thus has "the creative partnership between American inven-   5
tor/entrepreneurs and the brilliant wordsmiths and idea-men,"
capitalized on the sensual power of TV and the emotional insecu-
rity of the public, creating an industry based on false needs and
false hopes. It is this condition, added to all the frequently criti-
cized features of media advertising, that makes the article you
printed unworthy of your magazine, which has never before, to
my knowledge, allowed its pages to be taken up by blatantly self-
serving spokesmen for corrupt enterprises. I expect that an ob-
jective critique of these charlatans will appear in a forthcoming
issue. If it does not, you can expect to cancel my subscription.

Sample Responses to "Letter to the Editors"

Responder 1: Sandy

I get just as bored reading attacks on advertising as I am by
the ads themselves. This writer is all wrong, as I can tell you from

my experience. Maybe a mouthwash doesn't stop bad breath all day, but it lasts long enough in the evening to get through a date. My brother had a case of halitosis that wouldn't quit, and I told him it might hurt his chances of getting girls to go out with him. At first he thought I was just being sarcastic, but soon I noticed he was gargling with mouthwash every morning and before going out on dates. He also carries a tiny pocket spray to use throughout the day. The flavor of the mouthwash covers up his breath odors well enough to suit his friends, I guess, because he has become pretty popular.

I find most ads boring because they are repeated so often, and some are a little dopey--like the Charmin you mustn't squeeze. But I'm also bored by writers who think they're so smart because they can make fun of some advertisements. We can't have free TV and a lot of other things without ads, and so we might as well ignore the dumb ones and hope for a smile or two from the clever ones.

Responder 2: Maureen

You can't knock all ads. Some are really clever (the ads with James Garner and Charlie Chaplin), some are very cute (cat-food ads are my favorites, and I like the fat football player called "The Refrigerator", and travel ads are educational. But most ads are obnoxious. The characters are stupid, or the message is so obviously a lie--as if some cold medicine can cure all symptoms in half an hour. And the same ad is repeated over and over and over until I want to kick the tube in.

This letter criticizes advertising for inventing a need where we had no interest before. The writer has a point. I'm not fat by any means, and I'm pretty happy most of the time, although I know I'd look a little better if I lost about fifteen pounds. Then I see an ad for a diet drink with all those slender women catching all the good-looking men. Even the ads that sell cars and whatever show skinny women enjoying themselves and attracting men. After a long session in front of the TV, I come away a little depressed. Sometimes I swear I'll stop eating altogether, and that's silly. It's unreal. I'm me. No one's going to like me any better if I lose weight. They may throw me a few glances, but that's it--so it's not worth all the aggravation of dieting. But I can't convince myself of this when I am bombarded a million times with the Ideal Womanly Figure getting everything she wants.

Responder 3: James

When I think of the millions of dollars that companies spend to advertise their products, I get really mad. People are starving all over the world and in our country, too. We need housing for homeless persons. We need better medical care. We need to improve our educational system. But where does the money go? Into advertising. Millions of dollars are spent advertising hundreds of kinds of soap, even though they are all the same except for the smell. Instead of trying to find a way to stop crime or cure cancer, what big question do we want to know the answer to? That's right--Which cola tastes better? It makes me sick to think of all the millions being spent on selling people carbonated sugar water that rots our teeth and poisons our bodies with carcinogens. This writer is right. Brilliant people work day and night just to trick us into buying junk we don't need. We don't have to worry about the communists destroying America,

because advertising is doing it for them right now.

Considering the Responses

Response 1: Sandy

The class felt Sandy's response raised two questions: (1) Are most of the personal-care products advertised on TV useless? (2) Are advertisements as silly and misleading as some critics say, or are many ads really rather clever? Sandy's classmates advised her to limit her topic to one of the two questions.

1. If Sandy chooses to address the first question, can she develop a good essay by putting together a set of examples that describe her experiences with mouthwashes? Why or why not?
2. Do you think Sandy can refute the writer's negative view of advertising simply by giving positive examples of ads? Why or why not?

Actually, Sandy chose to address the second question, and the class advised her not to rely solely on examples of clever or intelligent ads. One student suggested that she first define what qualities make an ad "good" in her opinion. Sandy recognized the value of discussing her criteria, and so the main problem became one of balance. She had to decide how much of the essay should be devoted to her criteria and how much to examples that proved her point.

Response 2: Maureen

Maureen also had to make some choices regarding her topic. Either she could write about how TV ads cause viewers to feel unhappy with their self-image, or she could write about the anguish some people feel because of all the emphasis on being thin.

If Maureen chose the first topic, she could introduce other ways in which TV makes viewers dissatisfied with themselves or with their appearance. And if she chose the second alternative, she could similarly expand her topic by going beyond TV to include other sources of people's discontent with their looks or situation.

1. Advise Maureen about how to expand the first topic—how TV ads make people unhappy with their appearance.

2. What sources besides TV make people discontent with their looks and situation?
3. Which essay would you advise Maureen to write, and why?

Response 3: James

James reacted rather heatedly to the subject of advertising.

1. Do you think he can use all the ideas he raised in his response, or should he focus on a few of them? If you think he should limit his topic, which ideas would you advise him to use in developing a well-focused essay?
2. Would James do even better to address just *one* of the ideas in his response? Which idea do you think could be developed into the best essay, and why?
3. If you believe James could use the full range of ideas that appear in his response, suggest an order in which they could be presented effectively in his essay.

WORDS AS WEAPONS

RICHARD MITCHELL

Imagine that the postman brings you a letter from the Water   1
and Sewer Department or the Bureau of Mines or some such
place. Any right-thinking American will eye even the envelope
in the same way he would eye some sticky substance dripping
from the underparts of his automobile. Things get worse. You
open the letter and see at once these words: "You are hereby notified. . . . " How do you feel? Are you keen to read on? But you
will, won't you? Oh, yes. You will.

Here comes another letter. This one doesn't even have a   2
stamp. It carries instead the hint that something very bad will
happen to any mere citizen caught using this envelope for his
own subversive purposes. You open it and read: "It has been
brought to the attention of this office. . . . " Do you throw it out
at that point because you find it too preposterous to think that an
office can have an attention? Do you immediately write a reply:
"Dear So-and-so, I am surprised and distressed by the rudeness
of your first ten words, especially since they are addressed to one
of those who pay your salary. Perhaps you're having a bad day.
Why don't you write again and say something else?" You do not.
In fact, you turn pale and wonder frantically which of your mis-
deeds has been revealed. Your anxiety is increased by that passive verb—that's what it's for—which suggests that this damaging exposure has been made not by an envious neighbor or a
vengeful merchant or an ex-girlfriend or any other perfectly understandable, if detestable, human agent, but by the very nature
of the universe. "It has been brought." This is serious.

Among the better class of Grammarians, that construction is   3
known as the Divine Passive. It intends to suggest that neither

the writer nor anyone else through whose head you might like to hammer a blunt wooden spike can be held accountable for anything in any way. Like an earthquake or a volcanic eruption, this latest calamity must be accepted as an act of God. God may well be keeping count of the appearances of the Divine Passive.

Another classic intimidation with which to begin a letter is: 4 "According to our records. . . . " It reminds you at once, with that plural pronoun, that the enemy outnumbers you, and the reference to "records" makes it clear that they've got the goods. There is even a lofty pretense to fairness, as though you were being invited to bring forth *your* records to clear up this misunderstanding. You know, however, that they don't suspect for an instant that there's anything wrong in their records. Besides, you don't *have* any records, as they damn well know.

Such frightening phrases share an important attribute. They 5 are not things that ordinary people are likely to say, or even write, to one another except, of course, in certain unpleasant circumstances. We can see their intentions when we put them into more human contexts: "My dear Belinda, You are hereby notified . . . "conveys a message that ought to infuriate even the dullest of Belindas. Why is it then that we are not infuriated when we hear or read such words addressed to us by bureaucrats? We don't even stop to think that those words make up a silly verbal paradox; the only context in which they can possibly appear is the one in which they are not needed at all. No meaning is added to "Your rent is overdue" when the landlord writes, "You are hereby notified that your rent is overdue." What *is* added is the tone of official legality, and the presumption that one of the rulers is addressing one of the ruled. The voice . . . puts you in your place, and, strangely enough, you go there.

We Americans make much of our egalitarian society, and we 6 like to think we are not intimidated by wealth and power. Still, we are. There are surely many reasons for that, and about most of them we can do nothing, it seems. But one of the reasons is the very language in which the wealthy and powerful speak to us. When we hear it, something ancient stirs in us, and we take off our caps and hold them to our chests as we listen. About *that* we *could* do something—all it takes is some education. That must have been in Jefferson's mind when he thought about the importance of universal education in a society of free people. People who are automatically and unconsciously intimidated by the sound of a language that they cannot themselves use easily will never be free. Jefferson must have imagined an America in which all citizens would be able, when they felt like it, to address one another as members of the same class. That we cannot do so is a sore impediment to equality, but, of course, a great advantage to those who *can* use the English of power and wealth.

It would be easier to see bureaucratic language for what it is if 7 only the governors and bureaucrats did in fact speak a foreign tongue. When the Normans ruled England anyone could tell the French was French and English, English. It was the government that might, rarely, pardon you for your crimes, but it needed a friend to forgive you for your sins. Words like "pardon" and "forgive" were clearly in different languages, and, while either might have been translated by the other, they still meant subtly different acts. They still do, even though they are both thought of as English words now. Modern English has swallowed up many such distinctions, but not all. We still know that hearts are broken, not fractured. This is the kind of distinction Winston Churchill had in mind when he advised writers to choose the native English word whenever possible rather than a foreign import. This is good advice, but few can heed it in these days. The standard American education does not provide the knowledge out of which to make such choices.

Sample Responses to "Words as Weapons"

Responder 1: Marlene

I know how this writer feels. I got a letter from a department store that said I owed them fifteen dollars. The way they wrote the letter, you would have thought I owed them a million dollars. They used legal words, just like the ones the writer talks about--"You are hereby informed." The letter made me mad because I've bought a lot of things on credit at that store, and I've always paid my bills. I didn't even know I owed the money. You'd think that with my good record they could have sent a nicer letter. Instead they made me feel like some kind of crook. I should have sent them back a nasty letter, but I didn't. I just paid what I owed. I should have read this essay before. Then

I might have sent them a nasty letter. This essay really taught me something.

Responder 2: Harry

I say baloney to this essay. I owned a store for fifteen years in my old neighborhood. When I started out, I was Mr. Nice Guy. People would come into my store and ask for credit. They looked honest and nice, and they gave me some story about not having had a chance to get to the bank. They were always going to pay me tomorrow or in a couple of days. I played the sucker for so long that I was going into debt myself. When I finally wised up, I changed my attitude. I got tough with the deadbeats and told them, "No cash, no merchandise." People who owed me a lot, I threatened to get the law after them. You'd be surprised how fast all the parasites found out that they had money after all. That's why companies send letters like the ones the author says are so insulting to people. That's just too bad! If you don't scare the hell out of people, they'll never pay what they owe. I'm sixty-six years old, and one thing I've learned is that when it comes to money, you've got to be tough. Otherwise you'll go down the drain.

Responder 3: Leon

What's all this talk about English and writing? That's all I've heard since I started school. Teachers always talk about how important good English is, but who cares! I want to be an accountant. I do very good in accounting classes. I wish they'd stop wasting my time with all this required English. All I want to do is graduate and get a good job. I don't know what this guy is talking about with his "Divine Passive" and all that crap. If they forgot about all this English, I could graduate and get out of here a lot faster, and start making some money. So I'll never know how to write like a great writer--so what! As long as I do my job OK and make good money, everybody's happy. That's all I've got to say.

Responder 4: Caron

I see the author's point, and he's probably right when he says the wealthy and powerful use a certain kind of language to keep the rest of us in line. In fact language is used to separate classes and professions too. Middle-class people speak differently than lower-class people. Doctors and lawyers have their own languages. They use words that most people don't understand, and in this way they make it impossible for us to do without them. But I don't know if it would make a big difference if all of us used ordinary language. A rich and powerful man would still be respected and feared even if he spoke like an ordinary person. Sometimes politicians try to get people to vote for them by talking like Mr. or Mrs. Average Citizen. To me, they always sound phony. I can tell they're putting on an act to win votes.

Considering the Responses

Response 1: Marlene

Marlene ended her response by saying: "This essay really taught me something."

1. Based on Marlene's complete response, what do you think she meant by her last statement? Could the statement be used as the controlling idea for a complete essay? Why or why not?
2. If Marlene decides to write about what she learned from this essay, how could she use the essay itself to help plan her own essay?

Response 2: Harry

Harry's response was based on his experience as a store owner. Evidently this helped to shape his attitudes about creditors and made him sympathetic toward the kind of threatening language the author wants us to resist. During class discussion Harry said several times: "Business is business." When asked what he meant, Harry said that friendship and "being nice" have no place in business.

1. How might Harry develop an essay explaining what he means by "Business is business"? What kinds of explanatory support might he include besides his experiences as a store owner?
2. Is it possible to develop an essay that contradicts what Harry seems to mean by "Business is business"? How would you argue *against* the idea that humane considerations should have no place in business?

Response 3: Leon

Leon apparently thinks that required English courses have little value for him, since he wants to pursue a career in accounting. His response led the class to discuss the value of courses that are not directly related to a student's major field of study. Several students defended the idea that an educated person must know more than simply the fundamentals of a particular field or profession. These students argued that employers favor people who write and speak well and, furthermore, that getting ahead in a career often has as much to do with communication skills as with knowledge of the particular field.

Leon, with some support from other students, countered by saying that he had heard all that before and was tired of hearing it. He claimed that he had no ambitions to be a boss or an executive, and he doubted that he would ever use language well enough to be considered "executive material." All he wanted, he maintained, was the chance to get a decent job so that he could get married, buy a house, and drive a sports car. He wasn't interested in becoming a leader. He wanted to get out of school as quickly as possible and start earning money.

1. Leon decided to write an essay supporting his views about "useless" courses. Do you think he explored enough issues in his response and in class discussion to develop an effective essay? Why or why not?
2. Which of Leon's arguments is strongest, and why? Which is weakest, and why?

Response 4: Caron

Caron raised two issues. First she wrote about how language is used to separate people into different classes and different professions. Then she questioned the idea that the use of ordinary language by everyone would create a more democratic society. (Are rich and powerful people respected because they speak like rich, powerful people? Or are they re-spected simply because they have wealth and power?)

1. Which of these two issues would be easier to explore in an essay? Why?
2. Depending on your answer to question 1, how should Caron develop her essay?

CHILDREN'S INSULTS

PETER FARB

The insults spoken by adults are usually more subtle than   1
the simple name-calling used by children, but children's insults
make obvious some of the verbal strategies people carry into
adult life. Most parents engage in wishful thinking when they regard name-calling as good-natured fun which their children will
soon grow out of. Name-calling is not good-natured and children
do not grow out of it; as adults they merely become more expert
in its use. Nor is it true that "sticks and stones may break my
bones, but names will never hurt me." Names can hurt very
much because children seek out the victim's true weakness, then
jab exactly where the skin is thinnest. Name-calling can have
major impact on a child's feelings about his identity, and it can
sometimes be devastating to his psychological development.

Almost all examples of name-calling by children fall into four   2
categories:

1. Names based on physical peculiarities, such as deformi-
   ties, use of eyeglasses, racial characteristics, and so forth.
   A child may be called *Flattop* because he was born with a
   misshapen skull—or, for obvious reasons, *Fat Lips,*
   Gimpy, Four Eyes, Peanuts, Fatso, Kinky, and so on.
2. Names based on a pun or parody of the child's own name.
   Children with last names like Fitts, McClure, and Farb
   usually find them converted to *Shits, Manure,* and *Fart.*

3. Names based on social relationships. Examples are *Baby* used by a sibling rival or *Chicken Shit* for someone whose courage is questioned by his social group.
4. Names based on mental traits—such as *Clunkhead, Dummy, Jerk,* and *Smartass.*

These four categories were listed in order of decreasing offen-   3 siveness to the victims. Children regard names based on physical peculiarities as the most cutting, whereas names based on mental traits are, surprisingly, not usually regarded as very offensive. Most children are very vulnerable to names that play upon the child's rightful name—no doubt because one's name is a precious possession, the mark of a unique identity and one's masculinity or femininity. Those American Indian tribes that had the custom of never revealing true names undoubtedly avoided considerable psychological damage.

Sample Responses to "Children's Insults"

Responder 1: Larry

I remember a fat boy named Ralph who used to live in our neighborhood. My friends and I always referred to him as Fatty or The Whale. I don't know why he hung out with us, except maybe he was lonely and hoped we would eventually accept him. We were pretty nasty kids. We never stopped teasing Ralph, and I have to admit we really enjoyed it. We would make up jokes about how fat he was, and we played a lot of dirty tricks on him. When he finally blew up or started crying, we'd get even meaner, calling him much worse names.

I guess our insults really got to him because one day he ran away from home. It took the police a couple of days to find him. To tell the truth, we didn't feel bad about what happened to Ralph. In fact, we thought the whole thing was a terrific joke. I went around saying the police would have no trouble finding Ralph since he was too fat to hide for very long.

When I think about it now, I feel bad about how cruel we were to Ralph. But I sure didn't feel sorry for him at the time. I guess the writer is right when he says little children can be vicious.

Responder 2: Alice

I try to teach my daughter that it is a sin to say anything derogatory about another human being. The Lord does not want us to insult each other. But she tells me all the other children in her school use insults all the time, and she will occasionally hurt another child's feelings right before my eyes. Sometimes I think it is a hopeless task to be a parent these days. Between the influence of television and other children, I feel that I don't have much to say about the way my daughter is growing up. She already uses language that makes me blush. What will she be saying in another five years, when she is a teenager?

Responder 3: Donald

This writer referred to the old saying about sticks and stones; however, I believe he is not entirely correct. The surest remedy for an insult is to totally ignore it. When somebody attempts to unnerve my by using words like "stupid" or "asshole," I content myself with the thought that the words better describe the speaker. Ignoring such people works surprisingly well. If you remain unflustered, they will soon move on to another, more easily upset victim.

Considering the Responses

Response 1: Larry

Larry's response struck a familiar chord in the class. Nearly everyone recalled being either the insulter or the insulted in grade school, and in most cases the insults were aimed at some physical trait. Several classmates advised Larry to develop an essay showing how the children's cruelty caused Ralph to suffer so much that he ran away from home to escape their attacks. Such an essay would support Farb's contention that children are much nastier than most people want to admit.

Other classmates thought that this topic was too limited; it would show only that one boy, living near a particular group of very cruel children, suffered. They recommended that Larry try to figure out why he was so quick to injure someone. They assumed from the response that Larry and his buddies probably behaved this way toward any child who was as unpopular as Ralph was. They wanted him to offer a number of examples that would support the idea that "little children can be vicious."

1. Given Larry's generalization that children can be vicious, do you think that his essay should focus only on Ralph or on a number of examples to prove the point? Why?
2. If Larry's essay focuses only on Ralph's story, which ideas should he develop further, and what conclusion should he reach?
3. If Larry includes examples other than Ralph in his essay, should he explore *why* he and his friends were so mean, or will the examples alone prove that children are "vicious"?

Response 2: Alice

Alice's response offers several fertile topics for an essay, but the class immediately focused on her fear that as a parent she had too little control over her daughter's moral development. The students agreed readily that children today grow up too quickly and are exposed to too much too soon. As one student summed it up, "Anyone who has children these days has got to be crazy."

1. Do you think Alice should stick to the main ideas in her response by writing an essay about her daughter's use of insulting and foul language? Or should she develop an essay about the "hopeless task" of being a parent these days? Why?

2. What does Alice need to do if she decides to write about being a parent? What advice would you give her?

Response 3: Donald

No one in the class seemed to agree with Donald's method of handling verbal assaults. They said it would never work to ignore insults. Donald viewed their reactions as a challenge that he gladly accepted.

1. What should Donald do to expand his response into an effective essay? Will the use of examples prove his point? Why or why not?
2. Do you see any way that Donald can support his claim that "the surest remedy for an insult is to totally ignore it"?

ADDITIONAL READINGS

SILENCE

THOMAS MERTON

Life is not to be regarded as an uninterrupted flow of words 1 which is finally silenced by death. Its rhythm develops in silence, comes to the surface in moments of necessary expression, returns to deeper silence, culminates in a final declaration, then ascends quietly into the silence of Heaven which resounds with unending praise.

Those who do not know there is another life after this one, or 2 who cannot bring themselves to live in time as if they were meant to spend their eternity in God, resist the fruitful silence of their own being by continual noise. Even when their own tongues are still, their minds chatter without end and without meaning, or they plunge themselves into the protective noise of machines, traffic, or radios. When their own noise is momentarily exhausted, they rest in the noise of other men.

How tragic it is that they who have nothing to express are con- 3 tinually expressing themselves, like nervous gunners, firing burst after burst of ammunition into the dark, where there is no enemy. The reason for their talk is: death. Death is the enemy who seems to confront them at every moment in the deep darkness and silence of their own being. So they keep shouting at death. They confound their lives with noise. They stun their own ears with meaningless words, never discovering that their hearts are rooted in a silence that is not death but life. They chatter themselves to death, fearing life as if it were death.

TALKING LIKE A LADY: HOW WOMEN TALK

FRANCINE FRANK

FRANK ANSHEN

Perhaps the most common stereotype about women's   1
speech is that women talk a lot. If we take "a lot" to mean more
than men, we are faced with the surprising fact that there seems
to be no study which supports this belief, while there are several
which show just the opposite. One such study, by Otto Sonder,
Jr., is particularly interesting. Sonder organized discussion
groups which included women and men and assigned them specific topics. The discussions were recorded and transcribed, but
in the transcripts, the participants were identified only by letters,
as A, B, etc. Panels of judges who tried to identify the sex of each
speaker from these transcripts were correct about fifty-five percent of the time, a result which is better than chance, but not
overwhelmingly so. Closer examination of the data, however, reveals some interesting facts. A word count of the recorded discussions showed a clear tendency for the men who participated
in the study to utter more words than the women. In other
words, men, on the average, actually talked more than did
women. Even more interesting is the fact that individuals of either sex who talked a lot were more likely to be judged as males,
while taciturn individuals of either sex were more likely to be
identified as females. Not only does this study suggest that men
are more talkative, it also suggests that the judges "knew" this
fact and used it to make judgments about the sexual identity of
unknown speakers. Although, consciously, they would probably
subscribe to the cultural stereotype of the talkative woman, their
judgments show that they knew that the real situation is the direct opposite of the stereotype.

How can we reconcile this apparent contradiction between 2 our beliefs and our actions? It seems that people have an incorrect conscious stereotype of how much women and men talk, while at the same time having, at a less conscious level, the knowledge that men tend to speak more than women. When called upon to make judgments, they use their knowledge of actual behavior rather than the stereotype of presumed behavior. We are reminded of individuals in pre-Civil War America who thought slaves were lazy, in spite of the fact that they observed them doing backbreaking work from sunup to sundown.

Students of stereotypes believe that our preconceived notions 3 influence our expectations and responses during initial contacts with strangers. However, when we get to know people even slightly, we usually treat them as individuals and ignore the stereotypes. This is commonly recognized as the "Some of my best friends are . . ."syndrome. We may, for example, believe that girls are, in general, more social than boys, even though that may not be true of our own children or, indeed, of any children we know well; or we may believe that women are more talkative than men, although members of our family or circle of friends do not act that way.

HOW FATHERS
TALK TO BABIES

BARRY McLAUGHLIN

Much of what we know about the way children learn lan- 1
guage comes from studies in which researchers observe mothers
with their babies. . . . When mothers speak to their young children, their speech becomes slower, shorter, less complex, more
repetitious, uses fewer pronouns. In fact, this way of talking is
often called motherese.

Little is known about how fathers talk to babies, but one study 2
indicates they do not say much. Every two weeks during the first
three months of 10 babies' lives, Freda Rebelsky and Cheryl
Hanks recorded everything fathers said to their infants in a 24-
hour period. The fathers spoke to them an average of merely 38
seconds.

One of the few studies concerned with fathers' speech to 3
young children was conducted by William Corsaro of Indiana
University, who found that fathers asked more questions than
did mothers during interactions with their two-year-olds. Nearly
half of the fathers' utterances were leading questions: What is
this? (no response). Is this a camel? (no response). Can you say
that, camel? (no response). Camel?

Placed in the same situation, the children's mothers devoted 4
only 18 percent of their utterances to questions of this sort. Such
questions are one of the safest routes adults can take in conversation with small children. By asking leading questions, the adult
feels comfortable with the child and controls the conversation.

The father's tendency to use a controlling language style with 5
young children has been borne out of recent research I conducted with Caleb Schutz and David White. We found that fa-

thers used significantly more imperatives with their five-year-old children than mothers did in the same situation.

In our experiment we recorded the conversations of 24 parents 6 and their children while they were playing a table game called Capture the Hat. The game was new to the children, and the parents had to teach them the rules. What struck us immediately was the difference in teaching styles between the mothers and fathers. Mothers were involved with the children, they were careful about making rules clear, and they corrected mistakes and rule infractions. Fathers, on the other hand, were less involved; they often failed to cover the rules and tended to gloss over the children's mistakes or infractions. Although there were exceptions, fathers seemed uncomfortable and intent on getting the game over with. In fact, we found it difficult to find fathers who would participate in the study.

When playing the game, fathers appeared uncertain as to how 7 to talk to their children. They often talked down to them, saying, "All right, say you roll five. How would you move? Show me how many you would move. You would like this: One, two, three, four, five." In contrast, mothers tended to say the same thing more succinctly and less condescendingly: "Now, whatever number comes on the die, you get to move one of your hats that many places." Mothers did not count aloud because they knew the children could count spaces on a game board.

Although some fathers used speech that was too simple, un- 8 derestimating what their children understood, others used language that was too advanced. In such cases the children did not understand the game, but their fathers' concern was not to explain it; they wanted to get it over with. These fathers glanced around uncomfortably, allowed rules to be broken, and seemed generally uninterested in the task.

Indirect information on the way fathers talk to young children 9 comes from a study by Elaine Andersen at Stanford University, who had children aged between three and six play the role of parents. When the children pretended to be the father, their speech became shorter, their intonation changed (it became deeper, with less range in pitch), and they used more imperatives and fewer terms of endearment than when they played the mother.

Experimenter (taking the child's role): Tell me a story.   10
Child (in father's role): Mommy will.
Experimenter: No, I want you to.

Child: I'm going to sleep.
Experimenter: Please tell me a story.
Child: Ask your mother.
Experimenter: Please, please.
Child: All right. Sit down. Once upon a time. The end.

Other research suggests that the language of fathers to their 11 children is less attuned to the child's needs than is the speech of mothers. Fathers neither repeat nor expand the speech of young children who are learning to talk to the same extent that mothers do. Fathers are generally less skilled in motherese, although there has been so little research on fathers' speech to young children that we do not know, for example, whether this is true of fathers who are equally involved with the mothers in the child's upbringing. It appears that as long as most fathers leave the business of bringing up children to the mother, the language to which infants are exposed will continue to be principally the "mother tongue."

THE BEGGAR

ANTON CHEKHOV

Kind sir, be so good as to notice a poor, hungry man. I have 1
not tasted food for three days. . . . I have not a five-copeck piece
for a night's lodging. . . . I swear by God! For five years I was a
village schoolmaster and lost my post through the intrigues of
the Zemstvo. I was the victim of false witness. I have been out of
a place for a year now."

Skvortsov, a Petersburg lawyer, looked at the speaker's tat- 2
tered dark blue overcoat, at his muddy, drunken eyes, at the red
patches on his cheeks, and it seemed to him that he had seen the
man before.

"And now I am offered a post in the Kaluga province," the 3
beggar continued, "but I have not the means for the journey
there. Graciously help me! I am ashamed to ask, but . . . I am
compelled by circumstances."

Skvortsov looked at his galoshes, of which one was shallow 4
like a shoe, while the other came high up the leg like a boot, and
suddenly remembered.

"Listen, the day before yesterday I met you in Sadovoy 5
Street," he said, "and then you told me, not that you were a village schoolmaster, but that you were a student who had been expelled. Do you remember?"

"No-o. No, that cannot be so!" the beggar muttered in confu- 6
sion. "I am a village schoolmaster, and if you wish it I can show
you documents to prove it."

"That's enough lies! You called yourself a student, and even 7
told me what you were expelled for. Do you remember?"

Skvortsov flushed, and with a look of disgust on his face 8
turned away from the ragged figure.

"It's contemptible, sir!" he cried angrily. "It's a swindle! I'll 9
hand you over to the police, damn you! You are poor and hungry, but that does not give you the right to lie so shamelessly!"

The ragged figure took hold of the door-handle and, like a bird 10
in a snare, looked round the hall desperately.

"I . . . I am not lying," he muttered. "I can show documents." 11

"Who can believe you?" Skvortsov went on, still indignant. 12
"To exploit the sympathy of the public for village schoolmasters
and students—it's so low, so mean, so dirty! It's revolting!"

Skvortsov flew into a rage and gave the beggar a merciless 13
scolding. The ragged fellow's insolent lying aroused his disgust
and aversion, was an offence against what he, Skvortsov, loved
and prized in himself: kindliness, a feeling heart, sympathy for
the unhappy. By his lying, by his treacherous assault upon compassion, the individual had, as it were, defiled the charity which
he liked to give to the poor with no misgivings in his heart. The
beggar at first defended himself, protested with oaths, then he
sank into silence and hung his head, overcome with shame.

"Sir!" he said, laying his hand on his heart, "I really was . . . 14
lying! I am not a student and not a village schoolmaster. All that's
mere invention! I used to be in the Russian choir, and I was
turned out of it for drunkenness. But what can I do? Believe me,
in God's name, I can't get on without lying—when I tell the truth
no one will give me anything. Telling the truth one may die of
hunger and freeze without a night's lodging! What you say is
true, I understand that, but . . . what am I to do?"

"What are you to do? You ask what are you to do?" cried 15
Skvortsov, going close up to him. "Work—that's what you must
do! You must work!"

"Work. . . . I know that myself, but where can I go to get 16
work?"

"Nonsense. You are young, strong, and healthy, and could al- 17
ways find work if you wanted to. But you know you are lazy,
pampered, drunken! You reek of vodka like a pothouse! You
have become false and corrupt to the marrow of your bones and
fit for nothing but begging and lying! If you do graciously conde-
scend to take work, you must have a job in an office, in the Russian choir, or as a billiard-marker, where you will have a salary
and have nothing to do! But how would you like to undertake
manual labor? I'll be bound, you wouldn't be a house porter or
factory hand! You are too genteel for that!"

"What things you say, really . . ." said the beggar, and he gave 18
a bitter smile. "How can I get manual work? It's rather late for

me to be a shopman, for in trade one has to begin from a boy; no one would take me as a house porter, because I am not of that class. . . . And I could not get work in a factory; one must know a trade, and I know nothing."

"Nonsense! You always find some justification! Wouldn't you 19 like to chop wood?"

"I would not refuse to, but the regular wood-choppers are out 20 of work now."

"Oh, all idlers argue like that! As soon as you are offered any- 21 thing you refuse it. Would you care to chop wood for me?"

"Certainly I will. . . ."   22

"Very good, we shall see. . . . Excellent. . . . We'll see!"   23

Skvortsov, in nervous haste, and not without malignant plea- 24 sure, rubbing his hands, summoned his cook from the kitchen.

"Here, Olga," he said to her, "take this gentleman to the shed 25 and let him chop some wood."

The beggar shrugged his shoulders as though puzzled, and ir- 26 resolutely followed the cook. It was evident from his demeanor that he had consented to go and chop wood, not because he was hungry and wanted to earn money, but simply from shame and *amour propre,* because he had been taken at his word. It was clear, too, that he was suffering from the effects of vodka, that he was unwell, and felt not the faintest inclination to work.

Skvortsov hurried into the dining-room. There from the win- 27 dow which looked out into the yard he could see the woodshed and everything that happened in the yard. Standing at the window, Skvortsov saw the cook and the beggar come by the back way into the yard and go through the muddy snow to the woodshed. Olga scrutinized her companion angrily, and perking her elbow unlocked the woodshed and angrily banged the door open.

"Most likely we interrupted the woman drinking her coffee," 28 thought Skvortsov. "What a cross creature she is!"

Then he saw the pseudo-schoolmaster and pseudo-student seat 29 himself on a block of wood, and, leaning his red cheeks upon his fists, sink into thought. The cook flung an axe at his feet, spat angrily on the ground, and, judging by the expression of her mouth, began abusing him. The beggar drew a log of wood towards him irresolutely, set it up between his feet, and diffidently drew the axe across it. The log toppled and fell over. The beggar drew it towards him, breathed on his frozen hands, and again drew the axe along it as cautiously as though he were afraid of its hitting his galosh or chopping off his fingers. The log fell over again.

Skvortsov's wrath had passed off by now; he felt sore and 30
ashamed at the thought that he had forced a pampered, drunken,
and perhaps sick man to do hard, rough work in the cold.

"Never mind, let him go on . . ." he thought, going from the 31
dining-room into his study. "I am doing it for his good!"

An hour later Olga appeared and announced that the wood 32
had been chopped.

"Here, give him half a rouble," said Skvortsov. "If he likes, let 33
him come and chop wood on the first of every month. . . . There
will always be work for him."

On the first of the month the beggar turned up and again 34
earned half a rouble, though he could hardly stand. From that
time forward he took to turning up frequently, and work was always found for him: sometimes he would sweep the snow into
heaps, or clear up the shed, at another he used to beat the rugs
and the mattresses. He always received thirty to forty copecks
for his work, and on one occasion an old pair of trousers was sent
out to him.

When he moved, Skvortsov engaged him to assist in packing 35
and moving the furniture. On this occasion the beggar was sober,
gloomy, and silent; he scarcely touched the furniture, walked
with hanging head behind the furniture vans, and did not even
try to appear busy; he merely shivered with the cold, and was
overcome with confusion when the men with the vans laughed
at his idleness, his feebleness, and the ragged coat that had once
been a gentleman's. After the removal Skvortsov sent for him.

"Well, I see my words have had an effect upon you," he said, 36
giving him a rouble. "This is for your work. I see that you are sober and not disinclined to work. What is your name?"

"Lushkov." 37

"I can offer you better work, not so rough, Lushkov. Can you 38
write?"

"Yes, sir." 39

"Then go with this note tomorrow to my colleague and he will 40
give you some copying to do. Work, don't drink, and don't forget
what I said to you. Goodbye."

Skvortsov, pleased that he had put a man in the path of recti- 41
tude, patted Lushkov genially on the shoulder, and even shook
hands with him at parting. Lushkov took the letter, departed,
and from that time forward did not come to the backyard for
work.

Two years passed. One day as Skvortsov was standing at the 42
ticket-office of a theater, paying for his ticket, he saw beside him
a little man with a lambskin collar and a shabby cat's-skin cap.

The man timidly asked the clerk for a gallery ticket and paid for it with copeks.

"Lushkov, is it you?" asked Skvortsov, recognizing in the little 43 man his former wood-chopper. "Well, what are you doing? Are you getting on all right?"

"Pretty well. . . . I am in a notary's office now. I earn thirty- 44 five roubles."

"Well, thank God, that's capital. I rejoice for you. I am very, 45 very glad, Lushkov. You know, in a way, you are my godson. It was I who shoved you into the right way. Do you remember what a scolding I gave you, eh? You almost sank through the floor that time. Well, thank you, my dear fellow, for remembering my words."

"Thank you too," said Lushkov. "If I had not come to you that 46 day, maybe I should be calling myself a schoolmaster or a student still. Yes, in your house I was saved, and climbed out of the pit."

"I am very, very glad."   47

"Thank you for your kind words and deeds. What you said 48 that day was excellent. I am grateful to you and to your cook, God bless that kind, noble-hearted woman. What you said that day was excellent; I am indebted to you as long as I live, of course, but it was your cook, Olga, who really saved me."

"How was that?"   49

"Why, it was like this. I used to come to you to chop wood and 50 she would begin: 'Ah, you drunkard! You God-forsaken man! And yet death does not take you!' and then she would sit opposite me, lamenting, looking into my face and wailing: 'You unlucky fellow! You have no gladness in this world, and in the next you will burn in hell, poor drunkard! You poor sorrowful creature!' and she always went on in that style, you know. How often she upset herself, and how many tears she shed over me I can't tell you. But what affected me most—she chopped the wood for me! Do you know, sir, I never chopped a single log for you—she did it all! How it was she saved me, how it was I changed, looking at her, and gave up drinking, I can't explain. I only know that what she said and the noble way she behaved brought about a change in my soul, and I shall never forget it. It's time to go up, though, they are just going to ring the bell."

Lushkov bowed and went off to the gallery.   51

PART FIVE

ADDITIONAL
READINGS

WHAT'S IN A NAME?

LOIS SWEET

It was parents' visiting day. A week before, we'd waved 1
goodbye to our 8-year-old daughter as she left on a bus for camp.
We were dying to see her again.

When we asked for her, we were told there wasn't anyone 2
there by that name. Our hearts stopped. What could have happened to her?

Well, said the counsellor, there wasn't anyone there by that 3
first name. There was a girl with that last name.

When we found her, she calmly announced that she'd changed 4
her name. No longer was she to be known by the name we'd
given her at birth—Dechinta. She had become Rachel, the girl of
her middle name.

It may seem silly, but I take it seriously. Names are such state- 5
ments, such a form of self-identity, that any effort to change
them has to be considered.

Over the years, a lot of my friends have changed their names. 6
A number of them began to take an interest in their cultural
backgrounds and became horrified that their parents had angli-
cized their names in an effort to deny cultural differences. To my
friends, being pushed into the great bland melting pot felt more
like being drowned than saved. Their culture was a source of
pride and they demanded recognition for their "ethnic" names.

Then there have been what seem like hundreds of friends 7
whose marriages ended. Having taken their husbands' names at
marriage, deciding which name to use when they split up was a
problem. Some argued that reverting to their birth names would
create professional difficulties. After all, they'd established repu-
tations based on their husbands' surnames.

Photograph by David M. Grossman

Very Complicated

Others reclaimed their birth names, only to change again 8
when they remarried. It was very complicated. Whenever I
wrote a letter to one of them, I wasn't quite sure which name to
put on the envelope.

A handful of friends changed their names when they discov- 9
ered a life cause. One person illustrated the seriousness of his
newly found conviction with a modified name change. No longer
could we call him "Russ." He became "Russell" signifying that
there was no room in the relationship for either casualness or
false intimacy.

Still others chose to drop their last names completely in order 10
to flag their particular brand of radical feminism. Last names
were a patriarchal remnant, they said, created to establish male
ownership.

Although it takes a lot of effort to remember what to call 11
whom, I was among those who forced such an effort on others.
When I got married 15 years ago, it never occurred to me not to
take my husband's name. Ten years later, whose last name I was
using became an issue.

I discovered that a married name is only an assumed name and 12
that reverting to my birth name involved neither lawyers nor bu-
reaucracy. Although the name Sweet had been a plague during
childhood, it did belong to me. I decided to reclaim it.

Open to Change

Everyone, except relatives, has been open to the change. Nev- 13
ertheless, the step was worth it. It might have been an old name,
but it characterized a new me.

So what does a name change mean for an 8-year-old? Probably 14
that the child recognizes that her name reveals more about her
parents than about herself. The first name we gave our daughter
(which, granted, is unusual, but not made up), is an Athapaskan
Indian word meaning self-sufficiency. It says as much about our
generation as the names Pearl or Thelma said about our parents'.

Several years ago, when our daughter's kindergarten teacher 15
sent home a class list, we were struck with how much that generation of children were stuck with the "counter-culture" influence. Moonbeam, Airborn and names like them were in the majority. It's the unfaddish, un-made-up Biblical names like Rachel,
however, that wear like solid gold.

Changing names might be a bother for those who have to re- 16
member to use the new name, but it obviously has significance
for the person who's insisting on the change. Rather than a new
name bringing a new personality, I think a new name is a sign of

a new personality—or at the very least, of a profound personality change.

A point not lost on countries, let alone people, is that the right   17
to name the world for yourself is a matter of great political importance.

If I can respect name changes in my friends—and vice-versa—I   18
can respect it in my daughter. After all, families should be democratic.

I just hope it doesn't happen too often.   19

HOW COCAINE TOOK CONTROL OF MY LIFE

TONY ELLIOTT

I was fortunate. Facing the barrel of a coke dealer's .357   1
Magnum revolver brought me to my senses and helped me realize that I needed help, that cocaine had taken control of my life.
Len Bias and Don Rogers were not as lucky. They didn't get that
kind of warning.

Let me share with you how this problem started for me. There   2
were two related sources. First came the kinds of pressure that I
faced as an athlete growing up in the inner city.

I grew up in Bridgeport, Conn., in a neighborhood where drug   3
use was not looked down on by other kids and young adults. It
was even seen as a means of rebelling.

I was using drugs and alcohol before I became an athlete at the   4
age of 14. Being an athlete did not necessarily mean that drug use
was over. Your prestige among your peers didn't diminish. In
fact, I think my macho image was enhanced when people saw I
was able to use and still perform as an athlete. Boozing it up is
supposed to be a sign of manhood for the young athlete. Now it's
coke, the champagne of drugs. It's a status symbol. It gives you
the illusion of power and masculinity. It made me believe that
nothing could happen to me. I'm sure Len Bias and Don Rogers
felt the same way.

Like all high school athletes, I was asked to make sacrifices   5
that other kids did not have to make. We were told to give up
sex, partying and alcohol. I often felt that I was playing for the
coach and not for myself. I found myself trying to get away with
as much as I could. Avoid the exercise and drills if the coaches

weren't watching. Stay up as late as you could. Drink and use drugs if you could get away with it. I got away with it.

As a young adolescent, I had difficulty trying to confirm my 6 sense of identity. I desperately needed to be accepted. I always wondered if I was liked only because I was a football star or because I had drugs to pass around. The delusions are easy to build up but painful to take down.

As a star high school athlete, there were plenty of pressures 7 that went along with the attention. I often felt that the reputation of our entire school was being carried on my shoulders as I played each game. Was I going to be a hero this week or a zero? Drugs and alcohol were a welcome relief from this pressure from the coaches, schoolmates, the community and, most of all, from myself. I used drugs in response to sports success. The thrill of victory in competition, for me, is a natural high. I experienced the same euphoric feeling from cocaine that I felt during game conditions. Therefore, as an athlete, I feel that I was more susceptible to cocaine addiction than the average person. I feel that many athletes are. Those who have never tried it are very fortunate because after a while it is no longer enjoyable. It was like a demon in me that made life miserable as I constantly sought that euphoric feeling that was never there.

The second set of reasons for my drug use came from the fact 8 that as an athlete, all authority figures systematically removed responsibility from me off the field. I had fewer chores, I had to study less, I got away with more in school, I never had to make plans. Everything was done for me. All I had to do was play the game. This made it difficult for me to accept responsibility for my own behavior. They were wrong for doing this and I was wrong for allowing it to happen, but in the end I was the one who almost died.

I knew that my grades in school were directly related to my 9 performance on the field. If I played better, I could study even less. I began to understand the rules of the game.

In college, the system became even more exaggerated. I was 10 given money, apartments, cars. I didn't have to do anything but play ball. Nobody doubted my intelligence. But nobody asked me to study. I was a football star.

I was heavily into drug use by my senior year, 1981. I *knew* I 11 was invincible the next spring when I was drafted and signed by the New Orleans Saints. Not only was I signed but I got a $30,000 signing bonus!

As a professional, when the athlete returns to his community 12 the easiest way to keep ties with his former associates and to assure him that he has not forgotten "where he came from" is to use drugs or share his earnings with his friends by treating them to drugs. I spent the $30,000 in a two-week cocaine binge in my hometown.

Over a four-year period, I believe I spent close to a million dol- 13 lars on cocaine for me and my friends. I sold everything I had, ruined my first marriage, became a petty criminal, and finally peered down the barrel of my own personal Grim Reaper. Desperate, I had planned to hold up my dealer with a cheap pistol, but when the door opened I was on the other side of a .357 Magnum. At that time, a light went on and I was saved.

Yet I can see how Len Bias and Don Rogers didn't recognize 14 the imminence of their own "suicides." One night I sat alone with a pipe. There was a little bit of coke left when I began to feel sharp chest pains. I knew I was in trouble yet I chose to take that last hit and not deal with my heart. That's how powerful the stuff is. It's so powerful that Don Rogers took a dose just days after Bias's death. The ultimate tragedy of their deaths will be if we, as athletes and as a society, treat their deaths as isolated incidents. With millions of high school athletes abusing chemicals and alcohol, we are facing a monster near victory. Drug testing might help but it isn't the key. Education is. If the deaths of two physically gifted men at the top of their games doesn't scare us enough to make us see the monster eating our souls, what will?

I wish I knew the answer. I do know we have to be able to see 15 that it is a monster and that we are all its potential prey.

Note: Tony Elliott was allowed back into the National Football League in November 1984 as a result of his work speaking with young children on the subject of drug abuse.

F CO RT T PE'S SPL C D

MARTIN WINKLER

I am a performer of miracles. Minor miracles, to be sure, but 1
miracles nonetheless.

I am an official court reporter of the New Jersey Supreme 2
Court. I sit in a courtroom in Newark and I write every single
word spoken by anyone in that courtroom. I do not omit words
that are distasteful or improper or incomprehensible. I write
every word.

I sit on a not very comfortable chair, and I remain seated, un- 3
less I am bidden to come to the "side bar," where, standing, I
record the whispered colloquies between judge and lawyers,
straining to hear, wishing lawyers were obliged to cleanse their
breath before coming into court. Otherwise, I must stay in my
chair, regardless of physical need.

But a metamorphosis is in progress. I am on the verge of turn- 4
ing into a dinosaur in human form, and, shortly thereafter, of becoming extinct.

They want to replace me. 5

Not with a younger and perhaps more efficient human being, 6
but with a machine. A marvelous mechanical moron—a tape recorder. Guaranteed by its maker to do my job at least as well as I
do, at a fraction of the cost. A machine that needs no sick days,
no vacations, no pensions—and never has to go to the bathroom.

Isn't that wonderful? 7

No! 8

It's awful! 9

And I'm going to tell you why. 10

I admit to being highly prejudiced—and terrified at the pros- 11
pect of losing my job—but what I am about to say is true.

First of all, what is a tape recorder? 12

A tape recorder, no matter how sophisticated its gadgetry, is 13 nothing more than a mechanism that can only ingest noise. It does not give a damn whether that noise comes from a human voice, a siren or a jackhammer—a tape recorder will "swallow" *any* noise within range of its microphones. It is a very democratic machine, totally unbiased, with no power whatever to discriminate.

In this connection, it must be remembered that a courtroom is 14 not a recording studio. A courtroom is a place where, too often, several people are talking at once, where witnesses may mumble, whisper or speak in almost incomprehensible accents. Lawyers do not stand in one place as they question witnesses. Judges frequently hold hands over their mouths when they talk.

I pose the following rhetorical question: 15

Can a tape recorder ask to have a sentence repeated or a word 16 spelled?

Can a tape recorder, regardless of its multiple tracks, differen- 17 tiate between speakers?

Can a tape recorder read back verbatim? (Sure, it can be 18 played back—if the person "logging" the tape can find the right spot. But what will the jury hear? It will hear noise. Some of the noise will be understandable, but I could retire tomorrow if I had a dollar for every word the jurors couldn't decipher.)

Can a tape recorder transcribe itself? 19

Now ask yourself these same questions about a living, breath- 20 ing, *listening* court reporter.

And what happens when the judge calls the lawyers into his 21 chambers for a conference he wants "on the record" but out of the presence of the public?

And what happens if someone who is presently unemployed 22 gets a job as Person in Charge of Tape and decides to bring his scissors to work?

And what happens during a power failure—or if someone sim- 23 ply forgets to put the plug in the socket?

In the end, though, despite my irrefutable arguments, society 24 will probably turn me into a dinosaur.

Right now, on orders from the Supreme Court of my state, 25 there are tape-recording machines in all municipal courts, juvenile and domestic relations courts and district courts. And, under consideration at this moment, is a plan to install tape recorders in the superior courts of New Jersey for certain nonjury matters.

After that . . . ? 26

If the day comes when I am actually replaced by a machine, it 27 is my fervent hope that you will not be a litigant who writes a letter requesting a transcript of your trial proceedings.

Tape recorders take a very long time to answer their mail. 28

THE TROUBLE
WITH VIDEO GAMES

FRANK DEFORD

In the suburban town where I live there has been—as there   1
has been in a lot of places across the country—a fuss about electronic video games. In my town, a promoter sought permission
to construct a monstrous emporium to house scores of these
quarter-eaters, and a great many citizens came out violently in
opposition. Really.

Some of this was, of course, no more than a case of routine   2
generational hysteria, the sort of knee-jerk response we can expect from a certain segment of the adult population anytime anything new and mysterious comes along that appeals to the young.
That's life. That's the way the middle ages. But somehow we
have survived as a nation and as a planet these past three decades despite grim grown-up assurances circa 1955 that rock 'n'
roll would be the ruination of mankind. Alas, the same old flesh-
pot world destroyed poor Elvis Presley, not he us.

It has also been difficult for me to think of video games as new-   3
fangled instruments of the devil, inasmuch as pinball games long
preceded them. It seems to me that video games are to pinball
about what big Prince metal rackets are to little old wooden
ones. The products may be modified, but the arcades, like the
tennis, remain much the same as ever.

Really.   4

I don't use the above word just for the heck of it. "Really" is   5
the word that arcade children—which is to say, all children—use
these days instead of that quaint old word we formerly fell back
on, "yes," as in: Will you marry me?/Really.

The flip side of "Really" is "Not Really." "Not Really" is what 6
young people say now when they mean "no." (The first mistake
we made was starting to call kids "young people," but I digress.)
This generation simply can't bear to have the word "no" employed, lest someone might get around to saying "no" to them.
Really. I discovered recently that not even young policemen can
bring themselves to say "no." Not long ago, I asked one fuzzy-
cheeked constable if I might park for a while in a no-parking
zone.

He replied, "Not really." 7

Really. 8

Possibly there's some connection between young people play- 9
ing video games all the time and their not being able to say "yes"
or "no."

But then, adults themselves are often no prizes when it comes 10
to lucid, logical discourse. Most of the complaints I hear lodged
against video games are couched only in what I call the alternative negative. That is: These games are bad because otherwise
children would be doing something *more valuable with their time.*

I seize up when I hear that argument, because it is my experi- 11
ence that children, no less than adults, never make choices that
way. We never say, "Well, this afternoon I was planning to read
Plato for a while, visit some local shut-ins, then give blood and go
over to the orphan asylum and cheer up all the tykes, but instead
I'm going to do something altogether worthless." No, it's the human condition to decide in advance to do something utterly
worthless, and then to zero in on the specifics.

If kids weren't becoming mushbrained playing video games 12
they would only be engaged in some other equally scurrilous or
pointless activity. I doubt whether the quarter-chompers keep
them away from homework or Little League or choir practice.

Who knows? Maybe children who infiltrate arcades are actu- 13
ally being saved from much worse fates. The entrepreneur who
was fighting to get the electronic emporium licensed in my town
passed out bumper stickers that asked Pac Man or Pot? *Reductio
ad absurdum?* Don't be so sure. Take the example of drive-in the-
aters in my day and age. Many grownups said these passion
pits—passion pits!—were instruments of the devil, worse even
than rock 'n' roll. Now drive-ins are going out of business, and
what have we got in their stead? Coed dormitories, expansion
teams, and $9.95-a-night motels. Think about that. See what I
mean?

Why, Billie Jean King even avers that the precocity of young 14
athletes today may be accounted for by the extraordinary con-

centration they develop playing Space Invaders, Zaxxon, Donkey Kong, and what have you from an early age.

Maybe each generation needs its own games no less than it needs its own music and clothes and heroes. I remember Pete Dawkins, the West Point Heisman Trophy winner, Rhodes Scholar, now a general in Uncle Sam's Army, studiously assuring me late one night that Frisbee was the ultimate athletic expression of our generation. And I hung on every word. 15

But that makes me think, too. Dammit, Frisbee is creative. It isn't chess. Not really. It isn't even canasta, and possibly it's even on the low side of *Family Feud*, but it is you and the Frisbee all alone against the world. And pinball: Pinball games require a certain imaginative dexterity. They may even be a metaphor of life (or for drive-ins; one or the other), because the trick with pinball games is to know how to stretch, even to sorta kinda exceed the limits . . . but ever so gingerly—to caress some extra points out of the machine without ever quite tilting the whole shebang. Pinball teaches you to skirt, to fudge, to finagle, to take sensible risks. Here was the situation: You were not supposed to bang a pinball machine *at all*, but you knew you couldn't win replays without goosing it some. There was as much an art to playing pinball as there was to, say, growing up. 16

And herein lies the difference. Video games are not just sophisticated pinball machines; they are not just larger tennis rackets. They are a whole different way of looking at life. Video games sparkle and flash, ring and sing, gurgle and shine, but that's all tinsel. The quiddity of video games is that they are patterned. Did you know that? You can go to a store and buy books that show you what the patterns are. They can't tilt! It's all rote. That's why you read about these video idiot savants playing one machine for 40 or 50 hours in a row. They can't tilt! You could get street-smart playing pinball, but with the video games you can only learn how to get in a groove, how to become, in effect, an extension of the equipment. 17

And that's not playing. No game can be played that way, and I don't care whether it's golf or basketball or bumper pool or Frisbee or spin the bottle or cops and robbers. 18

Go to any arcade and watch the young people playing video games and you will see why they are instruments of the devil. Games should be fun. Even when too much emphasis is placed on winning, half the people come away happy. But nobody ever wins at video games. Not really. It's just a grind, paying two bits for the privilege of being part of a machine. And the kids' faces show it. There is a joylessness to these dens. It always looks 19 to me as if everybody is taking the SATs or something, only you get bells and stuff instead of having to press down hard with a pencil.

You see, the critics have missed the point. It has nothing to do 20 with whether the games are addictive. A lot of people are addicted to baseball, and that's not so bad. It has nothing to do with whether the games are seductive. From time to time we all need to be seduced away from the finer, better things in life. It has, ultimately, nothing even to do with whether these games are too much fun. No, you see, it's the other way around. Video games aren't excessively fun. Rather, they may not be fun at all. They are programmed not only to take quarters but also to suck up the imagination. And that is the ultimate cruelty for a child: That his very games must be serious toil. The one thing these video games deny children is their childhood. Really.

TELEVISION: THE PLUG-IN DRUG

MARIE WINN

Real People

It is not only the activities that a family might engage in to- 1
gether that are diminished by the powerful presence of television
in the home. The relationships of the family members to each
other are also affected, in both obvious and subtle ways. The
hours that the young child spends in a one-way relationship with
television people, an involvement that allows for no communication or interaction, surely affect his relationships with real-life
people.

Studies show the importance of eye-to-eye contact, for in- 2
stance, in real-life relationships, and indicate that the nature of a
person's eye-contact patterns, whether he looks another
squarely in the eye or looks to the side or shifts his gaze from side
to side, may play a significant role in his success or failure in human relationships. But no eye contact is possible in the child-tel-
evision relationship, although in certain children's programs
people purport to speak directly to the child and the camera fos-
ters this illusion by focusing directly upon the person being
filmed. (Mr. Rogers is an example, telling the child "I like you,
you're special," etc.) How might such a distortion of real-life relationships affect a child's development of trust, of openness, of
an ability to relate well to other *real* people?

Bruno Bettelheim writes: 3

Children who have been taught, or conditioned, to listen passively
most of the day to the warm verbal communications coming from the
TV screen, to the deep emotional appeal of the so-called TV personality,
are often unable to respond to real persons because they arouse so much

less feeling than the skilled actor. Worse, they lose the ability to learn from reality because life experiences are much more complicated than the ones they see on the screen. . . .

A teacher makes a similar observation about her personal 4 viewing experiences:

"I have trouble mobilizing myself and dealing with real people 5 after watching a few hours of television. It's just hard to make that transition from watching television to a real relationship. I suppose it's because there was no effort necessary while I was watching, and dealing with real people always requires a bit of effort. Imagine, then, how much harder it might be to do the same thing for a small child, particularly one who watches a lot of television every day."

But more obviously damaging to family relationships is the 6 elimination of opportunities to talk, and perhaps more impor- tant, to argue, to air grievances, between parents and children and brothers and sisters. Families frequently use television to avoid confronting their problems, problems that will not go away if they are ignored but will only fester and become less easily re- solvable as time goes on.

A mother reports: 7

"I find myself, with three children, wanting to turn on the TV 8 set when they're fighting. I really have to struggle not to do it be- cause I feel that's telling them this is the solution to the quarrel— but it's so tempting that I often do it."

A family therapist discusses the use of television as an avoid- 9 ance mechanism:

"In a family I know the father comes home from work and 10 turns on the television set. The children come and watch with him and the wife serves them their meal in front of the set. He then goes and takes a shower, or works on the car or something. She then goes and has her own dinner in front of the television set. It's a symptom of a deeper-rooted problem, sure. But it would help them all to get rid of the set. It would be far easier to work on what the symptom really means without the television. The television simply encourages a double avoidance of each other. They'd find out more quickly what was going on if they weren't able to hide behind the TV. Things wouldn't necessarily be better, of course, but they wouldn't be anesthetized."

The decreased opportunities for simple conversation between 11 parents and children in the television-centered home may help explain an observation made by an emergency room nurse at a Boston hospital. She reports that parents just seem to sit there these days when they come in with a sick or seriously injured child, although talking to the child would distract and comfort him. "They don't seem to know *how* to talk to their own children at any length," the nurse observes. Similarly, a television critic writes in *The New York Times:* "I had just a day ago taken my son to the emergency ward of a hospital for stitches above his left eye, and the occasion seemed no more real to me than Maalot or 54th Street, south-central Los Angeles. There was distance and numbness and an inability to turn off the total institution. I didn't behave at all; I just watched. . . ."

A number of research studies substantiate the assumption that 12 television interferes with family activities and the formation of family relationships. One survey shows that 78 percent of the respondents indicated no conversation taking place during viewing except at specified times such as commercials. The study notes: "The television atmosphere in most households is one of quiet absorption on the part of family members who are present. The nature of the family social life during a program could be described as 'parallel' rather than interactive, and the set does seem to dominate family life when it is on." Thirty-six percent of the respondents in another study indicated that television viewing was the only family activity participated in during the week.

In a summary of research findings on television's effect on 13 family interactions James Gabardino states: "The early findings suggest that television had a disruptive effect upon interaction and thus presumably human development. . . . It is not unreasonable to ask: 'Is the fact that the average American family during the 1950s came to include two parents, two children and a television set somehow related to the psychosocial characteristics of the young adults of the 1970s?' "

Undermining the Family

In its effect on family relationships, in its facilitation of paren- 14 tal withdrawal from an active role in the socialization of their children, and in its replacement of family rituals and special events, television has played an important role in the disintegration of the American family. But of course it has not been the only contributing factor, perhaps not even the most important one. The steadily rising divorce rate, the increase in the number of working mothers, the decline of the extended family, the breakdown of neighborhoods and communities, the growing isolation of the nuclear family—all have seriously affected the family.

As Urie Bronfenbrenner suggests, the sources of family break- 15 down do not come from the family itself, but from the circumstances in which the family finds itself and the way of life imposed upon it by those circumstances. "When those circumstances and the way of life they generate undermine relationships of trust and emotional security between family members, when they make it difficult for parents to care for, educate and enjoy their children, when there is no support or recognition from the outside world for one's role as a parent and when time spent with one's family means frustration of career, personal fulfillment and peace of mind, then the development of the child is adversely affected," he writes.

But while the roots of alienation go deep into the fabric of 16 American social history, television's presence in the home fertilizes them, encourages their wild and unchecked growth. Perhaps it is true that America's commitment to the television experience masks a spiritual vacuum, an empty and barren way of life, a desert of materialism. But it is television's dominant role in the family that anesthetizes the family into accepting its unhappy state and prevents it from struggling to better its condition, to improve its relationships, and to regain some of the richness it once possessed.

Others have noted the role of mass media in perpetuating an 17 unsatisfactory *status quo*. Leisure-time activity, writes Irving Howe, "must provide relief from work monotony without making the return to work too unbearable; it must provide amusement without insight and pleasure without disturbance—as distinct from art which gives pleasure through disturbance. Mass culture is thus oriented towards a central aspect of industrial society: the depersonalization of the individual." Similarly, Jacques Ellul rejects the idea that television is a legitimate means of educating the citizen: "Education . . . takes place only incidentally. The clouding of his consciousness is paramount. . . ."

And so the American family muddles on, dimly aware that 18 something is amiss but distracted from an understanding of its plight by an endless stream of television images. As family ties grow weaker and vaguer, as children's lives become more separate from their parents', as parents' educational role in their children's lives is taken over by television and schools, family life becomes increasingly more unsatisfying for both parents and children. All that seems to be left is Love, an abstraction that family members *know* is necessary but find great difficulty giving each other because the traditional opportunities for expressing love within the family have been reduced or destroyed.

For contemporary parents, love toward each other has increas- 19 ingly come to mean successful sexual relations, as witnessed by the proliferation of sex manuals and sex therapists. The opportunities for manifesting other forms of love through mutual support, understanding, nurturing, even, to use an unpopular word, *serving* each other, are less and less available as mothers and fathers seek their independent destinies outside the family.

As for love of children, this love is increasingly expressed 20 through supplying material comforts, amusements, and educational opportunities. Parents show their love for their children by sending them to good schools and camps, by providing them with good food and good doctors, by buying them toys, books, games, and a television set of their very own. Parents will even go further and express their love by attending PTA meetings to improve their children's schools, or by joining groups that are acting to improve the quality of their children's television programs.

But this is love at a remove, and is rarely understood by chil- 21 dren. The more direct forms of parental love require time and patience, steady, dependable, ungrudgingly given time actually spent *with* a child, reading to him, comforting him, playing, joking, and working with him. But even if a parent were eager and willing to demonstrate that sort of direct love to his children today, the opportunities are diminished. What with school and Little League and piano lessons and, of course, the inevitable television programs, a day seems to offer just enough time for a good-night kiss.

PUNISHMENT
VERSUS DISCIPLINE

BRUNO BETTELHEIM

A parent who respects himself will feel no need to demand 1 or command respect from his child, since he feels no need for the child's respect to buttress his security as a parent or as a person. Secure in himself, he will not feel his authority threatened and will accept it when his child sometimes shows a lack of respect for him, as young children, in particular, are apt to do. The parent's self-respect tells him that such displays arise from immaturity of judgment, which time and experience will eventually correct.

Demanding or commanding respect reveals to the child an in- 2 secure parent who lacks the conviction that his way of life will, all by itself, over time, gain him the child's respect. Not trusting that respect will come naturally, this parent has to insist on it right now. Who would wish to form himself in the image of an insecure person, even if that person is his parent? Unfortunately, the child of insecure parents often becomes an insecure person himself, because insecure parents cannot inculcate security in their children or create an environment in which the children can develop a sense of security on their own.

To be disciplined requires self-control. To be controlled by 3 others and to accept living by their rules or orders makes it superfluous to control oneself. When the more important aspects of a child's actions and behavior are controlled by, say, his parents or teachers, he will see no need to learn to control himself; others do it for him.

How parents in other cultures try to inculcate self-control in 4 their children can be instructive. Consider, for example, a study designed to find out why young Japanese do much better academically than Americans. When the researchers studied maternal behavior they saw clear differences between the Japanese and the Americans. Typically, when young American children ran around in supermarkets, their mothers—often annoyed—told them, "Stop that!" or "I told you not to act this way!" Japanese mothers typically refrained entirely from telling their children what to do. Instead they asked them questions, such as "How do you think it makes the storekeeper feel when you run around like this in his store?" or "How do you think it makes me feel when my child runs around as you do?" Similarly, the American mother, wanting her child to eat what he was supposed to eat, would order the child to do so or tell him that he ought to eat it because it was good for him. The Japanese mother would ask her child a question, such as "How do you think it makes the man who grew these vegetables for you to eat feel when you reject them?" or "How do you think it makes these carrots that grew so that you could eat them feel when you do not eat them?" Thus from a very early age the American child is told what to do, while the Japanese child is encouraged not only to consider other persons' feelings but to control himself on the basis of his own deliberations.

The reason for the higher academic achievement of Japanese 5 youngsters may well be that the Japanese child in situations important to his mother is invited to think things out on his own, a habit that stands him in good stead when he has to master academic material. The American child, in contrast, is expected to conform his decisions and actions to what he is told to do. This expectation certainly does not encourage him to do his own thinking.

The Japanese mother does not just expect her child to be able 6 to arrive at good decisions. She also makes an appeal to her child not to embarrass her. In the traditional Japanese culture losing face is among the worst things that can happen to a person. When a mother asks, "How do you think it makes me—or the storekeeper—feel when you act this way?" she implies that by mending his ways the child does her, or the storekeeper, a very great favor. To be asked to do one's own thinking and to act accordingly, as well as to be told that one is able to do someone a favor, enhances one's self-respect, while to be ordered to do the opposite of what one wants is destructive of it.

What is a parent to do in the short run to prevent a child from 7 misbehaving, as children are apt to do from time to time? Ideally, letting a child know of our disappointment should be effective

and should lead the child to abstain from repeating the wrongdo-
ing in the future. Realistically, even if a child has great love and
respect for us, his parents, simply telling him of our disappointment, or showing him how great it is, will not always suffice to
remedy the situation.

When our words are not enough, when telling our child to   8
mend his ways is ineffective, then the threat of the withdrawal
of our love and affection is the only sound method to impress on
him that he had better conform to our request. Subconsciously
recognizing how powerful a threat this is, some parents, with the
best of intentions, destroy its effectiveness by assuring their children that they love them no matter what. This might well be
true, but it does not sound convincing to a child, who knows that
he does not love his parents no matter what, such as when they
are angry at him; so how can he believe them when he can tell
that they are dissatisfied, and maybe even angry at him? Most of
us do not really love unconditionally. Therefore any effort to
make ourselves look better, to pretend to be more loving than we
are, will have the opposite effect from the one we desire. True,
our love for our child can be so deep, so firmly anchored in us,
that it will withstand even very severe blows. But at the moment
when we are seriously disappointed in the child, our love may be
at a low point, and if we want the child to change his ways, he
might as well know it.

The action to take is to banish the child from our presence. We   9
may send him out of the room or we ourselves may withdraw.
Whatever, the parent is clearly indicating, "I am so disappointed
in you that I do not wish, or feel unable, to maintain physical
closeness with you." Here physical distance stands for emotional
distance, and it is a symbol that speaks to the child's conscious
and unconscious at the same time. This is why the action is so effective.

Sending the child out of sight permits both parent and child to   10
gain distance from what has happened, to cool off, to reconsider.
And that does help. But it is the threat of desertion, as likely as
not, that permanently impresses the child. Separation anxiety is
probably the earliest and most basic anxiety of man. The infant
experiences it when his prime caretaker absents herself from
him, an absence that, should it become permanent and the caretaker not be replaced, would indeed lead to the infant's death.
Anything that rekindles this anxiety is experienced as a terrible
threat. Hence, as long as a child believes, however vaguely, that
his very existence is in danger if his prime caretaker deserts him,
he will respond to this real, implied, or imagined threat with

deep feelings of anxiety. Even when he is old enough to know that his life is not in real danger, he will respond to separation from a parent with severe feelings of dejection, because to some degree he will feel as if he were endangered. The difference is that at an older age the fear is not of physical but of emotional starvation.

If we should have any doubt that physical separation can be an 11 effective expression of our disgust with a child's behavior, we can look to our children themselves to set us straight. The worst that a child can think of when he is disgusted with his parents is that he will run away. He makes such a threat because he is convinced that it is so terrible that it will compel us to mend our ways. Clearly, a child understands very well that when we threaten to distance ourselves from him physically we are threatening to distance ourselves from him emotionally. That threat makes a very deep impression.

We must be honest about our strong emotional reactions to our 12 children's behavior, showing our children how deeply we love them, on the one hand, and, on the other, letting them know when we are disappointed in them, provided we do not become critical or punitive. This is all just part of being ourselves. We need not make any claim to be perfect. But if we strive as best we can to live good lives ourselves, our children, impressed by the merits of living good lives, will one day wish to do the same.

THE MIRAGES OF MARRIAGE

WILLIAM J. LEDERER
DONALD D. JACKSON

The offices of marriage counselors, psychologists, and psy- 1
chiatrists are crowded with clients who are concerned over problems which mainly involve marriage, and who pay from twenty-
five dollars to fifty dollars an hour for assistance. But these
troubled people usually cannot identify their problems; even
worse, they usually do not sincerely seek solutions. What each
one wants is confirmation that he is correct and good, and that
his spouse is the one at fault!

One reason for this marital disenchantment is the prevalence 2
of the mistaken belief that "love" is necessary for a satisfying
and workable marriage. Usually when the word "love" is used,
reference is actually being made to romance—that hypnotic, ecstatic condition enjoyed during courtship. Romance and love are
different. Romance is based usually on minimum knowledge of
the other person (restricted frequently to the fact that being
around him is a wonderful, beatific, stimulating experience). Romance is built on a foundation of quicksilver nonlogic. It consists
of attributing to the other person—blindly, hopefully, but without much basis in fact—the qualities one *wishes* him to have,
though they may not even be desirable, in actuality. Most people
who select mates on the basis of imputed qualities later find
themselves disappointed, if the qualities are not present in fact,
or discover that they are unable to tolerate the implication of the
longed-for qualities in actual life. For example, the man who is
attracted by his fiancée's cuteness and sexiness may spend tormented hours after they are married worrying about the effect of

these very characteristics on other men. It is a dream relationship, an unrealistic relationship with a dream person imagined in
terms of one's own needs.

Romance is essentially selfish, though it is expressed in terms 3
of glittering sentiment and generous promises, which usually
cannot be fulfilled. ("I'll be the happiest man in the world for the
rest of my life." "I'll make you the best wife any man ever
had.")

Romance—*which most spouses mistake for love*—is not neces- 4
sary for a good marriage. The sparkle some couples manage to
preserve in a satisfying marriage—based on genuine pleasure in
one another's company, affection and sexual attraction for the
spouse as he really is—can be called love.

If romance is different than love, then what *is* love? We do best 5
to return to the definition of Harry Stack Sullivan: "When the
satisfaction or the security of another person becomes as significant to one as is one's own satisfaction or security, then the state
of love exists." In this sense, love consists of a devotion and respect for the spouse that is equal to one's own self-love.

We have already shown that people usually marry on a wave 6
of romance having nothing to do with love. When the average
American (not long from the altar) lives with the spouse in the intimacy of morning bad breath from too much smoking, of annoy-
ing habits previously not known, when he is hampered by the
limitations of a small income (compared with the lavishness of
the honeymoon), or encounters the unexpected irritability of pre-
menstrual tension or of business frustration and fatigue, a
change in attitude begins to occur. The previously romantic person begins to have doubts about the wonderful attributes with
which his spouse has been so blindly credited.

These doubts are particularly disturbing at the start. Not very 7
long ago, after all, the spouse believed that "love" (romance) was
heavenly, all-consuming, immutable, and that beautiful relationships and behavior were *voluntary* and *spontaneous*. Now, if
doubts and criticism are permitted to intrude upon this perfect
dream, the foundations begin to shake in a giddy manner. To the
husband or wife the doubts seem to be evidence that one of them
is inadequate or not to be trusted. The doubts imply that the relationship is suffering from an unsuspected malignancy.

To live with another person in a state of love (as defined by 8
Sullivan) is a different experience from whirling around in a tor-
nado of romance. A loving union is perhaps best seen in elderly
couples who have been married for a long time. Their children
have grown, the pressure of business has been relieved, and the

specter of death is not far away. By now, they have achieved a set of realistic values. These elderly spouses respect each other's idiosyncracies. They need and treasure companionship. Differences between them have been either accepted or worked out; they are no longer destructive elements. In such instances each has as much interest in the well-being and security of the other as he has in himself. Here is true symbiosis: a union where each admittedly feeds off the other. Those who give together really live together!

THE PURSUIT OF
LONELINESS

PHILIP SLATER

The Great Illusion

It's easy to produce examples of the many ways in which   1
Americans try to minimize, circumvent, or deny the interdependence upon which all human societies are based. We seek a private house, a private means of transportation, a private garden, a
private laundry, self-service stores, and do-it-yourself skills of
every kind. An enormous technology seems to have set itself the
task of making it unnecessary for one human being ever to ask
anything of another in the course of going about his or her daily
business. Even within the family Americans are unique in their
feeling that each member should have a separate room, and even
a separate telephone, television, and car, when economically
possible. We seek more and more privacy, and feel more and
more alienated and lonely when we get it. And what accidental
contacts we do have seem more intrusive, not only because
they're unsought, but because they're not connected with any familiar pattern of interdependence.

Most important, our encounters with others tend increasingly   2
to be competitive as we search for more privacy. We less and less
often meet our fellow humans to share and exchange, and more
and more often encounter them as an impediment or a nuisance:
making the highway crowded when we're rushing somewhere,
cluttering and littering the beach or park or wood, pushing in
front of us at the supermarket, taking the last parking place, pol-
luting our air and water, building a highway through our house,
blocking our view, and so on. Because we've cut off so much
communication with each other we keep bumping into each

other, so that a higher and higher percentage of our interpersonal contacts are abrasive.

We seem unable to foresee that the gratification of a wish   3
might turn out to be a monkey's paw if the wish were shared by many others. We cheer the new road that shaves ten minutes off the drive to our country retreat but ultimately transforms it into a crowded resort and increases both the traffic and the time. We're continually surprised to find, when we want something, that thousands or millions of others want it, too—that other human beings get hot in summer and cold in winter. The worst traffic jams occur when a mass of vacationing tourists start home early to "beat the traffic." We're too enamored of the individualistic fantasy that everyone is, or should be, different—that a man could somehow build his entire life around some single eccentricity without boring himself and everyone else to death. We all have our quirks, which provide surface variety, but aside from this, human beings have little basis for their persistent claim that they are not all members of the same species.

The Freedom Fix

Since our contacts with others are increasingly competitive,   4
unanticipated, and abrasive, we seek still more apartness and thus accelerate the trend. The desire to be somehow special sparks an even more competitive quest for progressively more rare and expensive symbols—a quest that is ultimately futile since it is individualism itself that produces uniformity.

This is poorly understood by Americans, who tend to confuse   5
uniformity with "conformity," in the sense of compliance with group demands. Many societies exert far more pressure on the individual to mold herself to play a sharply defined role in a total group pattern, but there is variation among these circumscribed roles. Our society gives more leeway to the individual to pursue her own ends, but since the culture defines what is worthy and desirable, everyone tends, independently but monotonously, to pursue the same things in the same way. Thus cooperation tends to produce variety, while competition generates uniformity.

The problem with individualism is not that it is immoral but   6
that it is incorrect. The universe does not consist of a lot of unrelated particles but is an interconnected whole. Pretending that our fortunes are independent of each other may be perfectly ethical, but it's also perfectly stupid. Individualistic thinking is unflagging in the production of false dichotomies, such as "conformity *vs.* independence," "altruism *vs.* egoism," "inner-directed *vs* other-directed," and so on, all of which are

built upon the absurd assumption that the individual can be considered separately from the environment of which he or she is a part.

A favorite delusion of individualism—one that it attempts, 7 through education and propaganda, to make real—is that only egoistic responses are spontaneous. But this is not so: collective responses—helping behavior, nurturance, supportiveness, the assumption of specialized roles in group tasks, rituals, or games—these are natural, not trained, even among animals. People are more *self-consciously* oriented toward others in competitive, individualistic societies—their behavior is calculated. They accommodate to others because they want to look good, impress people, protect themselves from shame and guilt, and avoid confronting people directly. In more organic and cooperative communities people respond spontaneously to impulses that are neither selfish nor unselfish, but more directly from the heart. Sometimes they look generous, sometimes grasping, but what's important is that the behavior is *to* others, not an effort to produce some sort of *effect* on others. Cooperative societies are unassuming—it's the competitive ones that are concerned with appearances.

THE EGALITARIAN ERROR

MARGARET MEAD
RHODA METRAUX

Almost all Americans want to be democratic, but many 1
Americans are confused about what, exactly, democracy means.
How do you know when someone is acting in a democratic—or
an undemocratic—way? Recently several groups have spoken
out with particular bitterness against the kind of democracy that
means equal opportunity for all, regardless of race or national or-
igin. They act as if all human beings did not belong to one species, as if some races of mankind were inferior to others in their
capacity to learn what members of other races know and have
invented. Other extremists attack religious groups—Jews or
Catholics—or deny the right of an individual to be an agnostic.
One reason that these extremists, who explicitly do not want to
be democratic, can get a hearing even though their views run
counter to the Constitution and our traditional values is that the
people who *do* want to be democratic are frequently so muddled.

For many Americans, democratic behavior necessitates an out- 2
right denial of any significant differences among human beings.
In their eyes it is undemocratic for anyone to refer, in the presence of any other person, to differences in skin color, manners or
religious beliefs. Whatever one's private thoughts may be, it is
necessary always to act as if everyone were exactly alike.

Behavior of this kind developed partly as a reaction to those 3
who discriminated against or actively abused members of other
groups. But it is artificial, often hypocritical behavior, nonetheless, and it dulls and flattens human relationships. If two people
can't talk easily and comfortably but must forever guard against

some slip of the tongue, some admission of what is in both persons' minds, they are likely to talk as little as possible. This embarrassment about differences reaches a final absurdity when a Methodist feels that he cannot take a guest on a tour of his garden because he might have to identify a wild plant with a blue flower, called the wandering Jew, or when a white lecturer feels he ought not to mention the name of Conrad's beautiful story *The Nigger of the "Narcissus."* But it is no less absurd when well-meaning people, speaking of the physically handicapped, tell prospective employers: "They don't want special consideration. Ask as much of them as you do of everyone else, and fire them if they don't give satisfaction!"

Another version of false democracy is the need to deny the existence of personal advantages. Inherited wealth, famous parents, a first-class mind, a rare voice, a beautiful face, an exceptional physical skill—any advantage has to be minimized or denied. Continually watched and measured, the man or woman who is rich or talented or well educated is likely to be called "undemocratic" whenever he does anything out of the ordinary—more or less of something than others do. If he wants acceptance, the person with a "superior" attribute, like the person with an "inferior" attribute, often feels obliged to take on a protective disguise, to act as if he were just like everybody else. One denies difference; the other minimizes it. And both believe, as they conform to these false standards, that they act in the name of democracy.   4

For many Americans, a related source of confusion is success.   5
As a people we Americans greatly prize success. And in our eyes success all too often means simply outdoing other people by virtue of achievement judged by some single scale—income or honors or headlines or trophies—and coming out at "the top." Only one person, as we see it, can be the best—can get the highest grades, be voted the most attractive girl or the boy most likely to succeed. Though we often rejoice in the success of people far removed from ourselves—in another profession, another community, or endowed with a talent that we do not covet—we tend to regard the success of people close at hand, within our own small group, as a threat. We fail to realize that there are many kinds of success, including the kind of success that lies within a person. We do not realize, for example, that there could be in the same class one hundred boys and girls—each of them a "success" in a different kind of way. Individuality is again lost in a refusal to recognize and cherish the differences among people.

The attitude that measures success by a single yardstick and   6
isolates the *one* winner and the kind of "democracy" that denies

or minimizes differences among people are both deeply destructive. Imagine for a moment a family with two sons, one of whom is brilliant, attractive and athletic while the other is dull, unattractive and clumsy. Both boys attend the same high school. In the interest of the slower boy, the parents would want the school to set equally low standards for everyone. Lessons should be easy; no one should be forced to study dead languages or advanced mathematics in order to graduate. Athletics should be noncompetitive; every boy should have a chance to enjoy playing games. Everyone should be invited to all the parties. As for special attention to gifted children, this is not fair to the other children. An all-round education should be geared to the average, normal child.

But in the interest of the other boy, these same parents would 7 have quite opposite goals. After all, we need highly trained people; the school should do the most it can for its best students. Funds should be made available for advanced classes and special teachers, for the best possible coach, the best athletic equipment. Young people should be allowed to choose friends on their own level. The aim of education should be to produce topflight students.

This is an extreme example, but it illustrates the completely in- 8 compatible aims that can arise in this kind of "democracy." Must our country shut its eyes to the needs of either its gifted or its less gifted sons? It would be a good deal more sensible to admit, as some schools do today, that children differ widely from one another, that all successes cannot be ranged on one single scale, that there is room in a real democracy to help each child find his own level and develop to his fullest potential.

Moving now to a wider scene, before World War I Americans 9 thought of themselves as occupying a unique place in the world—and there was no question in most minds that this country was a "success." True, Europeans might look down on us for our lack of culture, but with a few notable, local exceptions, we simply refused to compete on European terms. There was no country in the world remotely like the one we were building. But since World War II we have felt the impact of a country whose size and strength and emphasis on national achievement more closely parallel our own. Today we are ahead of Russia, or Russia is ahead of us. Nothing else matters. Instead of valuing and developing the extraordinary assets and potential of our country for their own sake, we are involved in a simple set of competitions for wealth and power and dominance.

These are expensive and dangerous attitudes. When democ- 10 racy ceases to be a cherished way of life and becomes instead the name of one team, we are using the word democracy to describe behavior that places us and all other men in jeopardy.

Individually, nationally, and, today, internationally, the mis- 11
reading of the phrase "all men are created equal" exacts a heavy price. The attitudes that follow from our misconceptions may be compatible with life in a country where land and rank and prestige are severely limited and the roads to success are few. But they are inappropriate in a land as rich, as open, as filled with opportunities as our own. They are the price we pay for being *less* democratic than we claim to be.

"All men are created equal" does not mean that all men are 12
the same. What it does mean is that each should be accorded full respect and full rights as a unique human being—full respect for his humanity *and* for his differences from other people.

HOW TO STAY ALIVE

ART HOPPE

Once upon a time there was a man named Snadley Klab- 1
berhorn who was the healthiest man in the whole wide world.

Snadley wasn't always the healthiest man in the whole wide 2
world. When he was young, Snadley smoked what he wanted,
drank what he wanted, ate what he wanted, and exercised only
with young ladies in bed.

He thought he was happy. "Life is absolutely peachy," he was 3
fond of saying. "Nothing beats being alive."

Then along came the Surgeon General's Report linking smok- 4
ing to lung cancer, heart disease, emphysema and tertiary core-
opsis.

Snadley read about The Great Tobacco Scare with a frown. 5
"Life is so peachy," he said, "that there's no sense taking any
risks." So he gave up smoking.

Like most people who went through the hell of giving up 6
smoking, Snadley became more interested in his own health. In
fact, he became fascinated. And when he read a WCTU tract
which pointed out that alcohol caused liver damage, brain damage, and acute *weltanschauung*, he gave up alcohol and drank die-
tary colas instead.

At least he did until The Great Cyclamate Scare. 7

"There's no sense in taking any risks," he said. And he 8
switched to sugar-sweetened colas, which made him fat and
caused dental caries. On realizing this he renounced colas in favor of milk and took up jogging, which was an awful bore.

That was about the time of The Great Cholesterol Scare. 9

Snadley gave up milk. To avoid cholesterol, which caused ath- 10
erosclerosis, coronary infarcts and chronic chryselephantinism,

he also gave up meat, fats and dairy products, subsisting on a diet of raw fish.

Then came The Great DDT Scare.   11

"The presence of large amounts of DDT in fish . . ." Snadley 12 read with anguish. But fortunately that's when he met Ernestine. They were made for each other. Ernestine introduced him to homeground wheat germ, macrobiotic yogurt and organic succotash.

They were very happy eating this dish twice daily, watching 13 six hours of color television together and spending the rest of their time in bed.

They were, that is, until The Great Color Television Scare.   14

"If color tee-vee does give off radiations," said Snadley, 15 "there's no sense taking risks. After all, we still have each other."

And that's about all they had. Until The Great Pill Scare.   16

On hearing that The Pill might cause carcinoma, thromboses 17 and lingering stichometry, Ernestine promptly gave up The Pill— and Snadley. "There's no sense taking any risks," she said.

Snadley was left with jogging. He was, that is, until he read 18 somewhere that 1.3 percent of joggers are eventually run over by a truck or bitten by rabid dogs.

He then retired to a bomb shelter in his back yard (to avoid be- 19 ing hit by a meteor), installed an air purifier (after The Great Smog Scare) and spent the next 63 years doing Royal Canadian Air Force exercises and poring over back issues of The Reader's Digest.

"Nothing's more important than being alive," he said proudly 20 on reaching 102. But he never did say anymore that life was absolutely peachy.

WHEN WE ARE OLD

SIR PETER MEDAWAR

Over the past thirty years, research on aging has raised the   1
serious possibility that life expectancy might someday be extended by as much as one fourth. Many different lines of research—on diet, metabolism, and the immune system, among
other things—are being pursued. One of the most promising of
these originated with Denham Harman, professor of medicine
and biochemistry at the University of Nebraska, who proposed,
in 1954, that the highly reactive molecular fragments known as
"free radicals," which are especially damaging to biological mi-
crostructures, might to some extent be counteracted by the increased consumption of antioxidants. These chemical compounds, of which vitamin E is the best known, occur naturally in
some foods and are added as preservatives to others—in most
countries in tiny and strictly regulated proportions.

Harman and many others are of the opinion that, just as small   2
amounts of antioxidants preserve foods, in larger amounts the
compounds might preserve human tissue. Many antioxidants
have since been tested for such an effect on laboratory animals,
and the increased longevity observed was equivalent, in Harman's reckoning, to an extension of the average human life expectancy from seventy-three to ninety-five years.

If antioxidants can be ingested safely by human beings, the   3
result is not expected to be an extra decade or two of zombie-like
existence, in which people would be alive only in the purely
technical sense (or alive enough, shall we say, to avoid becoming
transplant donors). Not at all. What the researchers hope for is a
prolonging of life such as would be achieved if the seven ages of

man were marked off on a length of rubber and the rubber were stretched. A seventy-year-old would have the address to life of a sixty-year-old, and an eighty-year-old that of a seventy-year-old.

How successful any treatment to prolong life might be is un- 4 clear. Growing old is a bad thing quite apart from the decline of bodily faculties and energies that it entails. Even if the process of senescence could be arrested temporarily, we would still suffer from the passage of years. Consider, for example, the likely consequences of extending a woman's reproductive life to the age of sixty, or beyond. The older a woman is at the age of reproduction, the longer her finite endowment of egg cells will have been exposed to influences that are inimical to it. Thus, even though a woman of sixty might be as physically fit as a woman of thirty, the likelihood of a chromosomal aberration, such as that which causes Down's syndrome, would have increased with her age. The etiology of cancer is a similar example. Researchers believe that a malignant tumor can start with the mutation of a chromosome following the body's exposure to ionizing radiation, a toxic chemical, or some other mutagen. Thus, the longer one lives, the longer one has to cross the path of such hazards, and the greater one's chances of contracting cancer.

Because it is not easy to see a remedy for these side effects of 5 old age, I fear that the incorporation of antioxidants into our diet will have a more modest result than proponents of the theory expect. But there are people who say that such research ought not to proceed at all. Their opposition compels us to ask, Is the extension of the life-span a possibility that we should welcome or a temptation that we should resist?

The case against efforts to increase longevity takes several 6 forms. It is said, for example, that the prolonging of life runs counter to biblical teaching. Yet "threescore years and ten" (*Psalms* 90:10) has no authority other than the opinion of a psalmist. In fact, the phrase is something of a cliché in the Bible, standing for quite a number but less than a hundred. Thus we are told that there were threescore and ten palm trees in Elim (*Numbers* 33:9); that when the house of Jacob entered Egypt, it comprised threescore and ten persons (*Deuteronomy* 10:22); that Jerubbaal had threescore and ten sons (*Judges* 9:2). It might be more in accord with the spirit of the Bible if the human life-span were construed to be that which, for better or worse, human beings cause it to be.

People also say that extending life is a crime against nature. I 7 consider this a despondent view, which rests on an implicit nostalgia for the supposedly healthy, happy, exuberant, and yea-say-ing savages that Jean-Jacques Rousseau spoke for—creatures whose life expectancy probably did not exceed twenty-five or thirty years. This attitude echoes the literary propaganda of the Romantic revival, and it is surely wider of the mark than Thomas Hobbes's assertion that the life of man in a state of nature is "solitary, poor, nasty, brutish, and short."

Human life has always been what human beings have made of 8 it, and in many ways we have improved on nature. It cannot be too strongly emphasized that all advances in medicine increase life expectancy; their efficacy is measured by the degree to which they do so. I am referring not only to insulin, penicillin, and the other spectacular innovations of medical history but also to aspirin (which lowers fever and reduces inflammation, besides relieving pain), adhesive bandages, and washing one's hands before eating. These too, have contributed years to our life-span.

The whole philosophy of the prevention of disease—and 9 where prevention fails, the cure—represents a deep and long-standing moral commitment to life, and the research in question here is its logical development. Thus, one could argue that, our commitment to the preservation of life having already been made, it is too late for us to cease to be ambitious.

Other objections to prolonging old age have to do with popula- 10 tion control and age distribution. For example, it is asked, Dare we propose to add to a burden that is almost insupportable now? Shall the resources of underprivileged nations be consumed at an even faster rate by the technologically more advanced peoples of the Northern Hemisphere and of the West generally—those who will be the first to take advantage of new medical procedures?

In partial extenuation, it can be said that the increase in popu- 11 lation would not be exponential, because it is unlikely that older people would choose to add to their families. Admittedly, though, they would have mouths, and they would use energy and other raw materials at the high rate characteristic of people in the developed parts of the world.

One hears that the likely increase in population size would 12 provoke wars, as if the linkage were an established truth. But it does not stand up to scrutiny. No one will challenge Europe's claim to the dunce's cap for political aggression and warmaking, yet war has been no more frequent in Europe over the past hundred years than it was in medieval times or in the fifteenth century or in the seventeenth, even though the population has grown steadily.

The threat of gerontocracy—government by an aged and prob- 13
ably for the aged—is less easy to dismiss. Certainly old people require special attention, and their rising numbers would lay an extra burden on social-welfare services in a caring society. That
burden would have to be shouldered mainly by the young. A vig-
orous elderly generation would also probably hold on to jobs that
otherwise would pass to the young, thereby exacerbating unem-
ployment. Who knows? A gerontocracy might have the nerve to
impose a special tax on jobholders below some minimum age,
and at the same time reward older jobholders with generous con-
cessions.

Without minimizing these last worries, I must point out that 14
the political and sociological effects of a population shift would
not be felt overnight. We should have between fifty and 200
years to adapt.

The process might completely overturn our present ideas 15
about work and retirement, but in reality such a revolution has
been in progress for the past 150 years, as the proportion of older
people in the population has grown with advances in medicine
and sanitary engineering. It is reasonable to assume we can solve
the problems of the future, since they are not qualitatively new.

Jane Austen wrote her novels around the turn of the nine- 16
teenth century, and they are a mine of information about the
manners and attitudes of her day. Consider, in particular, Austen's first published novel, *Sense and Sensibility*. The hero, Colo-
nel Brandon, is rated at thirty-five an old man and quite past it—
so much so that Marianne Dashwood, the eighteen-year-old girl
whose hand he seeks, regards his suit as a kind of geriatric cha-
rade. In the book the question arises of laying down a sum to
purchase a fifteen-year annuity for Marianne's mother, who is
described as a healthy woman of forty. The man who would
have to provide for the annuity protests, "Her life cannot be
worth half that purchase." So Austen seems able to take for
granted her readers' doubt that a woman of forty could live to be
as old as fifty-five.

Suppose someone had told Austen's contemporaries that their 17
life expectancy could be doubled. If they were to react as some
people do today, they would have held up their hands in horror
at the impiety of interfering with nature—at the very idea that a
man of thirty-five would not have one foot in the grave and that a
woman of forty would live another fifteen years! Yet the average
life-span of a century or more ago seems pathetically short from
the perspective of today. How can we be certain that a genera-

tion as close to us as we are to Jane Austen would not look upon our fears with pained condescension?

Some lines by the poet Walter Savage Landor, which have the 18 cadences of a requiem, seem to rebuke the wish to delay death:

> Nature I loved; and next to Nature, Art.
> I warmed both hands before the fire of life;
> It sinks, and I am ready to depart.

Perhaps this declaration is a Christian acquiescence to an inevitable fate, but to me it sounds spiritless. A person who is loved and in good health has reason enough to want to live a few years longer than might seem to be his due: to learn, for example, how the grandchildren turn out, and whether the flux of history corroborates or refutes his expectations. A writer will want to complete his book, or even turn his thoughts to another, and no gardener will willingly surrender his hope of taking part in the wonder and joyous expectations of another spring. From the point of view of biology, the strength of our hold upon life has been the most important single factor in bringing us to our present ages and, indeed, in the fact that human beings have evolved at all.

Some of the evils that confront mankind—the havoc of war, for 19 example—can be anticipated and guarded against. Others are more insidious. They are the outcomes of well-intentioned actions and could not have been predicted. I have in mind the deaths from cancer of the pioneers of x-radiography, who could not possibly have known that x-rays are among the most potent cancer-causing agents.

Likewise, overpopulation is the consequence of a reduction of 20 mortality, especially in childhood, through medicine and sanitary engineering, which has not been matched by a corresponding reduction in the birthrate.

All else being equal, I think that the risk of unforeseeable ca- 21 tastrophe will probably be sufficient to turn us away from the research to extend life. But what I *hope* will happen is this: perhaps a dozen enthusiasts for the prolonging of life will go ahead and try to prolong their own lives. If they become wise and oracular nonagenarians or centenarians, they will be counted among the benefactors and pathfinders of mankind. If senile dementia is their fate, they will have warned us off, and that would be an equally useful service.

My personal sympathies are with the daredevils who want to 22 try out these new procedures. This kind of adventurousness has always been in the character of science, as Sir Francis Bacon, the Lord Chancellor of England, the first and greatest philosopher of science, and a pious and reverent man, believed. In one of his essays, he wrote:

The true aim of science is the discovery of all operations and all possibilities of operations from immortality (if it were possible) to the meanest mechanical practice.

I count Bacon, therefore, as a man on my side.

TIME BUT NO PLAN

JAYNE ANNE PHILLIPS

I can't reconstruct things enough to know when I decided. I   1
guess it seems I was working toward the divorce for years, but I
was only trying to get to the point where I could support myself.
I never even considered divorce—not with kids at home. Maybe
I stopped thinking on purpose during those years and lived in the
day-to-day. No struggle because every minute was filled.

I try to remember. A few separate days, isolated from each   2
other by months or years, swim up. Then I have to think hard to
know what years those were. I know immediately how they *felt*,
the weather, the news. How old you and Billy were, your teachers in school, clothes you wore. Your face and Billy's face—exactly how you looked.

You know, I don't remember my own face then. I didn't really   3
see myself. Just the slash of red lipstick and a comb through my
hair. There are no photographs of me with you kids from the
time you were old enough to be photographed without me.
Every year there were school pictures with my first-grade
classes, and I always threw them away.

I went back to college when Billy was in kindergarten and took   4
a full course load, but nothing changed at home. I did all
the housework and meals and put you kids to bed with stories,
then stayed up till two or three reading and memorizing. Long
nights, with all the house in darkness and one light burning over
the kitchen table. I'd hear sounds outside and the breathing of
sleepers.

I'd always been afraid of being alone, but now there was no   5
fear or wondering. I *was* alone, though not surprised, not bitter.
My mother had been alone, hadn't she, except for me? I'd bor-

rowed the money to pay for classes and wanted to get straight A's, a perfect record. The one time I got a C on a mid-term, I sat in the rocker in my bedroom and wept. I remember you standing there, trying to reason with me, being very grown-up at eight years old. I suppose my nerves stayed frayed until the degree was finished, and never a word of encouragement from Mitch. No blowups, no fights; he knew it was important I start earning an income, but he grew more silent.

We never fought much. Once, I remember having to stand up to him. 6

What year was it? The news was full of scary headlines about Cuba, and Mitch maintained we'd never be in this fix if a Catholic hadn't been elected president. People around town were talking about fallout shelters. The VFW organized a Civil Defense League: classes at the post office one night a week for four weeks. Mitch took them in the summer, when those old rooms must have been airless. Then he taught the same class in September. He was working for a construction company then, selling aluminum buildings on commission. Always yelling at you kids, *Get the hell off the telephone! Don't you know I earn a living on this phone?* Things were easier when he was involved in the civil defense work; there were books and pamphlets and construction details. Which basements were to be used for town shelters: the courthouse, the high school, all the churches. 7

It would have been October, and grainy aerial photographs of Cuban missiles were appearing in the newspapers. People were alarmed and news was broadcast on the hour. I didn't care much; I remember thinking myself strange. I spent eight hours a day with six-year-olds bused fifteen or twenty miles from hollows back in the country. Did they have fallout shelters? They didn't have mittens or winter coats unless I could find enough at the Salvation Army. Civil defense seemed crazy to me but it was important to Mitch, so I kept quiet. He talked about building a shelter in the little room behind the garage, a utility room where he kept tools, where the hot-water tank was, and the big cabinet that held canned goods. A ladder up the wall led to the attic door, which had to be shoved open from underneath. You kids were never allowed in the attic—there was no floor except for a narrow walkway, just insulation between the boards. Every change of season, I'd find myself up there, opening Mother's big cedar chest in a corner under the eaves. Packing woolens away with moth balls or shaking out summer cottons, hoping they weren't all outgrown. 8

That night, I was in the attic, trying to find enough winter school clothes. Dresses with big hems, pants to let out, but there 9

would have to be new boots and coats. I had a whole pile of
woolens and thought I'd get you both to try everything on while I
finished ironing a basket of Mitch's shirts, and my blouses.
Teaching, I wore skirts and those Ship 'n' Shore cotton blouses
with roll-up sleeves and Peter Pan collars; two white ones, a pale
green one, a blue one. Those are the details I remember, colors
and clothes and the smell of chalk at the blackboard, going over
your homework at night—the red arithmetic book Billy had in
the sixth grade called *Fun with New Math*. No questions about the
meaning of things; you don't think that way if you have children.
The meaning is right in front of you and you live by keeping up
with it. *I have my house and my children* was a phrase I kept in
mind. Piling up clothes, I calculated which would do and which
wouldn't. The light in the attic was dim, one bulb glowing and
the sun setting outside with a gold tinge. Underneath that yellow
color was the cold of the fall coming on. It was a Sunday night
because I was thinking I had the week's lesson plans to do, and
thirty-five big jack-o'-lanterns to cut from orange construction
paper. I loved decorating that classroom and spent hours on a different display every month. Just that day I'd gotten two big rolls
of brown paper so the kids could trace each other's shapes and
color their own portraits. I could put the shapes up all around the
room, with the movable arms and legs holding vowel sounds,
and the jack-o'-lanterns for heads, each with a different expression. In October I was still teaching letter recognition to kids
from the country who hadn't seen many books, kids who'd
never seen themselves full length in a mirror. At Halloween, a
third of the class would be too poor to have costumes; I could
take staples and elastic string to school to make masks out of the
jack-o'-lantern faces. I'd ask Bess and Gladys for worn-out linens
again, and use torn sheets for capes. I stood there in the attic
with all these plans, looking at shirts I knew Billy couldn't wear;
in the half-finished top of the house, I felt as though I were standing behind the scenes of some production. I couldn't move for a
minute, the feeling was so strong. Nothing seemed real. I thought
of my mother hemming my dresses on the porch, letting down
hems one after another while I sat playing with soap bubbles, a
skinny dark sparrow of a kid.

I heard Mitch walking on the concrete floor below. He tapped 10
with his pencil on the water tank, a small reverberating sound
that echoed itself. I looked over the edge of the attic opening and
saw him figuring on a tablet, holding his OCD manuals and a
tape measure. He wore the same khaki clothes at home that he'd
worn at the plant, before Clayton died and the business was sold.
Now he wore shirts and ties to work and called on customers; I

think he hated selling. Too proud not to resent doing it, and at his age. He must have been fifty. I was thirty-five, but I didn't feel young. Looking at him from above, I felt so distant I could have been watching from another planet. He stood inspecting the door to the patio, so involved he was unaware of the light on over his head. He turned abruptly and strode away into the garage.

I stepped back, switched off the light, and took up the bulky 11 clothes in the dark. The ladder was difficult. I held on with one hand and was halfway down when I got stung. Hornets always nested in the attic in summer, but I'd supposed they were gone by now. It was ludicrous; I wasn't willing to drop the clothes on the dirty floor and then sort them all again, and I couldn't move my hand. I called to Mitch but he must not have heard. So I climbed down while the hornet kept stinging me, unable to see over bundled wools and corduroys, and walked into the kitchen where I could put them down.

My hand felt as though it were on fire; there would be some 12 welts. Mitch came in and I stepped behind the heaped ironing board to give him room in the narrow kitchen.

He put a list on the table. "I can make an airtight shelter back 13 there—rig up an air-pipe vent and hand pump through one of the windows, then brick them up with cement block. We've got the water tank we could siphon to supplement to containers, and I'll need about a hundred sandbags to block the doorways."

"Isn't there room for us in the town shelter? We're only two 14 miles away."

"They recommend having your own if you can." He put the 15 manuals on the ironing board in front of me. "You need to read these."

"How can we afford—" 16

He nodded once. "I'll need your help on this." 17

What he meant was money. I looked down at the booklet and 18 saw a gray and yellow illustration of a man shoveling dirt onto a door. The door was propped at an angle against an outer wall. His sweater and the dirt were yellow, as though he were already covered with dust. *A Plan But No Time: Pile the dirt from the trench on top of the doors.* I scanned the words, not really seeing them. *Try to get in a shadow; it will help shield you from the heat.* The ironing board was piled high and the supper dishes were still on the table; my hand was throbbing and I felt almost dizzy with frustration. I turned a page and read: *Time But No Plan: Fill buckets, sinks, a bathtub, and other containers with water.*

"I can't read these," I said, "I'll be up until midnight as it is. 19 And the kids need coats this month. I can't give you any help."

For a minute he just looked at me. Then he leaned toward me 20 over the ironing board. He was a lot bigger than me and seemed huge. "Damn it to hell," he said. "I should know better than to expect help from you on a goddamn thing."

The door to the breezeway was behind me, but I wasn't going 21 to turn around and leave my own house. "You've got no right to talk to me like that. For your information, I've paid half the bills in this house and bought all the kids' clothes for two years."

"And don't you think you're goddamn great for every penny 22 you've spent!"

So we started. You remember his short fuse—breathing heav- 23 ily and shaking with rage in seconds. That's probably why he never raised a hand to you and left all the discipline to me—he got too angry to trust himself. I think I shoved the ironing board against him to get out from behind it. Then we were walking back through the house, just shouting. I was trembling but knew enough not to move too quickly; almost by instinct, he would have reached out and grabbed me.

I realized I was headed toward the back room, our bedroom, 24 and I walked into the bathroom and locked the door. *You'd better stay the hell in there*, he yelled. There was silence except for his voice. I imagined you and Billy in your rooms, listening. I heard you open your door ever so quietly and knew you were afraid.

I told him clearly, *I don't have to stay anywhere. There are laws* 25 *to protect me from men like you.* The words came out of my mouth as though I'd had them in my mind all along. Later I wondered if I'd heard my mother say them to my father.

You say I planned for years, but there was no plan. He was 26 earning less and less; I had to earn more and more. All those extension classes and summer courses to get the master's, almost a doctorate, then insisting we put that house on the market and move into town when you kids were in high school. Finally he agreed. You know, I told him I'd move out alone if he'd sign an agreement to pay for your college educations. But I would never have left you. I was only gambling.

I couldn't take it anymore, struggling on his ground. 27

THE BIRTHMARK

NATHANIEL HAWTHORNE

In the latter part of the last century there lived a man of sci- 1
ence, an eminent proficient in every branch of natural philosophy, who not long before our story opens had made experience
of a spiritual affinity more attractive than any chemical one. He
had left his laboratory to the care of an assistant, cleared his fine
countenance from the furnace smoke, washed the stain of acids
from his fingers, and persuaded a beautiful woman to become
his wife. In those days when the comparatively recent discovery
of electricity and other kindred mysteries of Nature seemed to
open paths into the region of miracle, it was not unusual for the
love of science to rival the love of woman in its depth and ab-
sorbing energy. The higher intellect, the imagination, the spirit,
and even the heart might all find their congenial aliment in pursuits which, as some of their ardent votaries believed, would as-
cend from one step of powerful intelligence to another, until the
philosopher should lay his hand on the secret of creative force
and perhaps make new worlds for himself. We know not
whether Aylmer possessed this degree of faith in man's ultimate
control over Nature. He had devoted himself, however, too unre-
servedly to scientific studies ever to be weaned from them by
any second passion. His love for his young wife might prove the
stronger of the two; but it could only be by intertwining itself
with his love of science, and uniting the strength of the latter to
his own.

Such a union accordingly took place, and was attended with 2
truly remarkable consequences and a deeply impressive moral.
One day, very soon after their marriage, Aylmer sat gazing at his

wife with a trouble in his countenance that grew stronger until he spoke.

"Georgiana," said he, "has it never occurred to you that the mark upon your cheek might be removed?" 3

"No, indeed," said she, smiling; but perceiving the seriousness of his manner, she blushed deeply. "To tell you the truth it has been so often called a charm that I was simple enough to imagine it might be so." 4

"Ah, upon another face perhaps it might," replied her husband; "but never on yours. No, dearest Georgiana, you came so nearly perfect from the hand of Nature that this slightest possible defect, which we hesitate whether to term a defect or a beauty, shocks me, as being the visible mark of earthly imperfection." 5

"Shocks you, my husband!" cried Georgiana, deeply hurt; at first reddening with momentary anger, but then bursting into tears. "Then why did you take me from my mother's side? You cannot love what shocks you!" 6

To explain this conversation it must be mentioned that in the centre of Georgiana's left cheek there was a singular mark, deeply interwoven, as it were, with the texture and substance of her face. In the usual state of her complexion—a healthy though delicate bloom—the mark wore a tint of deeper crimson, which imperfectly defined its shape amid the surrounding rosiness. When she blushed it gradually became more indistinct, and finally vanished amid the triumphant rush of blood that bathed the whole cheek with its brilliant glow. But if any shifting motion caused her to turn pale there was the mark again, a crimson stain upon the snow, in what Aylmer sometimes deemed an almost fearful distinctness. Its shape bore not a little similarity to the human hand, though of the smallest pygmy size. Georgiana's lovers were wont to say that some fairy at her birth hour had laid her tiny hand upon the infant's cheek, and left this impress there in token of the magic endowments that were to give her such sway over all hearts. Many a desperate swain would have risked life for the privilege of pressing his lips to the mysterious hand. It must not be concealed, however, that the impression wrought by this fairy sign manual varied exceedingly, according to the difference of temperament in the beholders. Some fastidious persons—but they were exclusively of her own sex—affirmed that the bloody hand, as they chose to call it, quite destroyed the effect of Georgiana's beauty, and rendered her countenance even hideous. But it would be as reasonable to say that one of those small blue stains which sometimes occur in the purest statuary marble would convert the Eve of Powers to a monster. Mascu- 7 line observers, if the birthmark did not heighten their admiration, contented themselves with wishing it away, that the world might possess one living specimen of ideal loveliness without the semblance of a flaw. After his marriage,—for he thought little or nothing of the matter before,—Aylmer discovered that this was the case with himself.

Had she been less beautiful,—if Envy's self could have found 8 aught else to sneer at,—he might have felt his affection heightened by the prettiness of this mimic hand, now vaguely portrayed, now lost, now stealing forth again and glimmering to and fro with every pulse of emotion that throbbed within her heart; but seeing her otherwise so perfect, he found this one defect grow more and more intolerable with every moment of their united lives. It was the fatal flaw of humanity which Nature, in one shape or another, stamps ineffaceably on all her productions, either to imply that they are temporary and finite, or that their perfection must be wrought by toil and pain. The crimson hand expressed the ineludible gripe in which mortality clutches the highest and purest of earthly mould, degrading them into kindred with the lowest, and even with the very brutes, like whom their visible frames return to dust. In this manner, selecting it as the symbol of his wife's liability to sin, sorrow, decay, and death, Aylmer's sombre imagination was not long in rendering the birthmark a frightful object, causing him more trouble and horror than ever Georgiana's beauty, whether of soul or sense, had given him delight.

At all the seasons which should have been their happiest, he 9 invariably and without intending it, nay, in spite of a purpose to the contrary, reverted to this one disastrous topic. Trifling as it at first appeared, it so connected itself with innumerable trains of thought and modes of feeling that it became the central point of all. With the morning twilight Aylmer opened his eyes upon his wife's face and recognized the symbol of imperfection; and when they sat together at the evening hearth his eyes wandered stealthily to her cheek, and beheld, flickering with the blaze of the wood fire, the spectral hand that wrote mortality where he would fain have worshipped. Georgiana soon learned to shudder at his gaze. It needed but a glance with the peculiar expression that his face often wore to change the roses of her cheek into a deathlike paleness, amid which the crimson hand was brought strongly out, like a bass-relief of ruby on the whitest marble.

Late one night when the lights were growing dim, so as hardly 10 to betray the stain on the poor wife's cheek, she herself, for the first time, voluntarily took up the subject.

"Do you remember, my dear Aylmer," said she, with a feeble 11 attempt at a smile, "have you any recollection of a dream last night about this odious hand?"

"None! none whatever!" replied Aylmer, starting; but then he 12 added, in a dry, cold tone, affected for the sake of concealing the real depth of his emotion, "I might well dream of it; for before I fell asleep it had taken a pretty firm hold of my fancy."

"And you did dream of it?" continued Georgiana, hastily; for 13 she dreaded lest a gush of tears should interrupt what she had to say. "A terrible dream! I wonder that you can forget it. Is it possible to forget this one expression?—'It is in her heart now; we must have it out!' Reflect, my husband; for by all means I would have you recall that dream."

The mind is in a sad state when Sleep, the all-involving, cannot 14 confine her spectres within the dim region of her sway, but suffers them to break forth, affrighting this actual life with secrets that perchance belong to a deeper one. Aylmer now remembered his dream. He had fancied himself with his servant Aminadab, attempting an operation for the removal of the birthmark; but the deeper went the knife, the deeper sank the hand, until at length its tiny grasp appeared to have caught hold of Georgiana's heart; whence, however, her husband was inexorably resolved to cut or wrench it away.

When the dream had shaped itself perfectly in his memory, 15 Aylmer sat in his wife's presence with a guilty feeling. Truth often finds its way to the mind close muffled in robes of sleep, and then speaks with uncompromising directness of matters in regard to which we practise an unconscious self-deception during our waking moments. Until now he had not been aware of the tyrannizing influence acquired by one idea over his mind, and of the lengths which he might find in his heart to go for the sake of giving himself peace.

"Aylmer," resumed Georgiana, solemnly, "I know not what 16 may be the cost to both of us to rid me of this fatal birthmark. Perhaps its removal may cause cureless deformity; or it may be the stain goes as deep as life itself. Again: do we know that there is a possibility, on any terms, of unclasping the firm gripe of this little hand which was laid upon me before I came into the world?"

"Dearest Georgiana, I have spent much thought upon the sub- 17 ject," hastily interrupted Aylmer. "I am convinced of the perfect practicability of its removal."

"If there be the remotest possibility of it," continued Geor- 18 giana, "let the attempt be made at whatever risk. Danger is nothing to me; for life, while this hateful mark makes me the object of your horror and disgust,—life is a burden which I would fling down with joy. Either remove this dreadful hand, or take my wretched life! You have deep science. All the world bears witness of it. You have achieved great wonders. Cannot you remove this little, little mark, which I cover with the tips of two small fingers? Is this beyond your power, for the sake of your own peace, and to save your poor wife from madness?"

"Noblest, dearest, tenderest wife," cried Aylmer, rapturously, 19 "doubt not my power. I have already given this matter the deepest thought—thought which might almost have enlightened me to create a being less perfect that yourself. Georgiana, you have led me deeper than ever into the heart of science. I feel myself fully competent to render this dear cheek as faultless as its fellow; and then, most beloved, what will be my triumph when I shall have corrected what Nature left imperfect in her fairest work! Even Pygmalion, when his sculptured woman assumed life, felt not greater ecstasy than mine will be."

"It is resolved, then," said Georgiana, faintly smiling. "And, 20 Aylmer, spare me not, though you should find the birthmark take refuge in my heart at last."

Her husband tenderly kissed her cheek—her right cheek—not 21 that which bore the impress of the crimson hand.

The next day Aylmer apprised his wife of a plan that he had 22 formed whereby he might have opportunity for the intense thought and constant watchfulness which the proposed operation would require; while Georgiana, likewise, would enjoy the perfect repose essential to its success. They were to seclude themselves in the extensive apartments occupied by Aylmer as a laboratory, and where, during his toilsome youth, he had made discoveries in the elemental powers of Nature that had roused the admiration of all the learned societies in Europe. Seated calmly in this laboratory, the pale philosopher had investigated the secrets of the highest cloud region and of the profoundest mines; he had satisfied himself of the causes that kindled and kept alive the fires of the volcano; and had explained the mystery of fountains, and how it is that they gush forth, some so bright and pure, and others with such rich medicinal virtues, from the dark bosom of the earth. Here, too, at an earlier period, he had studied the wonders of the human frame, and attempted to fathom the very process by which Nature assimilates all her precious influences from earth and air, and from the spiritual world, to create and foster man, her masterpiece. The latter pursuit, however, Aylmer had long laid aside in unwilling recognition of the truth—against which all seekers sooner or later stumble—that our great creative Mother, while she amuses us with apparently working in the broadest sunshine, is yet severely careful to keep her own secrets, and, in spite of her pretended openness, shows us nothing but results. She permits us, indeed, to mar, but seldom to mend, and, like a jealous patentee, on no account to make. Now, however, Aylmer resumed these half-forgotten investigations; not, of course, with such hopes or wishes as first suggested them; but because they involved much physiological truth and lay in the path of his proposed scheme for the treatment of Georgiana.

As he led her over the threshold of the laboratory, Georgiana 23 was cold and tremulous. Aylmer looked cheerfully into her face, with intent to reassure her, but was so startled with the intense glow of the birthmark upon the whiteness of her cheek that he could not restrain a strong convulsive shudder. His wife fainted.

"Aminadab! Aminadab!" shouted Aylmer, stamping violently 24 on the floor.

Forthwith there issued from an inner apartment a man of low 25 stature, but bulky frame, with shaggy hair hanging about his visage, which was grimed with the vapors of the furnace. This personage had been Aylmer's underworker during his whole scientific career, and was admirably fitted for that office by his great mechanical readiness, and the skill with which, while incapable of comprehending a single principle, he executed all the details of his master's experiments. With his vast strength, his shaggy hair, his smoky aspect, and the indescribable earthiness that incrusted him, he seemed to represent man's physical nature; while Aylmer's slender figure, and pale, intellectual face, were no less apt a type of the spiritual element.

"Throw open the door of the boudoir, Aminadab," said 26 Aylmer, "and burn a pastil."

"Yes, master," answered Aminadab, looking intently at the 27 lifeless form of Georgiana; and then he muttered to himself, "If she were my wife, I'd never part with that birthmark."

When Georgiana recovered consciousness she found herself 28 breathing an atmosphere of penetrating fragrance, the gentle potency of which had recalled her from her deathlike faintness. The scene around her looked like enchantment. Aylmer had converted those smoky, dingy, sombre rooms, where he had spent his brightest years in recondite pursuits, into a series of beautiful apartments not unfit to be the secluded abode of a lovely woman. The walls were hung with gorgeous curtains, which imparted the combination of grandeur and grace that no other species of adornment can achieve; and as they fell from the ceiling to the floor, their rich and ponderous folds, concealing all angles and straight lines, appeared to shut in the scene from infinite space. For aught Georgiana knew, it might be a pavilion among the clouds. And Aylmer, excluding the sunshine, which would have interfered with his chemical processes, had supplied its place with perfumed lamps, emitting flames of various hue, but all uniting in a soft, impurpled radiance. He now knelt by his wife's side, watching her earnestly, but without alarm; for he was confident in his science, and felt that he could draw a magic circle round her within which no evil might intrude.

"Where am I? Ah, I remember," said Georgiana, faintly; and 29 she placed her hand over her cheek to hide the terrible mark from her husband's eyes.

"Fear not, dearest!" exclaimed he. "Do not shrink from me! 30 Believe me, Georgiana, I even rejoice in this single imperfection, since it will be such a rapture to remove it."

"Oh, spare me!" sadly replied his wife. "Pray do not look at it 31 again. I never can forget that convulsive shudder."

In order to soothe Georgiana, and, as it were, to release her 32 mind from the burden of actual things, Aylmer now put in practice some of the light and playful secrets which science had taught him among its profounder lore. Airy figures, absolutely bodiless ideas, and forms of unsubstantial beauty came and danced before her, imprinting their momentary footsteps on beams of light. Though she had some indistinct idea of the method of these optical phenomena, still the illusion was almost perfect enough to warrant the belief that her husband possessed sway over the spiritual world. Then again, when she felt a wish to look forth from her seclusion, immediately, as if her thoughts were answered, the procession of external existence flitted across a screen. The scenery and the figures of actual life were perfectly represented, but with that bewitching, yet indescribable difference which always makes a picture, an image, or a shadow so much more attractive than the original. When wearied of this, Aylmer bade her cast her eyes upon a vessel containing a quantity of earth. She did so, with little interest at first; but was soon startled to perceive the germ of a plant shooting upward from the soil. Then came the slender stalk; the leaves gradually unfolded themselves; and amid them was a perfect and lovely flower.

"It is magical!" cried Georgiana. "I dare not touch it."   33

"Nay, pluck it," answered Aylmer,—"pluck it, and inhale its 34 brief perfume while you may. The flower will wither in a few moments and leave nothing save its brown seed vessels; but thence may be perpetuated a race as ephemeral as itself.''

But Georgiana had no sooner touched the flower than the 35 whole plant suffered a blight, its leaves turning coal-black as if by the agency of fire.

"There was too powerful a stimulus," said Aylmer, thought- 36 fully.

To make up for this abortive experiment, he proposed to take 37 her portrait by a scientific process of his own invention. It was to be effected by rays of light striking upon a polished plate of metal. Georgiana assented; but, on looking at the result, was affrighted to find the features of the portrait blurred and indefinable; while the minute figure of a hand appeared where the cheek should have been. Aylmer snatched the metallic plate and threw it into a jar of corrosive acid.

Soon, however, he forgot these mortifying failures. In the in- 38 tervals of study and chemical experiment he came to her flushed and exhausted, but seemed invigorated by her presence, and spoke in glowing language of the resources of art. He gave a history of the long dynasty of the alchemists, who spent so many ages in quest of the universal solvent by which the golden principle might be elicited from all things vile and base. Aylmer appeared to believe that, by the plainest scientific logic, it was altogether within the limits of possibility to discover this long-sought medium; "but," he added, "a philosopher who should go deep enough to acquire the power would attain too lofty a wisdom to stoop to the exercise of it." Not less singular were his opinions in regard to the elixir vitæ. He more than intimated that it was at his option to concoct a liquid that should prolong life for years, perhaps interminably; but that it would produce a discord in Nature which all the world, and chiefly the quaffer of the immortal nostrum, would find cause to curse.

"Aylmer, are you in earnest?" asked Georgiana, looking at 39 him with amazement and fear. "It is terrible to possess such power, or even to dream of possessing it."

"Oh, do not tremble, my love," said her husband. "I would 40 not wrong either you or myself by working such inharmonious effects upon our lives; but I would have you consider how trifling, in comparison, is the skill requisite to remove this little hand."

At the mention of the birthmark, Georgiana, as usual, shrank 41 as if a redhot iron had touched her cheek.

Again Aylmer applied himself to his labors. She could hear his 42 voice in the distant furnace room giving directions to Aminadab, whose harsh, uncouth, misshapen tones were audible in response, more like the grunt or growl of a brute than human speech. After hours of absence, Aylmer reappeared and proposed that she should now examine his cabinet of chemical products and natural treasures of the earth. Among the former he showed her a small vial, in which, he remarked, was contained a gentle yet most powerful fragrance, capable of impregnating all the breezes that blow across a kingdom. They were of inestimable value, the contents of that little vial; and, as he said so, he threw some of the perfume into the air and filled the room with piercing and invigorating delight.

"And what is this?" asked Georgiana, pointing to a small crys- 43 tal globe containing a gold-colored liquid. "It is so beautiful to the eye that I could imagine it the elixir of life."

"In one sense it is," replied Aylmer; "or, rather, the elixir of 44 immortality. It is the most precious poison that ever was concocted in this world. By its aid I could apportion the lifetime of any mortal at whom you might point your finger. The strength of the dose would determine whether he were to linger out years, or drop dead in the midst of a breath. No king on his guarded throne could keep his life if I, in my private station, should deem that the welfare of millions justified me in depriving him of it."

"Why do you keep such a terrific drug?" inquired Georgiana 45 in horror.

"Do not mistrust me, dearest," said her husband, smiling; "its 46 virtuous potency is yet greater than its harmful one. But see! here is a powerful cosmetic. With a few drops of this in a vase of water, freckles may be washed away as easily as the hands are cleansed. A stronger infusion would take the blood out of the cheek, and leave the rosiest beauty a pale ghost."

"Is it with this lotion that you intend to bathe my cheek?" 47 asked Georgiana, anxiously.

"Oh, no," hastily replied her husband; "this is merely superfi- 48 cial. Your case demands a remedy that shall go deeper."

In his interviews with Georgiana, Aylmer generally made min- 49 ute inquiries as to her sensations and whether the confinement of the rooms and the temperature of the atmosphere agreed with her. These questions had such a particular drift that Georgiana began to conjecture that she was already subjected to certain physical influences, either breathed in with the fragrant air or taken with her food. She fancied likewise, but it might be altogether fancy, that there was a stirring up of her system—a strange, indefinite sensation creeping through her veins, and tingling, half painfully, half pleasurably, at her heart. Still, whenever she dared to look into the mirror, there she beheld herself pale as a white rose and with the crimson birthmark stamped upon her cheek. Not even Aylmer now hated it so much as she.

To dispel the tedium of the hours which her husband found it 50 necessary to devote to the processes of combination and analysis, Georgiana turned over the volumes of his scientific library. In many dark old tomes she met with chapters full of romance and poetry. They were the works of the philosophers of the middle ages, such as Albertus Magnus, Cornelius Agrippa, Paracelsus, and the famous friar who created the prophetic Brazen Head. All these antique naturalists stood in advance of their centuries, yet were imbued with some of their credulity, and therefore were believed, and perhaps imagined themselves to have acquired from the investigation of Nature a power above Nature, and from physics a sway over the spiritual world. Hardly less curious and imaginative were the early volumes of the Transactions of the Royal Society, in which the members, knowing little of the limits of natural possibility, were continually recording wonders or proposing methods whereby wonders might be wrought.

But to Georgiana the most engrossing volume was a large folio 51 from her husband's own hand, in which he had recorded every experiment of his scientific career, its original aim, the methods adopted for its development, and its final success or failure, with the circumstances to which either event was attributable. The book, in truth, was both the history and emblem of his ardent, ambitious, imaginative, yet practical and laborious life. He handled physical details as if there were nothing beyond them; yet spiritualized them all, and redeemed himself from materialism by his strong and eager aspiration towards the infinite. In his grasp the veriest clod of earth assumed a soul. Georgiana, as she read, reverenced Aylmer and loved him more profoundly than ever, but with a less entire dependence on his judgment than heretofore. Much as he had accomplished, she could not but observe that his most splendid successes were almost invariably failures, if compared with the ideal at which he aimed. His brightest diamonds were the merest pebbles, and felt to be so by himself, in comparison with the inestimable gems which lay hidden beyond his reach. The volume, rich with achievements that had won renown for its author, was yet as melancholy a record as ever mortal hand had penned. It was the sad confession and continual exemplification of the shortcomings of the composite man, the spirit burdened with clay and working in matter, and of the despair that assails the higher nature at finding itself so miserably thwarted by the earthly part. Perhaps every man of genius in whatever sphere might recognize the image of his own experience in Aylmer's journal.

So deeply did these reflections affect Georgiana that she laid 52 her face upon the open volume and burst into tears. In this situation she was found by her husband.

"It is dangerous to read in a sorcerer's books," said he with a 53 smile, though his countenance was uneasy and displeased. "Georgiana, there are pages in that volume which I can scarcely glance over and keep my senses. Take heed lest it prove as detrimental to you."

"It has made me worship you more than ever," said she.   54

"Ah, wait for this one success," rejoined he, "then worship 55 me if you will. I shall deem myself hardly unworthy of it. But come, I have sought you for the luxury of your voice. Sing to me, dearest."

So she poured out the liquid music of her voice to quench the 56 thirst of his spirit. He then took his leave with a boyish exuberance of gayety, assuring her that her seclusion would endure but a little longer, and that the result was already certain. Scarcely had he departed when Georgiana felt irresistibly impelled to follow him. She had forgotten to inform Aylmer of a symptom which for two or three hours past had begun to excite her attention. It was a sensation in the fatal birthmark, not painful, but which induced a restlessness throughout her system. Hastening after her husband, she intruded for the first time into the laboratory.

The first thing that struck her eye was the furnace, that hot 57 and feverish worker, with the intense glow of its fire, which by the quantities of soot clustered above it seemed to have been burning for ages. There was a distilling apparatus in full operation. Around the room were retorts, tubes, cylinders, crucibles, and other apparatus of chemical research. An electrical machine stood ready for immediate use. The atmosphere felt oppressively close, and was tainted with gaseous odors which had been tormented forth by the processes of science. The severe and homely simplicity of the apartment, with its naked walls and brick pavement, looked strange, accustomed as Georgiana had become to the fantastic elegance of her boudoir. But what chiefly, indeed almost solely, drew her attention, was the aspect of Aylmer himself.

He was pale as death, anxious and absorbed, and hung over 58 the furnace as if it depended upon his utmost watchfulness whether the liquid which it was distilling should be the draught of immortal happiness or misery. How different from the sanguine and joyous mien that he had assumed for Georgiana's encouragement!

"Carefully now, Aminadab; carefully, thou human machine; 59 carefully, thou man of clay!" muttered Aylmer, more to himself than his assistant. "Now, if there be a thought too much or too little, it is all over."

"Ho! ho!" mumbled Aminadab. "Look, master! look!" 60

Aylmer raised his eyes hastily, and at first reddened, then 61 grew paler than ever, on beholding Georgiana. He rushed towards her and seized her arm with a gripe that left the print of his fingers upon it.

"Why do you come hither? Have you no trust in your hus- 62 band?" cried he, impetuously. "Would you throw the blight of that fatal birthmark over my labors? It is not well done. Go, prying woman, go!"

"Nay, Aylmer," said Georgiana with the firmness of which 63 she possessed no stinted endowment, "it is not you that have a right to complain. You mistrust your wife; you have concealed the anxiety with which you watch the development of this experiment. Think not so unworthily of me, my husband. Tell me all the risk we run, and fear not that I shall shrink; for my share in it is far less than your own."

"No, no, Georgiana!" said Aylmer, impatiently; "it must not 64 be."

"I submit," replied she calmly. "And, Aylmer, I shall quaff 65 whatever draught you bring me; but it will be on the same principle that would induce me to take a dose of poison if offered by your hand."

"My noble wife," said Aylmer, deeply moved, "I knew not the 66 height and depth of your nature until now. Nothing shall be concealed. Know, then, that this crimson hand, superficial as it seems, has clutched its grasp into your being with a strength of which I had no previous conception. I have already administered agents powerful enough to do aught except to change your entire physical system. Only one thing remains to be tried. If that fail us we are ruined."

"Why did you hesitate to tell me this?" asked she. 67

"Because, Georgiana," said Aylmer, in a low voice, "there is 68 danger."

"Danger? There is but one danger—that this horrible stigma 69 shall be left upon my cheek!" cried Georgiana. "Remove it, remove it, whatever be the cost, or we shall both go mad!"

"Heaven knows your words are too true," said Aylmer, sadly. 70

"And now, dearest, return to your boudoir. In a little while all will be tested."

He conducted her back and took leave of her with a solemn 71 tenderness which spoke far more than his words how much was now at stake. After his departure Georgiana became rapt in musings. She considered the character of Aylmer, and did it completer justice than at any previous moment. Her heart exulted, while it trembled, at his honorable love—so pure and lofty that it would accept nothing less than perfection nor miserably make itself contented with an earthlier nature than he had dreamed of. She felt how much more precious was such a sentiment than that meaner kind which would have borne with the imperfection for her sake, and have been guilty of treason to holy love by degrading its perfect idea to the level of the actual; and with her whole spirit she prayed that, for a single moment, she might satisfy his highest and deepest conception. Longer than one moment she well knew it could not be; for his spirit was ever on the march, ever ascending, and each instant required something that was beyond the scope of the instant before.

The sound of her husband's footsteps aroused her. He bore a 72 crystal goblet containing a liquor colorless as water, but bright enough to be the draught of immortality. Aylmer was pale; but it seemed rather the consequence of a highly-wrought state of mind and tension of spirit than of fear or doubt.

"The concoction of the draught has been perfect," said he, in 73 answer to Georgiana's look. "Unless all my science have deceived me, it cannot fail."

"Save on your account, my dearest Aylmer," observed his 74 wife, "I might wish to put off this birthmark of mortality by relinquishing mortality itself in preference to any other mode. Life is but a sad possession to those who have attained precisely the degree of moral advancement at which I stand. Were I weaker and blinder it might be happiness. Were I stronger, it might be endured hopefully. But, being what I find myself, methinks I am of all mortals the most fit to die."

"You are fit for heaven without tasting death!" replied her 75 husband. "But why do we speak of dying? The draught cannot fail. Behold its effect upon this plant."

On the window seat there stood a geranium diseased with yel- 76 low blotches, which had overspread all its leaves. Aylmer poured a small quantity of the liquid upon the soil in which it grew. In a little time, when the roots of the plant had taken up the moisture, the unsightly blotches began to be extinguished in a living verdure.

"There needed no proof," said Georgiana, quietly. "Give me 77
the goblet. I joyfully stake all upon your word."

"Drink, then, thou lofty creature!" exclaimed Aylmer, with 78
fervid admiration. "There is no taint of imperfection on thy
spirit. Thy sensible frame, too, shall soon be all perfect."

She quaffed the liquid and returned the goblet to his hand.   79

"It is grateful," said she with a placid smile. "Methinks it is 80
like water from a heavenly fountain; for it contains I know not
what of unobtrusive fragrance and deliciousness. It allays a feverish thirst that had parched me for many days. Now, dearest,
let me sleep. My earthly senses are closing over my spirit like the
leaves around the heart of a rose at sunset."

She spoke the last words with a gentle reluctance, as if it re- 81
quired almost more energy than she could command to pro-
nounce the faint and lingering syllables. Scarcely had they loi-
tered through her lips ere she was lost in slumber. Aylmer sat by
her side, watching her aspect with the emotions proper to a man
the whole value of whose existence was involved in the process
now to be tested. Mingled with this mood, however, was the
philosophic investigation characteristic of the man of science.
Not the minutest symptom escaped him. A heightened flush of
the cheek, a slight irregularity of breath, a quiver of the eyelid, a
hardly perceptible tremor through the frame,—such were the details which, as the moments passed, he wrote down in his folio
volume. Intense thought had set its stamp upon every previous
page of that volume, but the thoughts of years were all concentrated upon the last.

While thus employed, he failed not to gaze often at the fatal 82
hand, and not without a shudder. Yet once, by a strange and un-
accountable impulse, he pressed it with his lips. His spirit re-
coiled, however, in the very act; and Georgiana, out of the midst
of her deep sleep, moved uneasily and murmured as if in remon-
strance. Again Aylmer resumed his watch. Nor was it without
avail. The crimson hand, which at first had been strongly visible
upon the marble paleness of Georgiana's cheek, now grew more
faintly outlined. She remained not less pale than ever; but the
birthmark, with every breath that came and went, lost somewhat of its former distinctness. Its presence had been awful; its
departure was more awful still. Watch the stain of the rainbow
fading out of the sky, and you will know how that mysterious
symbol passed away.

"By Heaven! it is well-nigh gone!" said Aylmer to himself, in 83
almost irrepressible ecstasy. "I can scarcely trace it now. Success! success! And now it is like the faintest rose color. The light-

est flush of blood across her cheek would overcome it. But she is so pale!''

He drew aside the window curtain and suffered the light of natural day to fall into the room and rest upon her cheek. At the same time he heard a gross, hoarse chuckle, which he had long known as his servant Aminadab's expression of delight. 84

''Ah, clod! ah, earthly mass!'' cried Aylmer, laughing in a sort of frenzy, ''you have served me well! Matter and spirit—earth and heaven—have both done their part in this! Laugh, thing of the senses! You have earned the right to laugh.'' 85

These exclamations broke Georgiana's sleep. She slowly unclosed her eyes and gazed into the mirror which her husband had arranged for that purpose. A faint smile flitted over her lips when she recognized how barely perceptible was now that crimson hand which had once blazed forth with such disastrous brilliancy as to scare away all their happiness. But then her eyes sought Aylmer's face with a trouble and anxiety that he could by no means account for. 86

''My poor Aylmer!'' murmured she. 87

''Poor? Nay, richest, happiest, most favored!'' exclaimed he. ''My peerless bride, it is successful! You are perfect!'' 88

''My poor Aylmer,'' she repeated, with a more than human tenderness, ''you have aimed loftily; you have done nobly. Do not repent that with so high and pure a feeling, you have rejected the best the earth could offer. Aylmer, dearest Aylmer, I am dying!'' 89

Alas! it was too true! The fatal hand had grappled with the mystery of life, and was the bond by which an angelic spirit kept itself in union with a mortal frame. As the last crimson tint of the birthmark—that sole token of human imperfection—faded from her cheek, the parting breath of the now perfect woman passed into the atmosphere, and her soul, lingering a moment near her husband, took its heavenward flight. Then a hoarse, chuckling laugh was heard again! Thus ever does the gross fatality of earth exult in its invariable triumph over the immortal essence which, in this dim sphere of half development, demands the completeness of a higher state. Yet, had Aylmer reached a profounder wisdom, he need not thus have flung away the happiness which would have woven his mortal life of the selfsame texture with the celestial. The momentary circumstance was too strong for him; he failed to look beyond the shadowy scope of time, and, living once for all in eternity, to find the perfect future in the present. 90

PART SIX

IMPROVING YOUR WRITING

GETTING STARTED

Many students have trouble getting started writing, even after they have identified a topic that they want to write about. In talking with students about the problems of getting started, we learned how deeply frustrated some of them were. But we also were able to offer them some suggestions for overcoming the difficulties of putting their ideas on paper.

The most common problem is that many students believe that by identifying their topic—for example, "How Divorce Affects Children"—they have sufficient grounds for beginning to write. They start at once to look for an attention-grabbing opening sentence. Too often, unfortunately, the sentence that sounds fine in the writer's head loses some of its punch when it is transferred to paper. The usual solution is to scratch out that sentence and think of another, being sure to throw away the paper to destroy all traces of the false start. After discarding several attempts at an opening sentence, and filling the wastebasket with virtually unused paper, it's time for a snack, a short TV break, or a phone call. Later, the student returns to the drawing board to repeat this process in search of an elusive first sentence.

The trouble with this approach, apart from mounting frustration, is that the search for a good opening can divert your attention from your main goal, which is to express a particular *set of ideas* as effectively as possible. By itself, then, a good topic is seldom a sufficient basis for beginning to draft the essay.

From Topic to Thesis

Before trying to sum up your topic in a strong opening sentence, first you need to check your sense of direction. Decide what main idea, or *thesis*, you want to develop in the essay. Then, keep that general idea in mind as you jot down all the related ideas and examples that spring from it. By focusing on and expanding one major idea about your topic, you will get a fairly good sense of what you want to cover in your essay.

Selecting Your Thesis

Merely identifying a topic that you want to write about cannot provide the same degree of guidance that a thesis statement can, for a *thesis statement* goes beyond the topic and states the writer's point of view or attitude toward the topic. For example, if your topic is "How Divorce Affects Children," you might decide to emphasize the ideas expressed in the following thesis statement:

Photograph by David M. Grossman

Divorce seems to harm children between the ages of five and
ten much more that it harms teenagers or infants.

Notice how this statement sets real boundaries for an essay. It establishes age groups for comparison, and it suggests that divorce affects these groups differently. Now the writer should have little difficulty planning the essay, since the thesis statement calls for a description of the harmful effects of divorce on each age group. This naturally leads the writer to give evidence or state a theory that accounts for the differences described. The writer can move confidently to the next step, which is to organize this series of ideas into an effective outline for the essay.

Sometimes it is difficult to select a thesis. For example, you may disagree strongly with one of the readings in this book or with an opinion expressed by a classmate. Merely stating that you disagree, however, does not indicate the path that your own thoughts will take in the essay. To map out your course, we recommend that you try a technique called *brainstorming*, in which you quickly list any and all ideas that come to mind as you consider your topic. Do not censor yourself, saying "Oh, that's silly" or "It won't work" or "That doesn't fit my earlier response." Let *all* your thoughts flow freely for about five or ten minutes. Then, relax and look over the list to see whether any pattern appears. When you let down your guard this way, it often happens that your thoughts tend to veer in a particular direction, and you will see a thesis emerging from them.

Brainstorming is a bit like the practice of searching for a strong first sentence, except that you just jot down ideas and you *don't* discard all your false starts. Instead, you set aside a period of time in which you suspend all judgment and simply list every idea you have, no matter how unimportant it may seem. Surprisingly, many of the ideas will be related. When your brainstorming period is over and you consider the results as a whole, you will probably find a set of related ideas that suggest a thesis statement to guide your essay.

Remember that an important aspect of selecting your thesis is to consider your audience and your purpose for writing. The reading and responding process used in this book helps you to understand your audience, since you get feedback from other students when you share your initial response to an essay. During drafting, too, the reactions of your classmates can tell you whether or not you are reaching your audience effectively. Their comments also can help you define the purpose of your writing. Do you want to inform them about something, or do you hope to persuade them to agree with you? Their reactions to your ideas will tell you whether you are achieving your purpose. By considering your audience and how you want your writing to affect them, you will discover which ideas you want to emphasize in your thesis statement.

Stating Your Thesis

Merely saying that you disagree with someone ties you to that person's ideas. Your essay will be more interesting and original if you first make a positive statement that expresses your own ideas about the topic.

For example, about half of our students responded to Gordon Liddy's piece, "Without Emotion" (see Part One), by writing something like this: "I think Liddy was (wrong) (crazy) (evil) (foolish) to practice killing without emotion." But students who moved beyond mere judgments of Liddy to make strong personal statements found it easier to write solid, interesting essays. Here are some of their thesis statements:

Soldiers who suppress their sympathy for other people's suffering become machines, just like the Nazis did in Germany.

It's foolish to think you can train yourself not to feel compassion for your fellow human beings, because at some point you'll fall apart emotionally.

Killing innocent creatures is evil because it leads people to think murder and war are reasonable ways to solve problems.

Besides making it easier to write an effective essay, thesis statements like these result in essays that can stand alone. Readers do not have to know the passage from Liddy's book; they can react directly to the ideas presented in the essay.

Developing Your Thesis

By considering your audience, purpose, and topic, you have selected and stated a thesis. Now you need to gather and organize ideas to support your thesis. Again, the technique of brainstorming will help; set aside a few minutes in which you list all the ideas that come to mind without judging them. When the ideas stop flowing, take a deep breath and examine each item on your list. Does the first item relate in any way to your thesis statement? If it doesn't, cross it out, and move to the second item on your list. Examine each of your ideas in terms of your thesis statement. If you are writing about the effects of divorce on young children and teenagers, you can cross out any idea that doesn't fit—such as the legal aspects of divorce, or the high cost of a lawyer. Use your thesis statement to guide you in deciding which ideas support your point of view and which ideas are unimportant.

When you have crossed out all the unimportant ideas on your list, study the ideas that remain, and begin to explore them further. At this point you might like to try *freewriting*—write a few sentences about each item on your list, again without judging the results. For a brief period of time, let your ideas flow. If one sentence leads to another, go with it; find out where it leads. After freewriting, look over your sentences and group them into related ideas (for example, group all the sentences about divorce and young children). In this way you will develop a rough outline of ideas and details to support your thesis.

Drafting the Essay

After you have stated your thesis and have developed and outlined your ideas about it, you are ready to undertake the sentence-by-sentence writing of the essay. Although the problem of getting started has been resolved by first stating a thesis and preparing a rough outline of supporting ideas and details, you may still find yourself crumpling up sheets of paper to discard less-than-wonderful opening sentences. Many people seem to feel that almost anything they write is not good enough. Even if they get past the first sentence, the second or third one has them crossing out and discarding their efforts.

To avoid all this frustration, our advice is to write your first draft uncritically, without concern for the quality of your word choices and sentence structure. As you did during brainstorming and freewriting, write rapidly, just to record your ideas on paper, where they won't get lost (as they surely will if you struggle over every word and sentence in a quest for perfection).

"Writer's block"—the inability to write anything at all—often results from fear of failure. But no failure is possible during the drafting phase, since you alone will be the reader. So don't be too critical as you begin drafting. Wait until your first draft is finished before examining its content, organization, mechanics, grammar, and style.

Besides the danger of writer's block, another pitfall of trying to write a "perfect" first draft is that you are likely to lose sight of the thesis itself. Your main idea may then become just one of several ideas that seem equally important, leaving readers to wonder what you hoped to accomplish in your essay. Following is an example of how an introductory paragraph can go astray when the writer pays more attention to sentence structure and grammar than to the ideas he or she wants to express. Notice that each sentence is clear and well written; yet no main idea emerges:

In the beginning of the world, when God made the animals

and placed Adam and Eve in charge of them, all the Earth's

creatures lived together in peace. Things are different now. Hunting and fishing have become big sports because many people think animals were put on Earth just for their pleasure. And some scientists torture and even kill animals for "the advancement of civilization!" I gave up eating meat when I became old enough to realize how the meat came to my dinner plate. Some animals do serve a useful purpose, but the rest exist in Nature, just being their beautiful selves. No one should ever kill these animals, for they have just as much right to life as we do. I belong to several organizations that are working to stop the cruel killing of animals. But the government does little to help them. How can we call ourselves civilized if we keep on killing innocent creatures?

This paragraph goes off in so many directions that it does not point clearly in any particular direction. We can tell that the writer is fond of animals and believes that human beings abuse them in many ways. And if we have read "Without Emotion," we may also sense that the essay is a response to Gordon Liddy's writing. However, the writer has not focused on one specific statement about how people abuse animals. This relatively short essay cannot tackle all the problems at once. Yet the introductory paragraph mentions hunting as a sport, research experiments, slaughterhouses, and commercial hunting of endangered species. Each of these examples of killing leads to different arguments against them, even though all are linked by a common humanitarian point of view. Moreover, each category of abuse can be treated by the writer as a social problem, as a moral issue, or as a scientific matter.

To clear up the confusion and focus the essay, the writer's specific topic and point of view must both be spelled out in the form of a thesis statement early in the essay. This would guide both the readers and the writer, who at this point is trying to draft a well-organized piece of writing.

After a conference with the instructor, this student determined what the strongest topic was and from that developed a thesis statement. What most troubled the student was the commercial hunting of animals in order to use parts of their bodies—not for essential food but for vain, frivolous ends, such as fur coats, pet food, cosmetics, and aphrodisiacs. The main purpose of the essay, therefore, would be to convince readers to join the crusade against slaughtering wild animals for profit.

Next, the student drafted two fairly different opening paragraphs and read both to the class for reaction. Of the following two paragraphs, which one do you think has a stronger thesis and thus would lead to a better essay?

Last month my father received an appeal from Greenpeace, a worldwide environmental protection society, asking him to send money to help them stop the killing of whales and other endangered species. Dad threw the letter down and complained about all the junk mail we get. I told him this letter was not "junk"; these people are hoping to save innocent and beautiful creatures from extinction. I offered to donate some of my allowance if he would contribute the same amount. Eventually I convinced him that killing all these animals is a crime against Nature, like hunting the passenger pigeon to extinction a hundred years ago. I have earned a reputation at school as a conservation freak, but my work has raised a lot of money for conservation groups. And our conservation club at school is now working hard to convince the government to help preserve all living things on our planet.

We Americans have done a good deal for conservation, but a lot more remains to be done to protect Nature against all the greedy people who do not respect our wildlife. Ever since I was a Girl Scout, I have been concerned with animal welfare. At first, I was busy saving dogs hit by cars and curing wounded birds and animals I found in the woods. I didn't know about hunters who viciously slaughter whales and seals, or African poachers who kill elephants, rhinos, and gorillas for profit. When I learned about these awful things, I helped start a club that raises money and sets up protest marches in order to get our government to protect the future of our planet. My life's goal is to educate everyone to the

danger and the immorality of killing rare and beautiful animals

who have the same right as humans to live their lives in peace.

In using the reading and responding approach, be careful to distinguish between (1) writing a response, (2) brainstorming and freewriting, and (3) drafting the essay. The first step allows you to discover an interesting topic. The second step opens your mind and helps you to gather information related to your topic. The last step must be based solidly on the first two, developing in full your main idea about the topic. A well-formed thesis statement is the key to writing a successful first draft.

REVISING YOUR FIRST DRAFT

Every writer wishes that the first draft could be the last draft. Writing is difficult work, and the work never really ends because a word, sentence, paragraph, or essay can always be revised one more time. In addition, the elements and procedures of writing are intertwined: As you begin outlining your ideas, you also probably think about choosing the right word and even about spelling it correctly; or, as you look over your writing to check the spelling and grammar, you may suddenly realize that the essay is not organized as logically as you thought. Finally, when you write something, you *know* what you mean, and it may be difficult for you to see that other people—your readers—may not understand you. That's why we encourage you to share your early responses and first drafts with your classmates. Their questions and suggestions will help you to discover which aspects of your writing need revision.

Even the best writers know that revision is unavoidable, and they welcome the help of readers and editors along the way to their final draft. Whether you are an expert speller and grammarian or a writer who needs constantly to consult a dictionary and a handbook, "correctness" is only one part of effective writing—and only one part of effective revision. The main goal of writing is to express your point of view convincingly, and that should be your first concern in revising. Did you make yourself clear? Did your readers understand your main point and what you think about it? Was the information in your essay arranged logically and conveyed in effective language? When readers say "yes" to those three questions, you can be satisfied that revision is almost at an end. *Then* it's time to focus on the appearances of writing. Do the sentences in a paragraph flow smoothly? Is each sentence grammatical? Is each word spelled correctly? Finally, is your handwriting or typing neat and legible, so that the physical look of the essay doesn't distract readers from what you are saying?

Revision, then, is always possible, often necessary, and usually beneficial to your writing. To illustrate this point, the following pages present two examples of how students revised their essays after receiving written comments. Example 1 shows how an instructor's comments helped the student to revise, and Example 2 shows a revision based on a classmate's comments. As you study the first drafts, the comments, and the revised drafts, notice how these writers improved the expression of their ideas by taking readers' suggestions into account.

Example 1

First Draft

Misplaced Kindness

At first the story of how Mrs. Brown helped Mary made me

feel good because I enjoy reading about kind people. But then I began to think about the other students in Mrs. Brown's class who also needed help. Maybe they were not as needy as Mary, but they could have used some extra attention to make them good students instead of just average ones. When a teacher spends too much time and energy on the losers, the rest of the students have to improve all by themselves. Most of them cannot do it alone, and so that means Mrs. Brown was not a good example of a perfect teacher.

Many of the students in my classes were like Mary in some way or another, and most of the teachers especially in grade school gave extra time to these "difficult" students. That meant that the rest of us had to sit around very bored, or else we fooled around, while those teachers played Mommy to misbehaving children or those who did not really care about school. I resented the fact that these teachers did not help me to do better in math and science, my worst enemies.

The writer wants us to believe that Mrs. Brown's efforts paid off in a big way for Mary, but I would not bet any money on how well Mary ever did as a result of all that love and TLC. Some of the students in my classes who received extra attention are now unable to hold a job. What good did that special treatment do them? Furthermore, most of those losers never really wanted the extra help; they just did not dare refuse it. But the worst part of all this is that some of my friends who barely managed to pass are now running into trouble as they try to handle college work. If that extra help had gone to them, they would have made good use of it and would not be struggling to survive now.

I think that the article was meant to make teachers feel guilty if they are not giving all of themselves to their students, especially those at the bottom. This writer thinks she knows what is best, but she really does not understand the students. Doesn't she realize that most dropouts just plain do not like school? All they want to do is hang out. They actually resent teachers meddling in their personal lives. My advice to the teachers of the world is to concentrate on those who can really use their help. Let the losers stay lost.

Instructor's Comments about First Draft

Paragraph 1: Try to be more direct in your first sentence. What did you *think* of what Mrs. Brown did?

Can you be more specific about the other students' neediness? Your readers need to know what conditions you are focusing on. State your thesis more forcefully to express your point of view.

In last sentence, reconsider your word choice. The author never said that Mrs. Brown was *perfect*.

Paragraph 2: What do you mean by "we fooled around"? It doesn't add much to your point, and it makes the sentence a bit long and awkward. If you have details to add here, develop them more fully; readers won't know what you mean.

In the last sentence, it would help readers to know the extent of your difficulties in math and science. Did you fail these courses? What could the teachers have done to make you do better? Better than *what*?

Paragraph 3: The first sentence is too informal to tell us much, and the use of *TLC* assumes that readers will know what this term means. Express these ideas more clearly.

The entire paragraph covers too much ground. It has no single main idea. Finish your prediction of Mary's future before you discuss weak students you have known. Then, devote yet another paragraph to your friends in college. You cover too many ideas, but readers don't get a clear idea of what you mean.

Last paragraph: I think you are too harsh in judging the author. Don't forget that your first impression was highly favorable, as you say in the very first sentence of your essay. Tone down your criticism, and, if it seems reasonable, give Mrs. Brown a little credit. Did she do anything that you approve of?

Toward the end of the essay, take another look at your word choices. (1) You are not referring only to "dropouts." (2) Avoid slang phrases like "hang out"—try to be more formal to reach a wider audience. (3) In the last sentence, "really use" is vague and conversational; almost everyone can "really use" help, and so your conclusion is weakened by this phrase.

Entire essay: I found your essay very effective. Although I tend to agree with the author regarding Mrs. Brown's strategy with Mary, your essay showed me why it is so hard for most teachers to follow her example. They probably share your view to some extent.

Revised Draft

Misplaced Kindness

At first I agreed that Mrs. Brown was an excellent teacher because I felt sorry for Mary. But then I began to think about the other students in Mary's class who also needed help. They may not have repeated first grade and may not have been troublemakers, but they could have used extra attention to enable them to become good students rather than just average ones. When a teacher spends too much time and energy on the losers, the rest of the students have to improve on their own. And since most students cannot do this, they remain weak and may even lose interest in school. The more I thought about this story, the more I became convinced that Mrs. Brown was not an outstanding teacher.

When I was going to school, many of my classes contained students who were like Mary in one way or another, and most of the teachers, especially in grade school, gave extra time to these "problem" students. That meant that the rest of us had to sit around very bored, while these teachers played "mommy" to misbehaving children who were not really interested in school in the first place. When I had trouble getting even a C in math and science, I resented seeing teachers giving their time to students who usually failed anyway and did not care at all about learning.

This writer wants us to believe that Mrs. Brown's efforts were very beneficial to Mary, but I feel certain that Mary did not do any better because of all this love and attention. She probably went back to her old ways as soon as she left Mrs. Brown's class.

Other teachers would not spend so much time trying to improve Mary's self-image, and she would soon be misbehaving in order to get attention or because she felt inferior to the other children.

Most weak students do poorly because they are not interested in school subjects, and they have no ambition. Some of the people in my classes who received a lot of extra help over the years are now unable to find a job. What good did all that special treatment do for them? Furthermore, most of those losers never really wanted the extra help; they did not dare refuse it.

But the worst part of all is that some of my friends who barely managed to pass high school are now running into trouble as they try to handle college work. If more of that extra assistance for Mary had been given to them, they could have made good use of it and would not be struggling to survive now.

The writer intended to make teachers feel guilty if they were not giving all of themselves to those students who are having the greatest difficulty. What she says sounds nice because Mrs. Brown is so kind and Mary's behavior does improve. But the writer does not realize that most poor students just plain don't like school. All they want to do is hang out with their friends. They resent teachers meddling in their personal lives. My advice to teachers is to concentrate on those who can make the best use of their assistance. Let the losers stay lost.

This student read the instructor's comments before revising the first draft. As you can see, some of the revisions were based on the instructor's guidance, while others came from the student as part of the revision process.

1. How closely did the student follow the instructor's advice in revising the first draft? Which suggestions did the student accept, and which were rejected?

2. Which changes in the revised draft came from the student without the advice of the instructor? Do you think the student's revisions improved the essay? Why or why not?

3. In what way is the revised draft more effective than the first draft? Be specific in noting which ideas were improved by revision.

Example 2

First Draft

A Young Woman in Big Trouble

My own adolescence had its ups and downs, but for the most part I enjoyed growing up. Maybe things went well for me because I moved ahead at a normal pace, and I got along pretty well with my parents most of the time. On the other hand, my fourteen-year-old sister, Joann, seems to be having a very rough time. She hardly speaks to Mom and Dad, and she has fallen in with a wild bunch who are always getting into trouble of one kind or another. I wish some understanding person could see Joann's need for help and find some way to reach out to her. I believe Joann's tough attitude is just her way of keeping her personal pain hidden from the world. Somebody outside our family must get through to her before she wrecks her life.

Joann's problem goes back a long way. She came along when I was seven and my older sister Clare was nine. Mother had gone back to her job as a pediatric nurse and did not want to return to the role of housewife/mother. So babysitters were hired to care for Joann until she was old enough to go to kindergarten. None of them stayed very long. When I think back about Joann as a small child, I see a sour-faced brat, whose tears and shouts seemed fake about half the time.

School solved the babysitting problem because Clare and I could be assigned that job when we came home from school. I resented having to look after Joann, and I probably took my frustration out on her some of the time. Then she hit sixth grade, and everything changed.

When Joann, who wins the prize for good looks in our family, turned twelve, she became popular in school for the first time. Not with the teachers--she has never done well on report cards, especially in "attitude"--but with those girls who dress like Brooke Shields and act like they are eighteen. When Mother saw Joann's rapid transformation, she began criticizing her behavior, instead of just complaining as we had all been doing for years. Clare and I felt our parents were being a bit hard on Joann, but we were not worried then because we had fought with them about those things ourselves.

Recently, it became clear to us that the group of girls Joann hangs out with are even more rebellious than we had thought. They spend their afternoons and weekends with guys who are much older and wilder than is good for someone Joann's age. When Clare and I try to talk to Joann about the situation, she will not listen. She tells us to mind our own business.

Since I cannot see Joann responding to any of us, I desperately hope that someone she can respect will come along and take note of her troubled condition. She needs a true friend, and soon!

Classmate's Comments about First Draft

Paragraph 1: The way you begin seems wrong somehow—you're talking about *your* life, not your sister's, and it doesn't have much to do with her, either.

What kind of trouble was your sister "always getting into"? I know the teacher told us not to go into too much detail in our introductions, but she also said to be sure that readers know what you're getting at. I thought the trouble might be drugs at first—and you do mention that later—but I wasn't sure when I read the first paragraph.

The last half of the paragraph jumps around too much. You want someone to help Joann; then you explain her attitude; then you come back to wanting someone outside the family to help her. I think the last idea is a good way to end this paragraph, but you need to tell me why no one in the family can help. Give a clearer picture of her problem before you say what you think has to happen if she's going to get better.

Paragraph 2: I think the last sentence should go at the beginning, just after the first sentence.

Paragraph 3: You could say more about Joann—how she acted, how she must have felt.

Paragraph 4: I like the way you describe Joann and her friends. But why did your mother criticize her? What did she do wrong, other than act like a movie star? And what did your parents dislike about the other girls? What "issues" did they fight about?

Paragraph 5: What was so wild about these kids? What do you mean by "much older"—in their twenties?

What about your talks with Joann? What goes wrong? I think you need another paragraph to describe the way she turns off to you, and I think these two paragraphs should go up near the beginning of the essay so we can get a better idea of how much trouble Joann is in.

Last paragraph: This conclusion seems weak to me. You just sign off with a prayer for divine assistance. Why not go into more detail about the communication problem before you ask for an outsider to help your sister?

Revised Draft

A Young Woman in Big Trouble

My fourteen-year-old sister Joann seems to be having a very rough time growing up. She hardly ever speaks to Mom and Dad, and she and her friends have fallen in with an older group of guys who are always in trouble of one kind or another. Joann had an unhappy childhood and has developed a tough attitude to keep her personal pain hidden from the world. None of us can get through to her, and so I keep praying that she finds someone she can trust who will straighten her out before she completely wrecks her life.

Joann's problem goes back a long way. She was born when I was seven and my sister Clare was nine. When I think back about Joann as a small child, I always see a sour-faced brat whose tears and shouts seemed fake about half the time. At the time I hated her for being so bad tempered. But looking back now, I can see that she probably felt unwanted because no one in the family paid much attention to her unless she was making a very loud noise.

Mother had gone back to her job as a pediatric nurse after I started school, and she did not want to return to the role of housewife. So she hired babysitters for Joann until she was old enough for kindergarten. None of them stayed very long, and this may have left Joann feeling insecure. When she began going to school, Clare and I became the babysitters. However, this didn't help Joann, for I resented having to take care of her, and I took my frustration out on her some of the time. Clare was not much better. So the next six years weren't much better for Joann than the first six. Then she hit seventh grade, and everything changed dramatically.

When Joann, who wins the prize for good looks in our family, turned twelve, she became popular in school for the first time. Not with the teachers--she has never done well on report cards, especially in "attitude." She began hanging out with those girls who dress like Brooke Shields and act like they are eighteen. When Mother saw how Joann was changing, she began criticizing her behavior, including the way she dressed and her use of make-up. Both Mom and Dad were very critical of Joann's friends, who used foul language and hung around with a rough bunch of boys.

At first, Clare and I thought our parents were being too tough on Joann, and we were not worried about her because we had fought with our parents about similar issues ourselves. But recently, it became clear to us that the girls Joann goes around with are even more rebellious than we had thought. They spend their afternoons and weekends with guys who are much older than they are. Some have dropped out of high school, and all of them are involved with drugs and liquor.

When Clare and I try to talk to Joann about the situation, she will not listen. She tells us that she knows what she is doing and that she is in full control of her life. According to her, Clare and I missed out on all the excitement that is waiting for people who are brave enough to ignore all the myths that parents invent to control their children. Joann thinks our concern for her just shows how much we envy all the freedom she enjoys.

Mom and Dad have totally lost control of the situation. They cannot speak to Joann about anything without causing anger on both sides, and so they try to avoid her. Clare has very little time, for she is married and lives across town. So I am the only one who regularly talks to Joann, and then I can't mention the problems, or else she quickly tunes me out. I feel so terribly frustrated, having to stand by and watch my sister destroy her life this way. I guess we are all to blame--Mom and Dad for leaving her alone, and Clare and I for treating her like a bratty sister all those years. I just hope and pray it is not too late and that she can find a true friend who will get her to realize what is happening before she ends up in very serious trouble.

In this case, the student revised the first draft in response to a classmate's comments; the instructor made no suggestions at all.

1. What do you think of the classmate's comments? Were they as helpful as the instructor's comments were in Example 1? When you respond to a classmate's writing, are your comments as good as these? What can you learn from this classmate's response to the first draft?

2. Which of the classmate's comments would you have followed, and which would you have ignored? Why?

3. Look again at the first draft. What suggestions would you make to this writer? Put your comments in a form like the classmate's in this example. How would you advise this writer to proceed in revising the first draft?

A CHECKLIST FOR READING, RESPONDING, AND WRITING

Reading

Whether you are reading an assignment in this book or a classmate's first draft of an essay:

1. Relax and let your thoughts run free during your first reading.
2. Don't analyze what you are reading. Accept it—for now.
3. Pay attention to the ideas and feelings that you have as you read.

Responding to Reading

When you first respond to a reading selection or to a classmate's draft:

1. Record your strongest ideas and feelings about it without concern for the author's intentions or your instructor's expectations.
2. Record your response as soon as you finish reading the selection.
3. Share your response, either in class or as instructed.

Writing

After sharing your initial response with classmates, ask yourself the following questions to develop your thesis and draft your essay:

Selecting and Developing the Thesis

1. What point do I want to make about my topic? What do I hope to achieve? What does my audience know about the topic?
2. Is my topic focused enough, or do I need to limit it further?
3. Is my thesis clear and specific? Will my readers understand which aspects of the topic interest me and what my point of view is?
4. Should I use freewriting to develop my thesis further? Do I know all the ideas I want to explore in proving my point?
5. Do I need a classmate's reaction to my ideas at this point?

Drafting the Essay

1. Am I ready to start writing? Should I use brainstorming and freewriting to develop my ideas further?
2. Given my purpose and audience, how should I state my thesis in the introductory paragraph?
3. What is the best way to organize my supporting ideas and examples?
4. How should I state my conclusions in the last paragraph?
5. Can I improve the flow of ideas from thesis to supporting details to conclusion? Will my readers be able to follow my thinking?
6. Is my first draft ready for the instructor or classmates to read?

Responding to Writing

When you comment on a classmate's writing, questions like the following will help make your criticism constructive:

1. Do I agree or disagree with what the author is saying?
2. If I agree with the author's thesis, could I present the case any better? What other ideas would I include to support this thesis?
3. If I disagree with the author's thesis, what is the strongest case I can build against it? What ideas would I offer to support my objections?
4. What ideas can I offer to make this essay more effective?

Revising the Essay

After your instructor or classmates have reacted to your first draft of an essay, ask yourself these questions:

1. What comments did my readers offer that I want to consider in revising the essay? Which of their comments should I ignore?
2. Did my readers understand my thesis and feel that my supporting details and conclusions fit my thesis? Which ideas do I need to expand or clarify? Which ideas should I drop from the essay?
3. Did my readers object to any of the word choices I made?
4. Are all the sentences grammatically correct? Do they flow smoothly within each paragraph?
5. Have I made any mistakes in spelling, punctuation, or capitalization?
6. Am I ready to revise the essay and copy it neatly, or do I need further reaction from the instructor or classmates?

of Liveright Publishing Corporation. Copyright 1923 by Boni & Liveright. Copyright renewed 1951 by Jean Toomer.

Elizabeth Cady Stanton. "You Should Have Been a Boy!" from *Eighty Years and More*. Source Book Press, 1970.

Langston Hughes. "Salvation," from *The Big Sea* by Langston Hughes. Copyright 1940 by Langston Hughes. Copyright renewed © 1968 by Arna Bontemps and George Houston Bass. Reprinted by permission of Hill and Wang, a division of Farrar, Straus and Giroux, Inc.

Ruth Reichl. "There's Only Luck," first appeared February, 1981 in *New West/California*.

Arthur Bartlett. "Your Eyes Can Deceive You." Reprinted in *American Weekly*, 1951.

Sally Helgesen. "Growing Up in the Shadow of an Older Brother or Sister." Courtesy *Glamour*. Copyright © 1980 by The Condé Nast Publications, Inc.

Kate Chopin. "The Story of an Hour," from *The Complete Works of Kate Chopin*, edited by Per Seyersted, and published by Louisiana State University Press in 1969.

Isaac Asimov. "Intelligence." Copyright © 1972 by Communications Research Machines, Inc. Reprinted by permission of Isaac Asimov.

Jaime M. O'Neill. "No Allusions in the Classroom." Copyright 1985, by Newsweek, Inc. All Rights Reserved. Reprinted by permission.

Eric Zorn. "Memories Aren't Made of This." Copyright 1984, by Newsweek, Inc. All Rights Reserved. Reprinted by permission.

Louis Nizer. "How about Low-cost Drugs for Addicts?" Copyright © 1986 by The New York Times Company. Reprinted by permission.

M. Scott Peck. "Problems and Pain," from *The Road Less Traveled*. Copyright © 1978 by M. Scott Peck. Reprinted by permission of Simon & Schuster, Inc.

Gregory Bayan. "Reflections on a Hockey Helmet." Copyright 1984 by Gregory Bayan. Reprinted by permission of Gregory Bayan.

Karel Čapek. "The Last Judgment." Reprinted in *The Realm of Fiction: 61 Short Stories*, ed. by James B. Hall, from *Tales from One Pocket*. English translation by Norma Jeanne McFadden and Leopold Pospíšil especially for *Realm of Fiction* with permission of the Estates of Karel Čapek and Dilia. Copyright © 1965, 1970 by McGraw-Hill Book Company, Inc.

Richard Mitchell. "Words as Weapons," from *Less Than Words Can Say* by Richard Mitchell. Copyright © 1979 by Richard Mitchell. By permission of Little, Brown and Company.

Peter Farb. "Children's Insults," from *Word Play: What Happens When People Talk*, by Peter Farb. Copyright 1973 by Alfred A. Knopf, Inc.

Thomas Merton. "Silence," from *No Man Is an Island* by Thomas Merton, copyright 1955 by Our Lady of Gethsemani; renewed 1983 by the Merton Legacy Trust. Reprinted by permission of Harcourt Brace Jovanovich, Inc.

Francine Frank and Frank Anshen, "Talking Like a Lady: How Women Talk." Reprinted from *Language and the Sexes* by Francine Frank and Frank Anshen by permission of the State University of New York Press. Copyright 1983.

Barry McLaughlin. "How Fathers Talk to Babies," from "Second Look, The

Mother Tongue." From *Human Nature*, December 1978. Copyright © 1978 by Human Nature, Inc. Reprinted by permission of the publisher.

Anton Chekhov. "The Beggar." Reprinted with permission of Macmillan Publishing Company from *The Horse Stealers and Other Stories* by Anton Chekhov, translated from Russian by Constance Garnett. Copyright 1921 by Macmillan Publishing Company, renewed 1949 by David Garnett. Reprinted by permission of the literary estate of Constance Garnett and the Hogarth Press.

Lois Sweet. "What's in a Name? Quite a Lot." Reprinted with permission— The Toronto Star Syndicate.

Tony Elliott. "How Cocaine Took Control of My Life." Copyright © 1986 by The New York Times Company. Reprinted by permission.

Martin Winkler. " f Co rt T pe's Spl c d." Copyright © 1983 by The New York Times Company. Reprinted by permission.

Frank Deford. "Are Electronic Video Games Bad for Kids?" Reprinted courtesy of *Sports Illustrated* from the October 11, 1982 issue. © 1982 Time Inc. VIEWPOINT, by Frank Deford.

Marie Winn. "Television: The Plug-In Drug," from *The Plug-In Drug* by Marie Winn. Copyright © 1977, 1985 by Marie Winn Miller. Reprinted by permission of Viking Penguin Inc.

Bruno Bettelheim. "Punishment Versus Discipline," from *Punishment Versus Discipline* by Bruno Bettelheim. Reprinted by permission of Bruno Bettelheim and his agents Raines & Raines, 71 Park Avenue, New York. Copyright © 1985 by Bruno Bettelheim.

William J. Lederer and Donald D. Jackson. "The Mirages of Marriage." Reprinted from *The Mirages of Marriage* by William J. Lederer and Donald D. Jackson, by permission of W. W. Norton & Company, Inc. Copyright © 1968 by W. W. Norton & Company, Inc.

Philip Slater. "The Pursuit of Loneliness," from *The Pursuit of Loneliness*, revised edition, copyright © 1970, 1976 by Philip Slater. Reprinted by permission of Beacon Press.

Margaret Mead and Rhoda Metraux. "The Egalitarian Error," from *A Way of Seeing* by Margaret Mead and Rhoda Metraux. Copyright 1962 by Margaret Mead and Rhoda Metraux. Reprinted by permission of William Morrow & Company, Inc.

Arthur Hoppe. "How To Stay Alive." Copyright 1970 Chronicle Publishing Company, reprinted with permission of the author.

Sir Peter Medawar. "When We Are Old." Reprinted by permission of the author.

Jayne Anne Phillips. "Time but No Plan." From *Machine Dreams* by Jayne Anne Phillips. Copyright © 1984 by Jayne Anne Phillips. Reprinted by permission of the publisher, E. P. Dutton/Seymour Lawrence, a division of New American Library.

GUIDE TO
AUTHORS AND TITLES